AZTLÁN AND ARCADIA

Aztlán and Arcadia

Religion, Ethnicity, and the Creation of Place

Roberto Ramón Lint Sagarena

NEW YORK UNIVERSITY PRESS

New York and London

NEW YORK UNIVERSITY PRESS
New York and London
www.nyupress.org

References to Internet websites (URLs) were accurate at the time of writing.
Neither the author nor New York University Press is responsible for URLs that
may have expired or changed since the manuscript was prepared.

LIBRARY OF CONGRESS CATALOGING-IN-PUBLICATION DATA
Lint Sagarena, Roberto Ramón, 1967-
Aztlán and Arcadia : religion, ethnicity, and the creation of place / Roberto Ramón Lint
Sagarena.
pages cm
Includes bibliographical references and index.
ISBN 978-0-8147-4060-6 (cloth : acid-free paper) — ISBN 978-1-4798-5064-8 (paperback :
acid-free paper)
1. California, Southern—Historiography. 2. Aztlán. 3. Arkadia (Greece) 4. Indigenous
peoples—California, Southern—Ethnic identity. 5. California, Southern—Ethnic relations.
6. Historiography—Religious aspects. 7. Space—Religious aspects. 8. Regionalism—
California, Southern. 9. California, Southern—Relations—Mexico. 10. Mexico—
Relations—California, Southern. I. Title.
F867.L764 2014
305.8009794'9—dc23
2014009796

New York University Press books are printed on acid-free paper,
and their binding materials are chosen for strength and durability.
We strive to use environmentally responsible suppliers and materials
to the greatest extent possible in publishing our books.

Manufactured in the United States of America

10 9 8 7 6 5 4 3 2 1

Also available as an ebook

To Esmé, who made everything right

CONTENTS

ACKNOWLEDGMENTS

My interest in the subject matter of this book came about during a walk across the campus of Princeton University. As a provincial westerner who had never been east of Texas prior to arriving in New Jersey, I was initially impressed by the look of antiquity the collegiate Gothic architecture gave the campus, most especially the chapel. When I stopped to read the building's date stone I was surprised to find that the structure dated to the 1920s, making it of the same vintage as the Mission Revival apartment building I had lived in back in California. This encounter with historical fantasy inspired by religious architecture in the East caused me to think deeply about the nature of the built environment in the far West.

My pairing of and investment in the mythic traditions I have studied here is, no doubt, informed by the experience of having had a father who was dedicated to mentoring MEChA students in the early 1970s while our family lived on Ramona Street (the name an homage to the central character of California's Arcadian mythos). Many decades later, when I myself was mentoring MEChA students at the University of Southern California and living in a Spanish Revival bungalow, I proposed this book to Jennifer Hammer, the most patient and encouraging of editors.

I myself received from several exceptional scholars and good friends mentorship that was fundamental to this study. I am, as always, inspired by the scholarship and person of Albert Raboteau. His ability to draw out the complexity inherent in encounters between peoples serves as a model to a great many of us. His supportive friendship, in many ways, made this work possible. Davíd Carrasco strongly influenced my interest in and understanding of religion and architecture ultimately leading to this project. Although I grew up in both the United States and

Mexico, my experience of Mexico had been largely familial until Davíd made Mesoamerica and both Mexican and Chicana/o nationalism come alive for me in entirely new ways. Leigh Eric Schmidt's steady, reliable encouragement and guidance have been a gift. His rich understanding of American religious cultures helped me to better understand Protestant cultures in California.

This project took shape with a great deal of support over many years. It was encouraged in its earliest stages by Ann Taves, Thomas Tweed, Robert Wuthnow, Jim Sandos, Diane Winston, and John Giggie. James Boone's agile mind provided many insights that helped to frame my understanding of cross-cultural experiences. This book was greatly improved by Rudy Busto's remarkably keen and extensive commentary. I have also learned a great deal from conversations with Scott Sessions, Tom Bremer, Phoebe S.K. Young, Ben Johnson, Mark Wild, and Luis León.

I also owe particular debts of gratitude (again) to Leigh Schmidt, Laurie Maffley-Kipp, Mark Valeri, Sally Promey, Anthea Butler, Michael McNally, David Yoo, Tisa Wenger, Heather Curtis, Rick Ostrander, Catherine Brekus, and Katheryn Lofton as fellow collaborators in the Lilly Endowment's History of American Christian Practice Project. Richard Wrightman Fox and David Hall in particular provided directly helpful critiques on portions of this work. They have all been an invaluable cohort of colleagues and friends with whom to discuss the nature of religious practice and belief in relation to regionalism and ethnic formation.

Guidance and assistance from a number of librarians and archivists have been crucial to the completion of this work, most especially the remarkable staff of the Huntington Library, the Special Collections librarians at the University of California at Santa Barbara and Los Angeles, and the staff at Princeton's Firestone Library.

Many former colleagues at the University of Southern California provided support and encouragement along the way. George Sanchez took the time to provide me with a valuable critique of an early draft. I have long benefited from Bill Deverell's friendship. His scholarship and direct practical advice provided me with many valuable insights that have shaped this work. It is unlikely that this book would have made it to publication without the wisdom and strong encouragement of Ruthie Gilmore.

Gratitude for Jane Iwamura's camaraderie deserves its own line. Thank you so much, Jane.

More recently, my colleagues and students at Middlebury College have provided me with an energizing new workplace for which I am very grateful. Vermont exists in its own sort of borderlands and has proven to be an idyllic place from which to study the Southwest and northern Mexico.

Many years ago, shortly before his death, my father made a point of telling me (in a characteristically solemn tone) that I was very lucky to have Craig Harlan as a conversation partner. He was right, but he would never know that those conversations (and fruitful disagreements) with my then–future father-in-law would spur a transformation from life as a high school dropout and line cook to a life of privilege in the academy. The arc of that unlikely trajectory is also due in large part to Sallie Harlan, who remains our family's bedrock. Robert and Gene Irvin were a haven through both good and dark times; I miss them both. But it was their granddaughter, Anna Harlan, my partner of twenty-four years, who has made this rich life possible.

Detail showing the "Ancient Residence of the Aztecs" in Alta California from the *Mapa de los Estados Unidos de Méjico, según lo organizado y definido por las varias actas del Congreso de dicha República: y construido por las mejores autoridades*, New York, John Disturnell, 1847. This map accompanies the Treaty of Guadalupe Hidalgo, which marked the end of the Mexican-American War (1846–48) and the annexation of Mexico's northern territories.

Introduction

The [American] officers of these vessels, some of whom were men of superior character and education, fell permanently under the spell of the new land. They ate of her fruits; they basked in her sunshine; they breathed her "soft Lydian airs"; they looked upon her fair daughters; they enjoyed the generous hospitality of her people; they tasted the ease and peace of the life; and, like the lotus eaters of old, they forgot home and family and determined to remain forever in this Arcadia by the western sea. From this "peaceful invasion" came the matrimonial alliances between the Anglo-Saxon immigrants and the Spanish Californians, from which originated the old families which constitute our true aristocracy, occupying the same position as the Puritans on the other shore.
—Nellie Van de Grift Sanchez, *Spanish Arcadia* (1928)

Needless to say, all of us who reside in Aztlán, whether biologically Mexican or not, are part Mexican in a cultural-historical sense.
—Jack D. Forbes, "The Mexican Heritage of Aztlán" (1962)

Southern California's regional style manifests itself most uncannily in the many Mission Revival border patrol checkpoints that dot the local freeways; they sport red-tiled roofs and plaster walls that recall the romantic glory of California's Latin American past while standing as militarized guardposts of the state's present-day border with Mexico. This cognitive dissonance is implicitly, though less ominously, re-created in the ubiquitous presence of Mission and Spanish Revival architecture in everything from mansions and movie studios to bungalows and fast-food franchises. As Americans lay claim to California in the nineteenth and early twentieth centuries, there was considerable synergy between the creation of historical narratives that naturalized American possession of the land and the creation of regional architecture. As a result, aesthetically, much of California is built to be both celebratory of and yet divorced from its past, reinforcing a number of long-held but deeply problematic American cultural dispositions. These include an assumption of continuity between Spain's colonial enterprise and American expansion, a general *disinterest* in the history and legacy of the Mexican-American War (1846–48), and common portrayals and perceptions of ethnic Mexicans as familiar but nonetheless perpetually foreign in the United States.

Even as former portions of Mexico's Alta California were transformed into the United States' Southern California, however, the region's ethnic Mexican population increased, often dramatically. With the exception of brief downturns during repatriation campaigns in the 1930s, the Mexican-origin population of the United States has grown continuously since the end of the Mexican-American War. As both expatriate and native-born ethnic Mexicans made homes for themselves in this "*Mexico de afuera*" (greater Mexico), they created powerful regional and ethnic histories that existed appositionally (and oppositionally) to dominant narratives but were similarly given material form through aesthetic transformations of the vernacular landscape principally by way of murals, shrines, and commercial signage. These expressions of public history often worked explicitly to assert the legitimacy of the presence of ethnic Mexicans in the United States and to both maintain and re-define émigrés' relationships to Mexico.

This book offers a study of how religious history, iconography, and rhetoric have been put to work in these interrelated cultural projects. It examines them from the earliest efforts toward the Americanization of California to the assertion of countervailing definitions of place and identity made at various historical moments by Californios (Spanish Colonial and Mexican elites), Mexican-Americans, and Chicana/os. Most importantly, it illustrates how this range of efforts was shaped by tropes of religious conquest and reconquest common to nationalist idioms in both countries. Victory in the war with Mexico helped to reify the idea of the United States' providential right to span the continent and to conceive of far westward American expansion as a conquest of territories lost to imperial Spain. Throughout the settlement of what would become the Southwest, many Americans often understood themselves as following recuperatively (and at times literally) in the footsteps of the colonial project begun by Spanish missionaries. Many early Mexican nationalists, in contrast, portrayed their country's war for independence (1811–21) as an Indigenous yet Christian reconquest of the ancient Mexican Empire from a morally corrupt imperial Spain. While the subsequent American occupation and sundering of their nation (1848) challenged Mexicans to re-define themselves and their country in relation to an aggressive neighboring foreign power, the romantic use of the pre-Columbian past has remained fundamental to the articulation of national and ethnic identity by ruling elites, in Mexican popular culture, and among Mexican expatriates.

Both of these nationalist forms of historical expression reached peaks in their popularity during times of significant demographic change. In the decade following California's Gold Rush (1848–55) and its admission into the Union as a free state (1850), California's population more than tripled, largely in the northern mining areas. These rapidly growing communities of American arrivistes began to recast what had been Mexico's northern frontier into the United States' far West. These initial forms of Americanization gained considerable symbolic and material support through the efforts of newly arrived American Catholic clergy who took control of California's missions and through the work of sympathetic Protestants who sought to assimilate the colonial past and eventually encouraged the use of the historically Catholic church buildings as civic centers. These early transformations set the cultural stage for later arrivals in the 1880s, as real estate developers and rail lines brought many thousands more Americans and encouraged them to embrace romantic depictions of California's pastoral past created by Anglos and aging Californios alike. By the 1920s, Southern California's American postconquest history was largely codified, but the expansion of its urban centers and the rapid influx of an ethnic Mexican population encouraged many Americans to take part in an ever more fanciful embrace of Spanish colonial history and revivalist architectures.

Significantly, two great moments of increased out-migration from Mexico to the United States, those occurring in the 1910s–1920s and the late 1960s–1970s, coincided with a resurgence of Mexican indigenist nationalism. The first of these surges followed the Mexican Revolution, which began in 1910 as an uprising led by Francisco Madero against the dictatorial regime of Porfirio Díaz. By the time the decade-long war concluded, it had claimed at least a million lives. Resentments against foreign (principally U.S.) ownership of more than 20 percent of Mexico's land prior to the Revolution, as well as concerns over agrarian reform and the integration of the nation's indigenous population into modern Mexican society, fueled the rise of a powerful post-Revolutionary nationalism. This sentiment emerged in expressions of populist culture that celebrated the indigenous past and was inculcated in secular schools and in the public arts. However, the social displacement caused by the war's violence and a severe postwar economic downturn spurred Mexicans (notably including many Mexican Catholic priests and nuns fleeing anticlerical violence) to ride the rails northward in search of sanctuary and employment in the United States. Consequently, the hundreds of thousands of Mexican immigrants arriving in the United States during the 1910s and 1920s brought a strong sense of national and ethnic identity with them into lands that had been a part of Mexico just a few generations previously.

A subsequent era of large-scale migration to the United States began in the late 1960s with the passage of the Hart-Celler Immigration and Nationality Act (1965). This piece of civil rights legislation phased out the earlier national origins quota system favoring European immigration and stressed immigrant family reunification. Unintentionally, it ushered in a new era in which Mexico became the most common point of national origin for newly arriving peoples to the United States for decades to come. This change in U.S. immigration policy coincided with yet another popular renewal of the use of pre-Columbian tropes in Mexican nationalism that significantly affected Mexican culture abroad.

The hosting of the 1968 Olympics in Mexico City provided the impetus and opportunity for government officials to disseminate romantic representations of indigenous cultural patrimony, not only to the nation itself but also to the world. Subsequent archeological discoveries such as the dramatic unearthing of the massive stone sculpture of the goddess Coyolxauhqui, and the excavation of the Aztec *Templo Mayor* (both occurring in the very center of the capital in the 1970s) further incited public enthusiasm for the use of the pre-Columbian past in representations of Mexican-ness. However, this heightened national consciousness came into being against the backdrop of a number of repressive governmental actions, most notably the Tlateloloco massacre, which occurred ten days before the opening of the Olympic Games. During this event soldiers opened fire on activist students and civilians in one of the city's largest plazas, killing hundreds and arresting more than a thousand bystanders. In response to this and many other confrontations, Mexican activists increasingly employed indigenist nationalist emblems against the state, imbuing them with countercultural and revolutionary significance.

These events in Mexico as well as the increasing northward migration of politicized Mexican youth helped to give shape to the nascent Chicana/o movement in United States during the late civil rights era. In the process of creating a social space for themselves that would exist betwixt and between U.S. and Mexican national cultures, Chicana/os re-interpreted pre-Columbian iconography and mythology to fit contemporary concerns. Thus, Mesoamerican topoi became central to the elaboration of new and radical forms of ethnic self-ascription through artistic production and in constructions of place. This was accomplished most powerfully through the re-definition of Aztlán, the mythic homeland of the Aztecs, into a geographic metaphor for the Mexican lands lost to the United States and as a spiritual metaphor for the unity of all Chicana/os.

Although novel in form, this twentieth-century rendering of Aztlán re-inscribed nineteenth-century constructions of the border region as an extension of Mesoamerica put forward by both Mexicans and Americans in their attempts to integrate the northern/western frontier as parts of their respective national domains. As a multivalent metaphor referring to a largely indefinite physical location, the idea of Aztlán was invested with the symbolic power to transform any space where Chicana/os found themselves, regardless of national boundaries, into home. It provocatively located the legendary wellspring of Aztec/Mexican culture outside the nation in *el Mexico de afuera* (greater Mexico), serving as a counter to Mexican nationals' criticisms of expatriates for leaving their motherland and culture. Even more significantly, it provided a basis for claims of a deep spiritual link to indigenous culture and a prior and more legitimate connection to the land than that of Americans. Thus, the idea of Aztlán as the Chicana/o homeland implicitly undermined the dominant narrative taught in schools and lived in public spaces that portrayed Anglo Americans as the rightful heirs to a bucolic Spanish Arcadia on the shores of the Pacific.

However, there were significant and explicit critiques of American hispanophilia in California that predated the late-twentieth-century political use of the idea of Aztlán. In the late nineteenth century, Californios participated in the romanticization of the era of the "Spanish Dons" by Americans, but they also argued against early attempts to make easy claims of continuity between colonial Spanish and modern Anglo societies. As Mission and later Spanish Revival architectures became pervasive in Southern California, some Americans came to critique their connotation of luxury and leisure as being socially exclusive, and others critiqued them for their failure to remain "authentic" to the perceived style and simplicity of the missions.

In the aftermath of World War II, the vogue for mission-style bungalows was replaced by the popularization of ranch and other modernist architectural forms. It was then that journalist/historian/activist Carey McWilliams articulated the most influential critique of Americans' glorification of the Spanish mission era in California. He termed the prevalent understanding of mission history—that is, of the Spanish colonial period as a time of benevolent paternalism and contented Indigenous labor—the "Mission Legend." He argued that this mythic view of the past hid the true human cost of forced conversion and erased the Mexican past. Moreover, he contended that Americans' reverence for this imagined past constitutes a "Fantasy Heritage" and that its "function is to deprive the Mexicans of their heritage and to keep them in their place," defining them as foreigners by appropriating the region's history.[1]

The cultural consequences of dispossession McWilliams spoke of have long been examined from Chicana/o perspectives in works as diverse as Rodolfo Acuña's *Occupied America* (1972), Richard Griswold Del Castillo's *The Treaty of Guadalupe Hidalgo* (1972), David Weber's *Foreigners in Their Own Land* (1973), and John Chavez's *The Lost Land* (1984). More recently, Lee Bebout's *Mythohistorical Interventions* (2011) has examined, in part, the narrative legacy of the Chicana/o movement as it has confronted these same issues. Additionally, the study of the historical development of the "Mission Legend" has been deepened in a number of exemplary historical works that study the politics of public memory, most notably in William McClung's *Landscapes of Desire: Anglo Mythologies of Los Angeles* (2000), William Deverell's *Whitewashed Adobe* (2004), Matthew Bokovoy's *San Diego's World Fairs and Southwestern Memory* (2005), and Phoebe Kropp's *California Vieja* (2006).

This book similarly interrogates the creation of public histories in Southern California, but with a focus on the central role of religion in their development. It argues that the ways in which religious rhetoric was employed in the creation of Southern California as a region in the nineteenth century had a profound impact on a variety of social relations in the twentieth century. Inasmuch as the story of the formation of the Southwest and Southern California is about racial, ethnic, and national encounters, it is also about encounters between Protestant and Catholic cultures. The following pages show how, over time, increasingly positive Protestant assessments of Spanish Catholic missions and missionaries helped to "Americanize" Catholicism in broader U.S. culture and how, in a deeply related way, the emblematic use and transformation of religious iconography have been central to Chicana/o efforts to locate themselves socially and spatially.

In approaching the topic, this book relies on two basic premises. The first is that religious culture, language, and practice were central to the invention of traditions that helped various groups attempt to remedy the social and political traumas of the war with Mexico. A wide range of cultural practices inculcated these traditions (including parades, architectural styles, museum exhibits, and murals and other artistic productions), and these had deep social and political consequences, namely the enforcement of racial and ethnic social hierarchies as well as the formation of new identities and communities.

Second, the evidence I am presenting makes it clear that these Mexican and American invented traditions, one privileging an Indigenous past and the other a Spanish past, are interlinked in their vocabulary and mirror each other in their logic and rhetoric. Both spring from the historical facts of war and migration, both lay a spiritual as well as temporal claim to the same places, and both employ the vocabulary of colonial encounter. Thus, they exist in deeply proximate relation and are best understood when studied together.

This book brings these fundamentally related histories together through an interdisciplinary approach. Though this work is presented in the form of narrative history, its structure draws from a variety of models and methods. While it is a study of the uses of nationalist myths and symbols, its focus is on the lived and material consequences of these mythologies. In these cases, it is the interplay of competing nationalist myths that provides the deepest insights into the cultural and religious phenomena it considers. From geography and sociology, the insight that culture is spatial and that counterspaces can parody and undermine repressive spaces is key to framing the book's main points. In the manner of the study of lived practice in religious studies, it relies heavily on material and visual evidence as well as more conventional primary data from archival sources and literary productions. Beyond methodological concerns, topically it puts the field of American religious history into conversation with Chicana/o studies.

Ultimately, the principal concern of this book stems from the same question that motivated many of the historical actors described herein: What are the ways in which the history of the United States can be made to come to terms with its Latin American past? The question was crucial to late-nineteenth-century Californios making sense of their place in a new order, to East Coast transplants in Southern California attempting to create a regional identity, and to the children of twentieth-century Mexican migrants living in the cultural hyphen between nations. It remains a central question in Chicana/o and Latina/o studies but has often been neglected within the field of American religious history. This is due, in part, to common assumptions of a fundamental dissemblance between the Americas in part as a result of linguistic difference and perhaps also because of lingering biases favoring the study of Anglo-Protestant religious cultures. To be sure, canonical works on religion in the United States, from those of Herbert Bolton to those of Sydney Ahlstrom, have made attempts to integrate the Latin American past into a national historical narrative, but more typically American scholars have approached the problem by covering the Spanish colonial period as a discrete topic and not engaging the more recent inter-American past of the nineteenth and twentieth centuries. This book explores this question by showing how a variety of historical actors from both sides of the border have made sense of the past in Southern California, sometimes employing nostalgia, sometimes resorting to historical arrogation, and very often by making claims of religious and spiritual connection to place.

Chapter 1 begins with a discussion of commonly held historical beliefs and nationalist attitudes before and during the Mexican-American War in both countries. Mexican independence in the early nineteenth century saw the flowering of an indigenist or *indigenista* nationalism in Mexico that celebrated the Indigenous past (even as contemporary Indigenous peoples faced exploitation and oppression sanctioned by the state). This patriotic *indigenismo* married emerging forms of civil religion to Catholic Marian devotion through the cultus of the Virgin of Guadalupe, the nation's patroness. In the United States, the same period was marked by the dramatic rise of anti-Catholic nativism, which was principally directed against Irish Catholic immigrants but peaked with the rise of popular support for war with Catholic Mexico.

A variety of factors precipitated the invasion and occupation of newly independent Mexico by the United States. Among them were the incorporation of the formerly Mexican Republic of Texas into the Union, struggles over the expansion of slavery, the popularization of the idea of America's Manifest Destiny to expand to the Pacific, and Mexican officials' refusal to sell half of their nation's lands as solicited by U.S. President James K. Polk's administration. Ultimately, the conflict resulted in deep political instabilities in both countries; although the United States acquired nearly a third of its continental territory and gained access to trade in the Pacific, the war is also credited with accelerating the start of the U.S. Civil War (1861–65). However, subsequent commemorations of the shared experience of the war with Mexico also provided some northern and southern U.S. military men with a common ground upon which to try to repair the bonds broken by the War between the States.

The heart of chapter 1 turns on an analysis of early American impressions of Mexico's northern region and considers the various arguments that were made to assert the legitimacy of the American annexation of California. Soon after the war, many American clerics, historians, lawyers, and even poets popularized the idea that the nature and intent of California's initial colonization by the Spanish was strictly religious. In doing so, and despite common anti-Catholic biases, many Americans claimed a moral and spiritual continuity between the "civilizing" missionary work of the Spanish Franciscans and their project of settlement and development in the far West.

This emplotment of history became increasingly commonplace during the course of the late nineteenth century and was canonized in legal proceedings at The Hague. There, a series of legal battles between the American Catholic Church and the Mexican state over the ownership of a "Pious Fund" that had been set up to support the original missionization of Baja and then Alta California went before the international tribunal. The American Catholic Church claimed that because the Spanish settlement of California was a religious rather than a political enterprise, and because they were the new religious stewards of the missions, they had a right to sue the Mexican state for the financial support of the missions. Sets of favorable decisions for the American position in effect ratified the problematic though popular idea that the American conquest of California was similar to that accomplished by the Spanish—an allegedly strictly cultural and spiritual one. For nearly a century after the rulings, the Mexican government would make regular payments to the American Catholic Church for the maintenance of missions lost to the United States in the war.

Though the transition of lands and property from Mexican to American hands often took place in the context of deeply flawed legal disputes, the economic decline of Mexicans in California was portrayed as inevitable by American writers through the use of romantic and tragic literary tropes that were already common in literature that mourned the "passing" of Native Americans. The chapter concludes with a discussion of examples of this literary form as well as an analysis of Californios' own nostalgic recounting of their life stories in *testimonios*, or testimonials that were collected as oral histories.

The second chapter offers a treatment of the creation of Southern California as an American region within the context of post–Civil War reconstruction and the arrival of rail lines to the West. American migration to California greatly accelerated with the completion of the transcontinental railroad in 1869, and boom times were quickly followed by busts. Nonetheless, selling California as a place for health and profit proved attractive and lucrative. In the late 1800s California's marketability became dependent upon the state's rough frontier image being deliberately transformed into that of a more desirable and civilized destination. Rail companies that were invested in development mobilized considerable resources for the promotion of California: Agents were hired to write literature, give lectures, and create exhibits, all advocating settlement and tourism on the Pacific shores. Life in California was portrayed as a cure-all for the woes of Americans and European immigrants, be they related to ill health, financial misfortune, or crowded urban environments.

One of the most noteworthy tourists to arrive in California by rail in this period was Helen Hunt Jackson. This popular author transformed the region through her literary work, principally with the publication of the novel *Ramona*, which gave Americans a sense of Southern California as a place replete with pre-modern romance. Jackson's writing contributed to an already growing effort on the part of Americans to define the region through its pre-American features, namely its crumbling adobe buildings and Spanish place names, elements that were employed in the creation of a lasting and distinctive regional style.

The popularity of Jackson's depiction of California coincided with early deliberations about the style to be employed in the construction of the California building representing the state at the 1893 World's Fair Columbian Exposition in Chicago. In the creation of this first example of Mission Revival style, Southern Californians embraced an architecture that would connote their identity and that very quickly would become visual shorthand for Southern California itself.

Chapter 3 considers the encounter between American Protestantism and Catholicism in the celebration of California's Spanish Catholic past; it argues that events in California marked a turning point in denominational relations. As missions became civic monuments and as Spanish Franciscans were compared to and equated with English Puritans, elements of Catholic history were brought into the larger fold of America's national history. A powerful combination of cultural and economic interests worked hand in hand to promote this ecumenical history and saw to its dissemination through public school curricula as well as in architectural and performative expressions such as theatrical productions and citywide pageants.

This chapter also shows that at the same time that Southern California boosters were going to greater lengths to memorialize the region's

Spanish past, liberal nationalists in Mexico were promoting a cultural philosophy relying on *indigenismo* that celebrated Mexico's pre-Columbian cultures over and against their Iberian heritage. The expression of this form of Mexican nationalism in folk arts and muralism was well received in the United States even as postrevolutionary Mexican immigration to the United States was peaking. Upon arrival in Southern California, Mexican expatriates came face to face with Americans' appropriation of the region's Latin American past and found themselves in a culture in which that which was Spanish belonged and that which was Indigenous did not.

The chapter then charts the high point of American enthusiasm for California's colonial past in the wholescale architectural transformation of Santa Barbara, California, from a city originally modeled by Americans to resemble small New England towns into a community re-created in a uniformly Spanish Revival style. Santa Barbara's transformation was not only cast in the static shapes of the city's ornate buildings, it was (and is still) also performed in the city's "Old Spanish Days *Fiesta*." With Spanish Revival buildings serving as the sets, the pageantry of the Old Spanish Days festival acted out the city's reinvented connection to Spain.

The fourth chapter explores the evolution of a variety of expressions of ethnic Mexican self-ascription in the mid–twentieth century, first as Mexican Americans, later as Pachuca/os in youth culture, and then, employing an updated and recontextualized form of *indigenismo*, as politicized Chicana/os. Beyond simply creating appellations for themselves, ethnic Mexicans in the United States established a hybrid transnational *heritage*, one that asserted their communities' presence through new ways of representing the region's history and culture. This was achieved in no small measure through the widespread creation of murals displaying the emblems of ethnic Mexican identity, most notably and with greatest impact through abundant depictions of the Virgin of Guadalupe, an icon combining, race, religion, and nationality. This book ultimately argues that this lasting tradition has transformed many of Southern California's urban environments as dramatically as regionalist boosters did before them, but in a manner that re-orients the focus of the state's genealogy from Spain to Mexico.

1

Conquest and Legacy

Conciudadanos unidos podemos salvar a nuestra patria en sus necesidades. Pero si por desgracia nos dividimos, seremos victimas de cualqier enemigo que despondra de nuestras vidas y de nuestras fortunas. Unamosnos pues y aseguramos integro el territorio nacional, a cuya defensa estare siempre con vosotros cuanto como ciudadano y amigo. (Fellow citizens, together we can save our homeland in its time of need. But if lamentably we divide ourselves, we will be victims of whichever enemy takes charge of our lives and fortunes. Let us unite then and assure the integrity of the nation's territories, at whose defense I will always be with you all both as citizen and as friend.)
—Governor Pio Pico, "Carta a los Ciudadanos," August 31, 1845

A simple-minded and an indolent people passed their days upon this fruitful soil and beneath these sunny skies, seemingly, as if waiting the fulfillment of that great destiny which providence had marked out for the land, under the auspices of a new chosen people. What a change has followed! The good geni of the lamp could not in a like period of time have wrought a more wondrous result.
—Willard B. Farwell, "Oration delivered before the society of California pioneers at the celebration of their 8th anniversary of the admission of the state of California into the Union. San Francisco, Alta Job Office," 1859

[A]ccording to the traditions of the Mexicans, the progenitors of the Aztecs and others entered the country from the direction of California, thereby indirectly connecting that people with the ancient inhabitants of the States.
—William Gleeson, *History of the Catholic Church in California*, 1872

Aztecas Criollos and American Conquistadors

The Mexican-American War (1846–48), through which the United
States acquired roughly a third of its national territory, was a war of
conquest, and wars of conquest act as quickening agents on social
change. They add urgency to the redefinition of social and geographic
identities as both the vanquished and the conqueror confront the task
of inventing traditions that re-create order from disrupted conventions.
Because new social orders are built on historical narratives that claim
continuity with a sustaining past, who is counted as an ancestor in these
invented traditions matters a great deal.[1]

After the war, both sides contended with radically transformed
national geographies and weakened federal governments. Far from
uniting either country, the conflict widened political divisions and
precipitated civil wars in both nations. Americans faced the further
problem of formulating a history that could explain their presence
in territories acquired through military action without calling into
question the legitimacy of American rule. Concomitantly, ethnic
Mexicans remaining in the annexed territories were challenged to define
themselves and their heritage in the face of tremendous loss and rapid
cultural change.

In various ways, both Americans and Mexicans made claims of historical and cultural continuity with Latin America's earliest Indigenous
and colonial pasts in making sense of their postwar present. As this final
leap in the United States' continental expansion took place shortly after
the fall of Spain's empire in the Americas, many Americans saw their
country as eclipsing colonial Spain but following in its imperial footsteps, a vision supported by the acquisition of Florida from Spain, the
premises of the Monroe Doctrine, the rhetoric of Manifest Destiny, and
the occupation of Mexico. For Mexicans, on the other hand, the recent
struggle for independence from Spain (1810–21) had bequeathed an
indigenista understanding of the essential character of the new nation,
one that looked to the Indigenous past for that which was uniquely
Mexican.[2]

This dominant form of Mexican nationalism was a product of the
centuries-long colonial experience. *Criollos* (people of Spanish descent
born in the Americas) were ranked lower socially than Iberian-born

Peninsulares though they had a common ancestry. Resentments against this colonial arraignment as well as a desire for far-reaching historical roots on their home continent led *Criollos* to articulate a history that privileged the Indigenous past. Although colonial *indigenistas* would glorify pre-Columbian Indigenous peoples, they were not seeking to restore, or even necessarily celebrate, living contemporary Indigenous cultures. Instead, they were creating a past for themselves in the Americas that was altogether separate from their Iberian heritage.

The most strident *indigenistas* were liberal *Criollo* clergy with a strong missionary interest in Indigenous cultures. However, these early chroniclers of New Spain made sense of the Indigenous past through the lenses of classical European history and Christian theology. Throughout the three centuries of Spanish colonial rule, a large register of influential priests portrayed pre-Columbian Aztec culture as an equivalent classical antiquity of Mexican history, regularly comparing the Aztec empire to those of the Greeks and Romans—often quite favorably.[3] Aztec rulers were seen as inspiring figures who personified classic virtues, pre-Columbian Indigenous governance was often cast in the same light as the Athenian senate, and, by the late nineteenth century the quest for a national art would come to embrace a classicist visual vocabulary in the portrayal of Indigenous figures.[4]

However, even as they romanticized Mexico's pre-Columbian past, *indigenista* clergy commonly understood Indigenous religions as corruptions of Christianity. Many clerics argued that a literal interpretation of scripture made it necessary for at least one of the apostles to have evangelized the Americas centuries before the arrival of the Spaniards, reasoning that if Jesus had sent his apostles to preach the gospel throughout the world, then surely God would not have allowed the peoples of the Americas to remain ignorant of Christianity. This argument supported the popular idea that the Americas had originally been evangelized by the apostle Saint Thomas, who was believed to be known to Indigenous peoples as the god Quetzalcoatl, the same deity identified with Hernán Cortés at the time of his arrival.

Other evidence seen as pointing to an early evangelization included a cross motif that regularly appears in Aztec and Mayan art, a common myth of a great flood that destroyed the Earth, and shared ritual practices that included confession, fasting, and the tonsure of priests.

Indigenous religions could thus be understood as a continuation, albeit corrupt, of an early Christianity. This Christian genealogy provided Mexicans of all racial, ethnic, and social backgrounds with a powerful claim of a religious connection to the far Indigenous past and thus to the continent.

Iberian Christianity and pre-Columbian religions were symbolically linked by the clergy shortly after the initial conquest of Tenochtitlán though the cultus of the Virgin of Guadalupe. It would be difficult to overstate the importance of this Marian devotion to the development of modern Mexican identity, from the national to the individual level. The pious legend of the apparition of the Virgin of Guadalupe recounts a series of apparitions of Mary to an Aztec/Mexica neophyte named Juan Diego in 1531 at Tepeyac hill, in the Valley of Mexico. This immensely popular apparition narrative tells us that a young woman surrounded by light appeared to Juan as he was en route to attend mass. Speaking in Náhuatl (the language of the Aztec/Mexica), she revealed herself as Mary and requested that a temple be built at the site so that she could be with her beloved people. As directed, Juan Diego presented himself to the clergy and conveyed Mary's request. Initially, he was rebuffed by a skeptical bishop (Juan de Zumráraga) who required proof of the apparition. Then Mary appeared to him again and promised a sign that would convince the bishop. She instructed him to gather out-of-season flowers atop Tepeyac and carry them in his *tilma* (cloak) back to the bishop. Upon the delivery of the flowers, his *tilma* unfurled and revealed the miraculous image of Guadalupe as powerful visual evidence, thereby convincing the bishop and establishing her cultus.[5]

While Guadalupan devotion was criticized by some Franciscans as functioning as a cover for the continuation of Indigenous religions, the cultus grew rapidly and flowered in the nineteenth century as it provided the religious emblem for Mexican independence and nationalism. The popularity of the devotion stemmed from its ability to provide *Criollos* with an American (as opposed to European) Marian apparition and Indigenous peoples with cultural continuity, as Tepeyac had been a significant Aztec/Mexica religious site. Moreover, the *tilma* image of Guadalupe is racially ambiguous and has been the object of multivalent interpretation as depicting a *Criolla*, Aztec, or *Mestiza* woman, encouraging pious people from all three groups to see her as a mirror of themselves, as a mediatrix, and ultimately as an emblem of their admixture.

The significance of the apparition of the Virgin of Guadalupe to the idea of an early indigenous Christianity was most radically expressed by the priest Servando Teresa de Mier, a central figure in the development of Mexican nationalism and a leading voice among those calling for Mexican independence from Spain. On December 12, 1794, the feast day of the Virgin of Guadalupe, Mier gave a remarkable sermon condemning the popular understanding of the apparition's pious legend. He claimed that the Virgin did not appear to Juan Diego in 1532 as was generally believed. Rather, she had appeared much earlier to Saint Thomas, and the miraculous cloth image actually belonged to Thomas, not to Juan Diego. Mier told stunned clergy that just as Thomas was known as Quetzalcoatl, the Virgin of Guadalupe, the mother of God, was also known to the Aztec/Mexica as a number of goddesses: Teotenantzin, Tonacayona, Coyolxauhqui, and Coatlique.[6] His radically *indigenista* sermon conjoined the celebration of the classic pre-Columbian past and assertion of Christian origins for Aztec/Mexica religion.

The political significance of these claims was revolutionary. By arguing for a Christian America that predated the arrival of the Spanish, Mier and other *indigenistas* were doing away with the single most important juridical justification for the Spanish conquest: the conversion of Indigenous peoples to Christianity. Mier maintained that if the conquistadors had recognized Aztec religion as having its roots in Christianity, the conquest *could* have been peaceful. Hence, through their violence, the Spaniards had sinned deeply against the very religion that they professed. *Indigenistas* thus made use of their claims about Indigenous religious belief to rhetorically undermine the legitimacy of Spanish colonial rule and strengthen their claims of connection to a pre-Columbian heritage all at once. In this *indigenista* schema, what tied *Criollos* to Mexico and allowed them to make its past their own was a religious connection with pre-Columbian Indigenous Christians.

The idea that a call for Mexican independence was a justified response to the fundamental injustice of the conquest not only was articulated in books and sermons but also became a mobilizing political theme. The fathers of Mexican independence, priests Miguel Hidalgo and Jose Maria Morelos, both regularly portrayed revolution as an indigenous reconquest or *reconquista* of Mexico. Hidalgo famously took up a banner of the Virgin of Guadalupe as the standard for the Mexican cause, forever linking her image to the Mexican nation. As he and other nationalists rejected the colonial designation of "New Spain," they adopted the Náhuatl term *Anáhuac* that originally referred to the valley of Mexico and the Aztec empire, using it to speak of all of Mexico. In 1813, Morelos convened the first Mexican congress, *el Congreso de Anáhuac*, at Chilpancingo, Guerrero, and asserted national independence from Spain. Connecting that declaration of Mexican independence to the Aztec/Mexica past, he solemnly pronounced to his fellow revolutionaries that nearly 300 years after the fall of Tenochtitlán, "We are about to re-establish the Mexican Empire."[7]

During the course of the wars for independence, Hidalgo and Morelos were both executed, and conservative *Criollos* with less enthusiasm for the Indigenous past carried the early independence movement forward. Still, *indigenismo* remained a powerful cultural idiom for the new nation. In the years before the war with the United States, the celebration of this nationalist heritage was carried from the nation's center to its farthest periphery.

In the far northern frontier, the *indigenista* spirit found expression as Mexican territorial governments were formed to replace Spanish colonial governance. In Alta California, the newly appointed Governor Jose Maria de Echeandia, fresh from central Mexico, attempted to link this northernmost region with the nation's Aztec patrimony. On July 7, 1827, Echeandia and the governing deputation he had assembled approved a plan to change the name of Alta California to that of the Aztec emperor Moctezuma. This renamed territory was to be given a coat of arms that would display "an olive and an oak tree on its sides and containing in its center the figure of a plumed Indian with bow and quiver crossing the straits of Anian."[8] The image of the crossing of the strait suggested that while the region was peripheral to the Valley of Mexico today, it was the site of the original passage of Indigenous peoples into the Americas and, as such, an important part of the nation's Indigenous heritage. By becoming an originary site of the Aztec/Mexica past, the formerly Spanish territory of California could become Mexican.

The deputation's plan was sent to Mexico City for approval, but there is no record of a response from the central Mexican government, nor is there evidence that the plan was greeted with any enthusiasm by the general population of California. By the end of Echeandia's brief tenure in 1831, residents of California had developed their own discrete regional identity as Californios, complicating their identity as Mexicans.[9] Less than twenty years later they would face even greater challenges to their identity as they experienced invasion and subjugation by Americans.

In their transformation of Mexico's North into the American Southwest, many Americans became very aware that owning place requires owning history. During the first three decades after the war, Americans cultivated an understanding of the Southwest that would eventually cohere into a powerful historical mythology connecting an idealized past to the American present. While this history was revolutionary in its adoption of Catholic Spanish colonizers as American forebears, it developed organically from the existing cultural rhetoric with which many Americans had made sense of the war with Mexico.

Prior to the war, the legacy of the Black Legend (a tradition of anti–Spanish Catholic propaganda dating back to the Reformation), resentments against large-scale Irish Catholic immigration, and simmering tensions within Protestant culture made the mid–nineteenth century a time of strong anti-Catholic prejudice in the United States. Yet, these prejudices coexisted with a "religiously nostalgic" undercurrent of Protestant enthusiasm for medieval Catholic history that only grew as the century went on.[10] While the contemporary presence of poor Catholic immigrants and the alleged machinations of "Romanism" were disparaged and considered threatening to American democracy, the imagined nobility and simplicity of the Catholic Middle Ages were seen as a romantic antithesis to the ills of modernity and industrialization.[11]

Ironically, this enthusiasm led nineteenth-century Americans to take advantage of the newly available speed and economy of steamship travel to tour the pre-modern monuments of Catholic Europe. These tourists regularly published travel accounts laden with admiration and envy for European antiquity that were devoured by eager readers back home. Americans longed for a weighty history of their own that would pull their center of cultural gravity from the Old World to the New, and the war with Mexico provided the opportunity to create just that.[12]

At the outbreak of the war, common American perceptions of Mexico as an ancient place replete with ruins encouraged a vision of American troops as gallant knights crusading in an exotic land. While the cult of chivalry was established most strongly among American southerners, it also fueled the imaginations of northerners; Nathaniel Hawthorne, for instance, saw "chivalrous beauty" and the "spirit of young knights" in the American soldiers preparing for duty in Mexico. The diaries of young American soldiers themselves also often displayed this romantic and nostalgic understanding of their role in the war.[13]

The timely publication of William H. Prescott's *History of the Conquest of Mexico* in 1843 provided American imaginations with a wildly popular script for conceptualizing the war. Prescott's positive depiction of the exploits of the Spanish conquistadors offered an alluring historical drama that American soldiers could reenact and make their own. Just as Prescott's Cortés was a civilizer of the "superstitious and barbaric" Aztecs in the 1520s, Americans saw themselves as a latter-day civilizing force in Mexico in the 1840s. They celebrated the fact that their fleet followed the path of Cortés's campaign, landing as he did on a Good Friday in Veracruz and tracing the same overland route to the Mexican capital. The American reading of the war as a replaying of the Spanish Conquest, even resulted in redefinitions of Mexico City and its built environment. Americans commonly referred to the city as "Montezuma's Capital" and its baroque colonial buildings as "the Halls of the Montezumas."[14] By referencing the Capital in this manner, the Huey Tlatoani's (Mexica/Aztec ruler) already misspelled name came to stand in for and de-historicize all Mexica/Aztec/Mexican political figures.

The equation of American soldiers with civilizing knights not only worked to lend a historical patina to the campaign against Mexico, it also served as a rhetorical defense of American wartime ethics by supporting American assumptions about the benevolence and honor of their army. One journalist wrote, "We rejoice less at the success of our army than at that chivalric generosity, that enlightened moderation, and fraternal beneficence which ally both officers and men to the best days of knighthood."[15] Emma Willard, a prolific historian and feminist reformer, enthusiastically echoed this sentiment in 1847, claiming that the American conquest of Mexico City was not carried out as that of "Carthage and other cities were by the Romans—to be destroyed, or to become the sport of petty tyrants and a lawless soldiery." Much of the nation agreed with Willard's assessment that American soldiers truly behaved like "knights of old" in their treatment of the vanquished Mexicans.[16]

During the occupation of Mexico City, officers of the U.S. Army established an exclusive social club that they named "The Aztec Club of 1847" in commemoration of their capture of "Montezuma's Capital." Its roster of original members reads like a *Who's Who* of American military history; among its 110 founders were Joseph Hooker, George McClellan, Philip Kearny, Pierre G.T. Beauregard, Robert E. Lee, and Ulysses S. Grant. After the withdrawal of the American forces from Mexico City in 1848, the Aztec Club was adjourned and during the Civil War its members divided ranks into the Confederate and Union armies. Remarkably, the club was revitalized in the 1870s, principally through the efforts of President Ulysses S. Grant and other northern Republicans. Their aim, in large part, was to promote camaraderie among the nation's military elite. After the divisiveness of the Civil War, the club provided its members with a neutral identity as heroic and "chivalrous" veterans of the campaign against Mexico.

On January 6, 1880, members of the Aztec Club gathered at Delmonico's restaurant in Manhattan for a fete in honor of their president, Major General Robert Patterson.[17] That evening, more than thirty years after the war, General Zealous Bates Tower paid tribute to the members' triumphs in Mexico. He told the assembled men,

Our own Poet historian, Prescott, with his vivid imagination, has portrayed in glowing colors the brilliant exploits of that Castilian Knight, who, with a handful of his followers, made the first conquest of Mexico. His history reads like a romance of olden days. Yet it tells a true tale of a most adventurous invasion of the Aztec Nation, which, in spite of its "*Noche Triste*," was in the end crowned with a success even now seemingly miraculous.

Our own army also had its nights of sadness, followed however by a glorious morning, whose light of splendor, like the "Sun of Austerlitz," bore upon its cheering rays that inspiration of valor that enforced victory, and planted our Nation's banner high above the Halls of the Montezumas.

Though there be no Prescott to make a romance of the history of its achievements, there are those who hold the opinion that, for boldness of

conception, and for daring and valorous execution, the second conquest
of Mexico was in no way surpassed by the first.[18]

Tower's speech clearly illustrates the importance of comparative
assessments in the construction of American historical mythology.
By envisioning themselves as following in the footsteps of the Spanish
conquistadors but besting their predecessors' martial skill and bravery,
Americans built up the glory of their achievements and the temporal
reach of their own history. The idea of an American "second conquest" of
Mexico not only made narrative sense of the Mexican-American War and
helped to reunify the American military after the Civil War, it also became
crucial in the development of southwestern regionalism. It held great
resonance for Americans who migrated to and settled in the territory
because it offered them a ready-made connection to the region's past.

As a result, when the Mexican *Norte* became the American
Southwest, the region's newly articulated history was patterned by the
wartime imagination; the binary Spanish/Aztec distinctions common
during the war became crucial to early definitions of place. As the
Americans played the role of latter-day conquistadors, the territory they
acquired was cast as the land of the defeated Aztecs. Indeed, Americans
understood much of the Southwest as an extension of Mesoamerica.
Rather than work to undermine the region's adoption into the United
States, however, this understanding reinforced comparisons and
imagined connections between Spanish and American conquests and
dominion over Mesoamerica.

Americans literally mapped Mesoamerica onto the southwestern ter-
rain. The American-made Disturnell Map, used to illustrate the new
political boundaries established by the Treaty of Guadalupe Hidalgo
(formally ending hostilities), tied the Southwest to Mesoamerica by
locating Aztlán, the mythic Aztec homeland, in present-day Utah.[19] But
this was only one of the many Aztláns that Americans located in the
early Southwest. A mining camp named Aztlán, for example, was considered as a possible site for the first capital of Arizona, but the honor
was instead conferred upon the town of Prescott, named after the influential historian himself.[20]

Both during and after the war, Americans were captivated by the
Indigenous architecture of the Southwest, especially by that which lay

in ruins. Places such as Pecos, Acoma, and Zuni were routinely taken to be locations of the ruins of Aztec civilization. In 1846, soldiers from General Kearny's army came upon a large adobe building near a settlement of Pima Indians and assumed that it was Montezuma's house or the "*Casa Montezuma*." Even common stones fired the imagination— Major William H. Emory reported that "about the ruins" he encountered on the Gila River lay "quantities of the fragments of agate and obsidian, the stone described by Prescott as that used by the Aztecs to cut out the hearts of their victims." Flawed but enthusiastic interpretations like these left their mark on the American Southwest by inspiring place names such as Aztec Ruins National Monument, Montezuma's Castle National Monument, and the latter's related Montezuma's Well.[21]

American excitement over southwestern "Mesoamerican" ruins did not do away with racism toward Amerindians and their ancestors who had built them. It did however, spur interest in determining the origins of Native American peoples and evaluating their cultural achievements. The American Ethnological Society eagerly read soldiers' travel accounts of Mexico and the Southwest at their meetings on the East Coast. While early ethnologists often accepted the soldiers' common conflation of Aztec and other Indigenous cultures, many argued against the grand portrayal of the Aztecs received from Prescott's *History*. Robert Wilson's *New History of the Conquest of Mexico* (1859), for example, was largely an effort to stem the influence of Prescott's epic depiction of the Aztecs. Writers such as Wilson, Lewis Morgan, and Adolph Bandelier all evinced a common sensibility, arguing that an Aztec civilization of the level described by Prescott and his Spanish sources was simply impossible given the "primitive" evolutionary state of Amerindian culture.[22]

William Gleeson, an Irish-American Catholic priest and historian serving in California, did not share these ethnologists' skepticism about the colonial Spanish clergy's accounts of Mesoamerican civilization. Nonetheless, Gleeson did hold the belief common to nineteenth-century ethnologists that the major accomplishments of Indigenous civilizations could be ascribed only to foreign influence.[23] He devoted half of his extensive *Catholic History of California* (1872) to the presentation of evidence that "Christianity was introduced into America by the Irish, on the Atlantic border, at or before the tenth century." Gleeson claimed that these Irishmen came to be known as the "Tolmecs" [sic] who were "the fountains or source whence were derived the knowledge and refinement enjoyed by [Indigenous peoples]." He believed that the mounds of Ohio, various ruins in the Southwest, and the Aztec empire itself were evidence of the westward proselytizing and civilizing campaign of these "Tolmec" [sic] Irishmen.[24]

Gleeson saw the lack of any permanent architecture built by California's Native American population as final proof for his thesis. He took this absence as evidence that, while Indigenous peoples may have crossed the Bering land bridge (across what is now the Bering Strait) from Asia into the western half of the Americas, civilization (and architecture) clearly came from the East.[25] However, California was far from an architectural *tabula rasa* when it was occupied by American troops. Although the wooden shelters of California's Indigenous population did not evoke the same interest or enthusiasm among Americans as the ruins of the southwestern deserts, the coastal chain of mission churches did.

In California, the presence of recognizably Spanish influences on the architectural landscape provided a rare opportunity for American settlers and developers. Here, they could lay claim to a domesticated version of the Old World, with "ancient" churches and balmy Mediterranean shores. In the minds of émigrés from the eastern United States, southern California's coast became an Iberian counterpoint to the traces of "Aztec" civilization read into the southwestern deserts.

The first decades of the American settlement of California centered largely in the North. These early years were defined by the Gold Rush and its attendant mass migration, the population boom in San Francisco, and the rise of a ruthlessly violent and xenophobic but also cosmopolitan culture.[26] Culturally and demographically, Southern California changed little in the first decade after the Mexican-American War; the few Americans living in Southern California during this period were largely southerners engaged in cattle ranching. But by the mid-1860s, migrations consisting largely of East Coast northerners from the Sierra Nevada gold fields into the region effected great changes and began the American appropriation of Southern California in earnest.[27]

Despite the initial foreignness of its *ranchos*, *presidios*, and Franciscan missions, the distinctiveness of Southern California's built environment was employed in the creation of a new regional history that re-defined the formerly Mexican region into a Spanish arcadia. This was accomplished largely thorough the production of a constellation of historical narratives that maintained wartime enthusiasm for Spanish history in order to valorize California's Spanish era over Native American "pre-history" and the recent Mexican past. Just as the Aztec Club encouraged unity among elite veterans through the promotion of a common past that adopted Spanish forebears and celebrated victory over Mexico, in Southern California northerners created a regional history that did the much the same; it accommodated both southerners and northerners as heirs of a Spanish past in opposition to Mexican elements in the present. In time, this retelling of California's history came to work powerfully and persuasively in the distinctions people made between one another, the stories Americans told themselves about the legitimacy of their presence in the region, and most enduringly in the way in which they created, controlled, and understood their lived environment.

Inventing California: Missions and Missionaries

The first description of California to reach general audiences in the United States was in Henry Dana's autobiographical adventure story *Two Years Before the Mast*, published in 1840. Although the novel's initial popularity was due to its captivating portrayal of life at sea, it continued to sell well for decades to a large audience of westward-traveling migrants eager for descriptions of California.

Dana's reader's first glimpse of California is of its architecture as visible from the deck of the aptly named American merchant ship, *The Pilgrim*, as it sails into the Santa Barbara Channel. Like those of most mid-nineteenth-century American visitors to California, Dana's assessments of secular adobe buildings were mostly critical, but he viewed the adobe mission with great enthusiasm. Over time, American fascination with the missions would grow dramatically, in part because the buildings were quick to ruin; it often took much less than one hundred years for the unfired adobe bricks to literally be undone by the elements. The rapid disintegration of these churches provided ripe material for American imaginations, as the ruins offered both historical solemnity and great interpretive possibilities.[28]

Santa Barbara's mission was built in 1815, the same year that Dana was born in Cambridge, Massachusetts. But, to the nineteen-year-old's eyes, "The Mission [was] a large and deserted looking place, the outbuildings going to ruin, and everything giving one the impression of decayed grandeur."[29] This alluring vision of decay became common to American narratives about the missions because it added an ethical dimension to their history, deepening the buildings' appeal. The fact that these "stately monuments" were falling into disrepair was taken by many Americans as an obvious sign of the moral failures of Mexican rule. Most commonly, the American apportionment of blame for their fall was carried out in critical commentaries about the Mexican authorities' secularization of the missions.

The term *secularization* refers to the process of raising a Catholic church from mission to parish status and replacing the regular clergy of the founding religious order (e.g., Jesuits or Franciscans) with secular (diocesan) clergy. While secularization was a regular occurrence in the development of parishes in colonial Mexico, its implementation was often politically motivated. The Spanish Crown held much greater influence over the national church through its control of the election of Spanish bishops than it did over the powerful and independent religious orders. From the first decades of the colonization of Mexico in the sixteenth century until Mexican independence in 1821, the Spanish Crown vied with missionary orders, most notably the Franciscans and the Jesuits, for authority and temporal power in the New World. Thus, the secularization of mission churches offered the Crown a mechanism for curbing the strength of the religious orders.[30]

In 1749, King Ferdinand VI of Spain ordered a large-scale campaign to secularize all missions under his dominion in the New World. This edict was followed by the expulsion of the Jesuit order from the Spanish empire in 1767 and a series of other reforms limiting the privileges of the clergy. As a result, the power and influence of the religious orders declined, and the nature of missionization in the final years of the Spanish Empire in the Americas was permanently transformed. Under these new policies, secularization came to connote the establishment of tax-paying settlements and the transfer of authority over Indian neophytes from ecclesiastical to civil authorities.[31]

Initially, the missions of Alta California had been founded largely to defend the Spanish frontier against Russian and British incursions.[32] As the last major Spanish missionization effort after the institution of Ferdinand's secularization reforms, their future was clouded from the first. The document that ordered their establishment, the *Reglamento De La Nueva California* (1773), also contained the orders for their prompt secularization and transfer to civil rule.[33] The secularization of the missions of Alta California began in earnest in the early 1830s, shortly after Mexican independence in 1821 and the founding of the last mission in California's chain, San Francisco Solano, in 1824.[34]

Dana first saw Santa Barbara's mission only a few months after it had been secularized, inviting him to offer an American evaluation of the role of Mexican "misrule" in the "tragedy" of secularization. Dana wrote,

> Ever since the independence of Mexico, the missions have been going down; until at last a law was passed, stripping them of all their possessions, and confining the priests to their spiritual duties; and at the same time declaring all the Indians free and independent *Rancheros*. The change in the condition of the Indians was, as might be supposed, only nominal; they were virtually slaves, as much as they ever were. But in the Missions the change was complete. The priests have now no power, except in their religious character, and the great possessions of the missions are given over to be preyed upon by the harpies of the civil power. . . . The change had been made but a few years before our arrival upon the coast, yet in that short time the trade was greatly diminished, credit impaired, and the venerable missions going rapidly to decay.[35]

Dana's writing is remarkable as a statement of both reproach and regret about the decline of Catholic order in Mexican California by a Harvard-educated Protestant New Englander. Here, he manages to draw from the Black Legend, his own observations about the harsh realities of mission life faced by Native American neophytes, and contempt for Mexican civil authority to simultaneously cast aspersions on the clergy as slaveholders and still empathize with them and their churches as "victims" of Mexican rule.

Dana's reading of the decline of the missions became a powerful and influential model for later American authors. Early American reviews of the Franciscans' interactions with Native Americans at the missions were mixed, but even authors who, like Dana, were appalled at their treatment saw the secularization of the missions as a terrible crime. Those with a more sympathetic view of the priests saw secularization as an even more heinous act. For example, a decade later, during the war with Mexico, Joseph Revere, a grandson of Paul Revere, described the secularization of the missions in much the same way as Dana had, but he also bemoaned the loss of the influence of the Catholic clergy upon the indigenous population. In his wartime diary, *A Tour of Duty in California* (1848), he wrote,

> Upon a small elevation at no great distance, we saw the ruined towers of an old church, and also some walls built of adobe, which had evidently enclosed extensive and commodious buildings, now fallen into utter decay. This was the ancient mission of Carmel, which in common with all the other missions, had been suppressed by an act of the Mexican Congress for reasons which I am unable to disclose.
>
> This consecrated spot, so long the abode of holy men, is now the property of a private person, and has fairly "gone to grass." Whether the surrounding Indians are any the worse Christians, or the more trouble-some neighbors, may be easily guessed by those who know that Catholic missionaries exert a more wholesome influence over the aborigines than any others.[36]

Positive assessments of the Franciscan missionaries, like Revere's, became increasingly common after the war as the missions were adopted as American ruins by settlers and tourists. The fact that the 1869 (and subsequent) editions of Dana's book revised his numerous references to the mission Indians as slaves to the more neutral term *serfs* is telling of changes in late-nineteenth-century American attitudes toward California's early Catholic missionaries.[37]

As romantic American portrayals of the Spanish Franciscans and their missions proliferated, animus toward the Mexican implementation of secularization grew in direct proportion. This trend accelerated, and by the 1870s American authors in California commonly portrayed the missions and missionaries in positive terms, praising their paternalism toward the Indians and damning the effects of "greedy" Mexican secularization.

These tropes formed the basis of a genre of mission history that has remained immensely popular and influential for well over a century. An early example of this literature is Elizabeth Hughes's *The California of the Padres; or Footprints of Ancient Communism*, published in 1875. In standard form, Hughes praised the mission system by telling her readers, "The Indians had all their wants supplied, and lived in peace and plenty," and bemoaned the fact that the missions' endowment, the California Pious Fund, was taken by the "hungry office-seekers and politicians" of the Mexican government. Further, "as the Fathers lost their influence on the community . . . everything went into decay."[38]

Hughes's book is noteworthy for its clear division of California's colonizers along secular and religious lines. In a move away from the military glamour of Prescott's *History*, she wrote,

> Who were [California's] conquerors? Ask Cortez. No, the proud Spaniard turns away humiliated. In the serene mansions of the just made perfect, shall we invoke the benignant presence of [Padres] Salva Tierra [*sic*] and Ugarte.[39]

She praised "our friends the padres" for achieving this conquest "in the face of the greatest difficulties, not so much by power of force as by the feminine power of love and inspiration."[40]

Like many authors after her, Hughes would clearly ascribe negative aspects of Spanish colonization to secular greed and idealize the religious altruism of the padres as the valuable and instructive historical legacy that Americans should claim. Unlike the military Spanish conquest of Mexico, the Spanish conquest of California was imagined as a spiritual conquest. This refinement of the American understanding of Spanish colonization had great historiographic implications. Just as the American "second conquest" of Mexico City was understood as having been carried out benevolently by gallant soldiers following the model of Cortés, the American conquest of California was portrayed as an echo of a Spanish Franciscan conquest—that is, as a legitimate, peaceful, and inevitable progressive transition toward greater civility, industry, and piety.

The elevation of the padres' motives and methods over those of the conquistadors offered a resolution to the tensions that were present in earlier, more negative assessments of the missionaries. While Dana and others saw the padres ambivalently, as both slaveholders and victims, forty years later Hughes would defend them as civilizers against those who "sneer at their treatment of the Indians." She did this through comparisons of the Native Americans' lot in the missions and under American rule to show that Americans were in no moral position to judge the padres. Hughes rhetorically asked, "[A]re the Indians any better off to-day, lying around the streets of Los Angeles like masterless dogs, and half of the time in the calaboose or the chain gang? There are races that seem never to rise beyond childhood and need wise training."[41]

Negative depictions of Native Americans were commonplace in the nineteenth century, but the promotion of Catholic priests in heroic terms was a delicate matter in times when anti-Catholic sentiments were commonplace in American culture. Like other early American promoters of California's mission history, Hughes felt compelled to reassure her largely Protestant audience that she was "no advocate of Romanism" and, without critical self-reflection about her racist views of Native Americans, urged that "we have to free ourselves of all prejudice, even against Romanism."[42]

While Hughes and other Protestants played a large part in the early popularization of the missions and the padres, influential Catholics also contributed to the reinvention of California's past. Among the most significant of these contributors was Santa Barbara's leading citizen, José de la Guerra y Noriega. A Spanish-born military leader and businessman, de la Guerra was also a very devout Catholic with tight bonds to the Franciscans of California's missions. As a result of his lasting friendship with the priests and his financial acumen, he was entrusted with the position of *sidico* or financial custodian of the entire mission chain of Alta California. He managed both the distribution of wealth among the missions and commercial trade between the missions and American merchants.[43]

One of the most memorable vignettes in Dana's *Two Years Before the Mast* is the description of the wedding of de la Guerra's daughter Anita to Alfred Robinson, the wealthy and well-connected commercial agent for *The Pilgrim*, the merchant brig on which Dana served. Through this new familial connection to Robinson, de la Guerra gained an opportunity to influence the institutional development of postwar Catholicism in California and, by extension, the attitudes of American Catholics toward California's past.[44]

As a businessman originally from New England and a wealthy convert to Catholicism, Alfred Robinson had made the acquaintance of John Hughes, the bishop of New York. In 1848, at Robinson's recommendation, Bishop Hughes wrote to de la Guerra inquiring about "the status of religion in that territory annexed to the United States."[45] The naïveté evinced in Bishop Hughes's questions (e.g., "Is there a resident Bishop in California?") and the fact that his query was directed to de la Guerra instead of to the local clergy are telling of the gulf that existed between the American and Mexican Catholic churches at the time.

The first bishop of the Californias, Francisco Garcia Diego y Moreno, had died in 1846, just prior to the Mexican-American War, leaving the bishop's seat vacant.[46] De la Guerra encouraged Bishop Hughes to promote the election of a Spanish-born bishop, claiming that "the Catholics of this country are almost all Spanish-American, with whom the Spaniards are in sympathy."[47] De la Guerra's recommendation is remarkable because as a peninsular Spaniard he had considerable first-hand experience of the animus many Mexican *Criollos* and Californios felt toward the Spanish.

Although the Mexican War of Independence had changed his citizenship from Spanish to Mexican, anti-Spanish sentiments after the war had cost de la Guerra a seat in the Mexican National Congress and had nearly forced his expulsion from Mexico.[48] During the Mexican-American War, but before the American victory, de la Guerra renounced his allegiance to Mexico and was returned his Spanish citizenship by the Spanish Vice Consul, Cesareo Lataillade (another son-in-law), in Santa Barbara.[49] As a result, de la Guerra became one of the very few Spanish-Americans in California following the American conquest. While mid-nineteenth-century Americans sometimes blurred distinctions between Spanish and Mexican peoples, these ascriptions mattered a great deal in postcolonial Latin America. Thus, it is unlikely that de la Guerra's advice to Hughes was a matter of simple mistranslation or miscommunication but rather should be read as a deliberate attempt to influence the future character of the Catholic Church in California.

Bishop Hughes took de la Guerra's suggestion and actively promoted the election of a Spanish-born priest as bishop of the Californias. Bishop Michael O'Connor of Pittsburgh spoke out against de la
Guerra's advice, telling his peers that he doubted the wisdom of send-
ing a bishop with Spanish blood among Mexicans who had no love
for Spain. The post was initially offered to Charles Pious Montgomery, but he declined it. Ultimately, the majority of American bishops
agreed with the assertion of Bishop James Van de Velde of Chicago
that there should be few complications from the appointment of a
Spanish bishop because California was now American and appointment would be made by the American Catholic Church and not by
Spain. In May 1850, Joseph Sadoc Alemany, a Catalan priest serving in
Ohio, was named bishop of the Californias. Initially, his see extended
into Mexico, to the tip of the Baja California peninsula to the south,
and over most of present-day Utah to the east.[50]

The selection of a Spanish-American bishop had profound consequences for the development of American views of California's Catholic past. In many ways, Bishop Alemany's Spanish-American identity
formed a bridge between the idealized Spanish padres and the contemporary American Catholic Church. The bishop's first concern upon
his arrival in California in 1850 was the assessment and gathering of
resources for the building up of his dioceses' infrastructure. The sale of
the missions' lands by the Mexican government after secularization had
left many former church buildings in private hands; like many Americans, Bishop Alemany argued strongly against the legitimacy of these
transactions. One of Alemany's first acts as bishop was to petition the
U.S. government for the return of the missions from their "illegitimate"
owners, and, in time, President Abraham Lincoln signed legislation
that did exactly that.[51]

While the appropriation of the missions marked a relatively
easy victory for Alemany, a second goal, the acquisition of the
missions' endowment, proved a more elusive prize. The Pious Fund
of the Californias was established in 1697 by wealthy Spanish donors
promoting the Jesuit missionization of Baja California, but it was also
used to establish the Franciscan missions of Alta California. With the
expulsion of the Jesuits from New Spain in 1767, the administration of
the Pious Fund was transferred first to the Spanish colonial government

and, after independence, to the Mexican government. The Fund consisted of both gold coin and profitable ranches, but because of post-independence political turmoil, successive Mexican administrations came to rely on "loans" from its considerable assets. By 1842, Mexican President Antonio López de Santa Ana had completely incorporated the Pious Fund into his government's coffers, ending all Mexican support for California's missions.[52]

In 1853, Bishop Alemany traveled to Mexico City and "demanded . . . that satisfaction be made to our church in California, that as successor to Bishop Garcia Diego, I justly demanded for my own missions and for my Church what Mexico owed from the Pious Fund to my diocese; and that they should cease also to oppose my administration in Lower California."[53] The Mexican response was predictably cool, reminding the bishop that the Church in California was no longer actively pursuing the conversion of pagans, the stated purpose of the Fund. That same year, a petition from the Mexican Church to the Vatican for the division of the bishopric of the Californias was honored, and Alemany's see was divided along national lines, ending his jurisdiction in Mexico.

Upon his return to the United States from this disappointing trip, Alemany sought the counsel of attorney John Thomas Doyle to assess the possibility of legal recourse against the government of Mexico for the recovery of the Pious Fund. However, because of the legal complexity of making claims against the Mexican government after the war, it wasn't until 1870 that the case was brought before the Mixed American and Mexican Claims Commission in Washington, D.C.[54] The Pious Fund Case put American historiography on trial. Both Doyle, representing California's Catholic bishops, and Manuel Azpiroz, the counsel for the Mexican government, were avid historians, and the case proceeded slowly as each side presented competing interpretations of reams of colonial documents and receipts. It took five years of deliberations for the case to be resolved.[55]

The final opinion of Manuel de Zamacona, the Mexican claims commissioner co-presiding in the case, was a strong critique of Doyle's presentation of a standard American reading of California's history. He argued that the American interpretation was flawed because it rested on two fallacies. The first was that Americans wrongly believed the missionary work supported by the fund was a strictly religious undertaking. This belief was incorrect because it did not recognize

> the religious means used by the Spanish Government to colonize and extend its dominions. Without bearing in mind this undeniable fact, we run the risk of regarding the conquest and colonization of the Spanish Americas, as a merely spiritual work in which the political power of the monarchs of Spain becomes eclipsed behind the activity and apostical zeal of the Missionaries . . . [and that] the undertaking of the first missionaries in California was more of an affair of the Government than of the Church; that the persons of whom donations were obtained, made them for establishments already founded, for the principal and known purpose of continuing and consolidating the Spanish conquests in the north-western part of Mexico.[56]

However, de Zamacona acknowledged that the American reading was understandable because the duality of functions inherent in Spanish colonization efforts

> cannot be easily understood by those who profess and practice the religious theory which recognizes Christ only, as the head of the Church; but in some Catholic and monarchical countries in the eighteenth century, there was, besides the visible head represented by the pope, a certain ecclesiastical and spiritual authority vested in the temporal sovereigns.[57]

In other words, he believed that nineteenth-century American Protestants espousing the separation of church and state would have a rather difficult time understanding the nature of colonization in Catholic New Spain.

The second supposed fallacy he cited was that the American Catholic claimants believed they were heirs to the Pious Fund, which had served to secure the Mexican frontier. He argued that the American Catholic Church did not constitute a legitimate successor to the Mexican Church in California precisely because it inherited its position as a result of the war with Mexico. He argued that the Spanish as well as the Mexican Catholic Church were of a national character; from which it follows that even if it be proved that the Missions of California, their endowment and administration were within the sphere of the Church, it could not be claimed, as these claimants insist, that the present American Catholic Church of Upper California is the heir and successor of the Mexican Catholic Church.[58]

However, William H. Wadsworth, the American commissioner, supported Doyle's case and largely ignored the Mexican counselor's arguments in his rather brief final opinion.[59] Unsurprisingly, the fact that the case was heard by only the two commissioners meant that their decisions came down to a tie along national lines.

Sir Edward Thornton, Great Britain's ambassador to the United States, was asked to act as umpire and cast a tie-breaking opinion. The case was re-argued, and in November 1875 Thornton sided with the American commissioner in favor of the American Catholic Church. The net amount awarded to Alemany's archdiocese was $904,070 (Mexican gold dollars), which the Mexican government paid in full over thirteen years.[60] However, in 1902 the issue of unpaid interest on the Fund was brought before the Arbitration Tribunal of The Hague, and Mexico was once again made liable for payment, this time in the amount of $43,050.99 in Mexican pesos to be paid annually in perpetuity.[61]

While the financial award was an important gain for the coffers of the American Catholic Church in California, the Pious Fund Case had a broader impact by further securing the two "historical fallacies" cited by de Zamacona into the American understanding of the history of the missions. It had now been established, with the authority of an international tribunal, that California's Spanish missionaries were pious men whose deeds and ambitions were wholly religious and distinct from those of the Spanish and Mexican civil authorities. Moreover, the American Catholic Church (and by extension all Americans in California) could see themselves as legitimate heirs to the Spanish missionary project after a dark period of decay under Mexican rule. The fact that the Pious Fund Case coincided closely with the one hundredth anniversaries of many of the missions provided the opportunity to publicly circulate these newly endorsed versions of California's history.

The 1877 centennial celebration of the founding of Mission Saint Francis de Asis (better known as San Francisco's Mission Dolores) was the first to occur after the Pious Fund Case was settled. It was a grand affair that attracted a crowd of more than 5,000 people, including such dignitaries as California's governor (the "president of the day") and the Mexican, Spanish, Russian, Portuguese, Chilean, and Costa Rican consuls. The presence of civil and religious dignitaries as well as a large Protestant showing among the celebrants speaks to the broad appeal and importance that the history of the missions and the padres already held for Californians at the time.[62]

Archbishop Alemany opened the festivities with a speech honoring the missions' founders. After providing numerous examples of the protection and instruction of Native Americans by priests in the Americas, he cited Prescott's depiction of Queen Isabella as the "Indians' excellent friend and protector" as final proof of the benevolence of the Franciscans' conquest of California. Alemany presented the Spanish conquest of California as the inheritance of Americans by telling his audience,

> Well may California be proud of her heroic disinterested Christian pioneers, who in a short time transformed numberless barbarous tribes into comparatively well-civilized Christian communities; and well may we echo to-day with sweet strains of joyous melody the solemn Te Deum intoned here for the first time one Hundred years ago.[63]

By establishing the Franciscans as California's pioneers, with no reference to lay Spanish or Mexican settlers, Alemany reiterated the argument that California's conquest had been a strictly religious one. By doing so he was able to make a more powerful and less contentious claim to his audience about the legitimate succession of the American Catholic Church to the missionary fields of the early Franciscans.

Alemany's oration was followed by a poem written by Miss Harriet M. Skidmore and recited by B. P. Oliver. Skidmore's poetic tribute to the missions is noteworthy for its division of their history into the pattern that supported a vision of a spiritual or moral renewal of California by Americans. Rhetorically this historical narrative became "a drama of the triumph of good over evil, of virtue over vice, of light over darkness."[64]

It ascribed ethical values to divisions of time—a glorious beginning was posited, this falls victim to criminal neglect, and is followed by a final period that marks a triumphal return to the original state of grace or virtue. Skidmore follows this tripartite romantic form perfectly, beginning with an image of admirable piety among mission neophytes:

> Within the rude adobe shrine,
> What holy calmness dwelt!
> How fervent was the Savage throng
> That round its altar knelt!
> How lowly bowed the dusky brows
> When, through the sunset glow,
> Rang out the sweet-toned Angelus,
> One hundred years ago!

This turns into a period of decline due to secularization,

> Pure Eden-like simplicity,
> Forever passed away!
> For o'er the Missions came at last,
> A fierce tyrannic sway—
> A sacrilegious hand could dare
> To strike with savage blow,
> The band that brought Salvation's boon
> One hundred years ago!

Ultimately the American present is cast as a time of renewal and appreciation of the golden past:

> But we, who know how rich the gift
> The holy land bestowed
> Upon the land where stranger hosts
> Since made their fair abode—
> Aye, we who hail the beams of Faith,
> In radiant noonday glow,
> Will fondly bless the dawn that rose
> One hundred years ago![65]

Skidmore's poem distills the popular American narrative of California's mission history down to its basic elements. However, in order to become a compelling history, this "inherited" Catholic past had to belong to all Americans, most especially the Protestant majority.

The most well received, and lengthiest, speech of the celebration was given by John Dwinelle, who was an attorney, a historian, and a Protestant. His lecture provides insight into the curious ecumenism present in American versions of the missions' history. Dwinelle told the assembled celebrants that

> Precisely one hundred years ago, in the year 1769, the colonization of California had its beginning; but it was a religious, not a civil or political colonization; and its origin, aims and results are to be treated as the work of the Roman Catholic Church. As a Protestant, with my fellow Protestants, I come here not to sing fulsome praises to the Roman Catholic Church, but to render her a due meed of honor.[66]

This opening statement displays the principal elements of the rhetorical strategy employed by Protestants to overcome any incongruities that might be perceived in their celebration of the Catholic missions' history. The most problematic of these was the elaboration of a positive stance toward Catholicism. Dwinelle's "meed of honor" to the Catholic Church bears quoting at length. He began,

> A hundred years ago how feeble was the Catholic Church in the United States! To-day how strong she is—strongest among the strong. A hundred years ago proscribed, her name a reproach! To-day, proud in the consciousness of her strength, her children are free to ask for everything—to receive it. They can be legislators, Governors, Senators and Judges: one of them was chief justice of the Supreme Court for twenty five years. . . . Where is she stronger at this day than in the United States? Where are her foundations broader, deeper, more solid? Where are her hospitals, her convents, her colleges, her churches in a more flourishing condition? . . . I believe that the Roman Catholics of California are more than compensated for all they have lost, in having their political destinies brought within the circle of the American Union. . . . Protestant as I am, I am not afraid to say that I rejoice in the strength and

prosperity of the Holy Apostolic Roman Catholic Church; and that when I predict that a hundred years from now she will be stronger than ever, and that her greatest strength will be in the United States, it is because my heart goes with the prediction; and when I consider that she has been the mother of all modern civilization, and the foster-mother of all free political institutions, I devoutly invoke the Almighty God that this great empire of freemen may empty into her lap the Horn of Plenty in its widest abundance.[67]

Dwinelle went beyond Elizabeth Hughes's defensive aspersions on prejudices against "Romanism" and cast Catholic history and Catholics as unquestionably American. Here, Catholic history becomes American history. In this remarkable speech, the United States is presented as the modern center of the Catholic world.

Having quickly resolved the problematic relationship between Catholicism and Protestantism in the United States, Dwinelle was free to employ the crucial narrative element for Americans: the repetitive insistence on the religious character of the original conquest of California. Dwinelle reiterated that "the colonization of California was not civil, but religious. Its plan was not so much to bring citizens into California, as it was to convert the native savages of California into Christians. . . . The religious character of this colonization is most emphatically and accurately described [by the] Hon. Alpheus Felch, one of the first judges on the United States Land Commission in California."[68]

Dwinelle's reliance on an American Land Commissioner as an authority on the nature of the Spanish colonization and conquest of California is quite revealing of what was at stake. With the establishment of the original colonization of California as a religious enterprise, the legitimacy of the presence of Mexican settlers who were not members of the clergy was undermined. In this schema, just as it was for early Mexican *indigenista* clergy, what ties one to territory and place is a religious connection.

Dwinelle underscored the connections between Americans and the Franciscans by painting the padres as industrious and refined men who might feel at home in upper-class American social clubs. He claimed that "the Franciscan Friars, who superintended these establishments, most of whom were from Spain, and many of them highly cultivated men, statesmen, diplomatists, soldiers, engineers, artists, lawyers, merchants, and physicians, before they became Franciscans, always treated the neophyte Indians with the most paternal kindness."[69] In contrast he claimed that Californio merchants could be "characterized by the exuberance of their noses, their addiction to the social game called monté, and the utter fearlessness with which they encountered the monster aguardiente." Motivated by "rancor and greed," these private traders "were both constant and persistent in their denunciations of the monks who had charge of the Missions."[70]

The implications of Dwinelle's presentation are made clear through his condemnation of the Mexican government's "theft" of the Pious Fund and the Californios' "criminal" secularization of the missions. If the original conquest of California was religious and Mexican settlers' culpability in the decline of religion was obvious in the secularization and decay of the missions, then Mexican civil society could be seen as both illegitimate and morally bankrupt. For Americans, their own conquest and occupation of California became legitimate precisely because they esteemed and valued the missions' presumed singular purpose and history.

Dwinelle ended his speech to great fanfare and an ovation by a very enthusiastic audience. After the applause and cheers of Americans had subsided, an aged Mariano Vallejo stepped up to the podium to provide an alternate view of the missions' history. After a tribute to the efforts of the Franciscan missionaries, he mounted a defense of Mexican civil authorities that turned the tables on the American historical presentations of the day and obliquely criticized the American conquest of Mexican California. Pausing after his discussion of the merits of the Franciscans, he said,

And, now, permit me to make a few remarks in defense of the good name of some of the individuals who governed this country during the Mexican Administration, whose reputation has been sometimes wantonly attacked; while nothing has ever been said against the Governors, under Spain who preceded them. . . . That the Mexican Governors robbed the Missions is an absurdity. . . . Castro, Gutierrez, Chico, Alvarado, Micheltorena, and lastly Pio Pico, all had to contend with revolutionary elements. The priests had disappeared, the neophytes had left the Missions and had gone away to the villages of the gentiles, and the government, under such circumstances, had to take possession of the lands which were claimed by the Missions, through the power which it possessed, and in order to defend the country against an *invasion with which it was threatened.*[71]

In short, Vallejo blamed the negative effects of the secularization of the missions on the American invasion of California. He argued that if not for the war, then perhaps the missions and their lands would not have been auctioned for proceeds to support the defense of the territory from hostile American invaders.

At base, Vallejo's most damaging assertion against the history presented by Americans was a denunciation of the idea that the colonization of California was strictly religious. He pointed out that

it is necessary to bear in mind that the Spanish flag waved over California, and that the priests did no more than comply with the orders of the King, at the same time that they looked for their own protection and that of the Missions, soldiers being constantly engaged in protecting the Missions, and in continuous campaigns for the purpose of keeping the Indians under subjection. Without those soldiers, the Indians would have risen immediately against the Missions, and all the white inhabitants would have inevitably perished.[72]

Vallejo held that, the opinion of Americans and their land commissioners aside, a strictly religious conquest could not have occurred and indeed did not.

Doubtless his American audience would have been given a great deal to think about had they understood Vallejo, but he delivered his comments in Spanish without a translator.[73] There is no record of a response from Bishop Alemany or any other Spanish speakers in attendance. While disregarding Mexican views of history, the English-speaking audience politely applauded his concluding remarks and admired the poise and dignity of the old "Don" as he left the stage.

Tragedy and Nostalgia: The Californios

Despite esteem for some elite Californios, such as Mariano Vallejo, American appraisals of California's Mexican population during and after the conquest were generally negative. The worst aspersions were cast on the region's Native Americans, commonly referred to as "Digger Indians," an appellation that implied a complete lack of civilization. However, Mexican *gente de razón*, the Californios, were also seen as fundamentally flawed and tragic individuals who were destined to pass away with the advent of a new, more vibrant American order.

Even Alfred Robinson, de la Guerra's son-in-law, who had renounced American citizenship in order to do business in Mexican California, wrote in 1846 that "the early Californians, having lived a life of indolence without any aspiration beyond the requirement of the day, naturally fell behind their more energetic successors."[74] Americans arriving after Robinson saw things in much the same light.

The trope of "indolence" became a centerpiece for American commentary on the Californios. Edwin Bryant's wartime impressions of life in Mexican California in *What I Saw in California (1846–47)* is rather standard in the form of its critique. He wrote,

> The whites are in general robust, healthy and well made . . . but most of them are entirely indolent, it being very rare for any individual to strive to augment their fortune. Dancing, horse riding, and gambling occupy all their time. The arts are entirely unknown and I am doubtful if there is one individual who exercises any trade; very few who understand the first rudiments of letters and the other sciences are unknown amongst them.[75]

Nevertheless, Bryant, like many young American bachelors writing early American accounts of the region, praised the energy and beauty of Californio women. These positive assessments were generally commensurate with social class, as these writers were often taken aback by poorer Mexican women's lack of "proper" decorum. Alternating between warmly admiring and cooler ethnographic tones, Bryant wrote,

> This beautiful species is without a doubt the most active and laborious, all their vigilance in the duties of the house, the cleanliness of the children, and their attention to their husbands, dedicating all of their leisure moments to some sort of occupation that may be useful towards their

maintenance. Their clothing is always clean and decent, nakedness being entirely unknown among either sex.[76]

Admiration for the domestic industry of disenfranchised Mexican women, however, often provided a comparative framework for criticizing Californio men, defining them as less capable and industrious than their "weaker" female counterparts.

While indolence among Californio men was often perceived as the root of other morally reprehensible habits such as gambling, dancing, and drinking, after the American conquest it was seen more broadly as a reason for the perceived failures of the Mexican era and the secularization of the missions. Consider the vehement statement against Californio culture made by William Redmond Ryan in his account of life in California during the early Gold Rush:

> For a space of nearly two centuries, the degenerated Spanish Race had held the whole country, never dreaming of its value, nor in their sluggishness, deeming the improvement and development of its resources possible. Though a people as eminently qualified by nature in every respect as their Anglo-Saxon conquerors, to aid the general cause of progress, their efforts have been confined to procuring the mere necessities of existence, to an indulgence in the enjoyments of a semi-savage life, and to a complete abandonment to the practices of some of the worst vices of civilization. . . . So engrossed were they in these pursuits—the majority of them frivolous—that it was not to be wondered that their missions and towns should gradually go deserted, and fall into ruins; at once a standing reproach to the people, for their negligence and effeminacy, and to the Mexican government, for its supineness, its reckless, narrow-minded policy, and its injustice. In the hands of any other people, these missions might have been made the legitimate instruments of improving the population, and of ministering no less to their physical necessities than to their spiritual requirements.[77]

By portraying the Mexican period as a time of idleness and frivolity, Americans could cast the Californios historically as only temporal placeholders, awaiting the arrival of their industrious "Anglo-Saxon conquerors" who would cultivate and make proper use of the land.

Charles Loring Brace in *New West: Or California 1867–1868* took this interpretation a step further, claiming not only that it was inevitable that the Californios, in their negligence and recklessness, would lose their land but that it should be taken away from them by any means necessary:

> The immense energy and restless impulse of the Yankee population are gradually but surely driving out the old Spaniards from their ill-farmed or neglected properties. It is rare anywhere in California that you pass a thrifty, well-kept farm, and hear that it is a Spaniard's or a Mexican's. As a general thing the Spanish owner has gambled, or drunk, or otherwise wasted his property, or has been passed by his neighbors in competition, or has lost large portions of his ranch by sharp legal practice among the Yankees. On a broad view, it is better for the whole country that his wide, half-cultivated, or abandoned farm should be broken up, even by an oppressive legislation; and, undoubtedly, his own original title was often hardly more equitable or legal than that of the [American] squatters on his neglected acres.[78]

Thus, the ends of American settlement warranted the means of confiscation of Californio lands. The trope of Latin indolence not only worked to justify American possession of the land, it also helped to define the Californios as a people hopelessly governed by irrepressible desires (to drink, to *siesta*, to gamble, etc.). This meant that the Californios were often cast as fundamentally flawed figures for whom tragedy was inevitable. From the beginning of the war this interpretation of the Californios became popular with American authors. However, most compelling to their American audiences were the stories of those Californios who attempted to live up to the American ideals of industriousness and honor but who nonetheless fell victim to their terrible fate.

Joseph Revere provided the first written example of this genre in an episode in *A Tour of Duty in California* (1848). Revere claims that "The Story of Ramon and Dolores" was recounted to him by Ramon's mother while he stayed as a guest in their camp on the Russian River. He tells his readers that he includes this story because it "has some bearing on the gambling customs of the Californians," but the narrative reads more deeply as an early American statement of the tragic nature of the Californio and is, therefore, worth recounting in detail.

Ramon Sepulveda, the youngest boy of a family of nine, labored hard to support his widowed mother and siblings on their rancho. His elder brothers, on the other hand, "though handsome and dashing fellows enough, and brave besides, as well as excellent vaqueros and skillful rancheros, were reckless gamblers, and thriftless in their management" of the family's property. They would often gamble away in one week a year's earnings to the "avaricious foreigners," the Americans, who "enrich[ed] themselves by administering to [the] evil passions" of the Californios, and encouraged their certain ruin. When his brothers gambled away his favorite horse, Ramon had had enough. He asked the beautiful Dolores to marry him and move out to the untamed Russian River to live in peace away from his reckless brothers. Ramon and Dolores built an adobe and lived happily for a few years raising two children. Then, inevitably, tragedy struck. A band of Californios went "into Ramon's neighborhood, ostensibly to catch horse-thieves, but really to obtain servants by capturing Indians." They attacked a Native American settlement, killing many women and children, but failed to capture any male servants. The Indians later gave way to "their outraged feelings, took vengeance on the settlers in the neighborhood, who had indeed no connection with the marauders, but were sacrificed . . . to atone for the guilty crimes of their compatriots." In the subsequent massacre, Ramon's innocent wife and children were killed. "General [Mariano] Vallejo was at that time *Comandante General*. He raised a party and, with Ramon, visited this scene of terrible disaster. They attacked the savages, and wreaked a most awful vengeance; but Ramon's cattle had all been driven away, and all the bodies of his little family lay buried in the blackened ruins of his once happy home. Poor, poor Ramon! Bereft at a single blow of wife, children, and property . . . [he was] not the blithe and frolicsome young cavalier he was before his sad bereavement. He [had] grown pensive and melancholy."[79]

Thus, even Ramon, a Californio who worked hard to live honorably, became a victim of his brothers' weaknesses and was consumed by the violence that surrounded him.

Shortly after the war, in 1854, a darker and even more violent portrayal of a tragic Californio appeared. *The Life and Adventures of Joaquín Murieta, the Celebrated California Bandit* by Yellow Bird (John Rollin Ridge) was inspired by contemporary stories of social bandits whose acts were conflated and attributed to a single Joaquin. Ridge's depiction of Joaquin was similar to Ramon's story in that his Murieta was, initially, a "mild and peaceable" young man. Just as Ramon left his paternal *rancho* because of his brothers' moral failings, the fictional Murieta left his birthplace of Sonora, Mexico, "disgusted by his degenerate countrymen." Furthermore, Murieta wanted to "try his fortunes among the American people, of whom he had formed the most favorable opinion . . . and [he was] fired with enthusiastic admiration of the American character."[80] However, he would soon discover that California

> was then full of lawless and desperate men, who bore the name of Americans but failed to support the honor and dignity of that title. . . . A band of these lawless men, having the brute power to do as they pleased, visited Joaquin's house and peremptorily bid him to leave his claim as they would allow no Mexicans to work in that region.[81]

When Murieta resisted, he was beaten and tied up, and the Americans "ravished his mistress before his eyes. They left him, but the soul of the young man was darkened."[82] When Murieta's younger brother is falsely accused of a crime and lynched, his "character . . . changed, suddenly and irrevocably . . . [and] he declared to a friend that he would live henceforth for revenge and that his path would be marked with blood. Fearfully did he keep his promise."[83] The drama of the book centers on Murieta's career as a bandit leader, robbing and killing dozens of Americans before he is eventually shot down by a group of California Rangers.[84]

Within a few years of the initial publication of Yellow Bird's *Joaquín Murieta*, the story had taken on a life of its own. It very quickly became a powerful folktale, and different versions of the story were regularly published, each more bloody and popular than the last. Eventually, as we will see, the character of Joaquin was re-imagined, re-defined, and given a radically different new life in poetry. But this early tragic narrative form, evident in the early story of Ramon and Dolores, and later refined in the legend of Joaquín Murieta and others like it, gained lasting popularity with American audiences for several reasons. First, the stories were lurid and dramatic romances that made for engaging, compelling reading. Second, this particular form of narrative allowed Americans to acknowledge their mistreatment of Californios and sympathize with them, but ultimately and inevitably to condemn them for the perceived frailty of their morals. Most of all, the immense popularity of these narratives reinforced the American understanding of Californios as a tragic people to whom bad things happened; some may have been indolent, some may have been violent, some may have tried to make a place for themselves in the new American order, but they were all doomed to failure, destined to pass away.

By the 1870s, Americans were beginning to secure their political and economic control of California, and most Californios who had been adults during the American conquest were entering middle or advanced age. As the Californios began to gray, American attitudes toward them changed dramatically; Americans began to see them less as obstacles to "progress" and more as picturesque historical characters.

Hubert Howe Bancroft saw that time was running out for the aged leaders of Californio society and that they were valuable resources for documenting the history of California. Throughout the 1870s, he hired agents to record the reminiscences of sixty-two leading Californios to provide him with material that would help to reconstruct the Mexican era for his monumental *History of California*. Although these documents themselves never received wide readership, the Californios' nostalgic portrayal of their past deeply influenced the tone of Bancroft's *History*.

The process of recounting their memoirs encouraged Californio elites to reimagine their past as an aristocratic golden era.[85] As the settlement of Southern California began to be actively promoted in the East, the Californios' nostalgic conception of their past became increasingly attractive and useful to Americans. It soon became crucial to the articulation of an alluring regional identity that emphasized luxury and affluence. The trope of carefree indolence began to take on a more positive cast as the lost wealth of the Californios was exaggerated and paired with utopian versions of the history of the missions. As a result, California became more and more clearly a "Spanish Arcadia."

This was a definition of place that was most actively promoted by those who stood to gain the most from it: land developers and rail companies.

Coda

The early history of the United States' annexation of northern Mexico, and specifically Alta California, illuminates a number of important facets of the cultural transformation of the region. It shows the dialogic interrelation of narratives of conquest and reconquest common in expressions of regionalism and nationalism in both the United States and Mexico, and it demonstrates how a variety of means, from the literary to the legal, were employed to codify American views of the missions' historical record and purpose. Moreover, it gives us an understanding of how emergent postwar cultures made use of nostalgic and tragic tropes in the creation of new social orders. These elements provide a rich field from which to begin to theorize interconnections between emerging forms of civic life, racial distinctions, and religious practices in the region.

As we have seen, the appropriation of place requires the creation of legitimizing myths and symbols that support new ways of conceiving of local history. It is often the case, and it was certainly true in California, that while inventive, these new histories are informed by extant ways of viewing the past. Just as *indigenista* rhetoric and Marian imagery celebrating an anticolonial reconquest helped to constitute early Mexican nationalism, in the United States the concept of Americans "following in Spanish footsteps" became a common and lasting way of understanding the nation's first foreign war, the acquisition of great tracts of land, and acts of aggression against ethnic Mexicans and Indigenous peoples.

The idea of Americans' re-playing Spanish Catholic history, originating as it did in the midst of mid-nineteenth-century nativism, was deeply interwoven with the logic of Manifest Destiny. Initially, claims of repeating the glorious military conquests of the past provided a sense of providential inevitability to martial successes. In subsequent decades, however, claims that Americans' annexation of California constituted a peaceful spiritual conquest provided a morally attractive narrative of missionary enterprise to those same victories. This transition from the language of military conquest to that of spiritual conquest is central to understanding the process of legitimization of the appropriation and invention of Southern California as an American region. The organizing principle for this rhetorical transition was the sustained American critique of the secularization of the missions under Mexican rule.

Just as declension narratives gave shape to Americans' understanding of Puritan culture in the East, the secularization of the missions provided a story of spiritual declension in the West. Remarkably, in the late nineteenth century Americans in California began to lay the groundwork for Spanish Franciscans to become the Puritans' historical analogues in the West. Even through the gulf of denominational and cultural difference, many Americans were able to see themselves as participating in a moral and civic revival through their appropriation and valorization of the Spanish Franciscan colonial past.

As we will see, this sense of continuity between the Spanish colonial past and the American present has framed dominant forms of civic life in the region for generations. Civic life is in essence participation in the creation and maintenance of one's community. As such, it requires individuals to recognize themselves as part of a larger social fabric and history. In the wake of the conquest and demographic transformation of California, not all peoples saw these emerging civic narratives as congruent with their understanding of history or the experiences of their communities. In this plural postwar society, multiple forms of civic life existed side by side, vying with but also informing one another. While some Californio elites actively participated in the creation of dominant forms of postwar civic life, for most Californios it was the war with the United States itself, not the secularization of the missions, that marked the most significant historical moment of social decline.

In the aftermath of the war, the remaining population of Californios native to the territory was bolstered by the arrival of Mexican miners drawn across the new national border by the Gold Rush. As a result of these migrations, the ethnic Mexican population in California was larger in the second half of the nineteenth century than it had been under Mexican rule. Thus, even as Americans manufactured expressions of ownership of place, they did so among an expanding ethnic Mexican population, which predictably resulted in increased racial and ethnic tensions. However, racism is rarely simple in its essentialist logic; it is sometimes explicitly critical and sometimes romantic. All at once, American writers cast the Californios as indolent and fabulously wealthy; they were astoundingly generous in some accounts, and in others their supposed greed was directly responsible for the collapse of the missions.

In a similarly unstable fashion, early ethnic ascriptions of Spanish and Mexican identity were often used interchangeably. However, distinctions between the two nomenclatures came into increasingly sharp focus as processes of racialization took their course, in part because of the nature of the historical project underlying postwar American civic life, which relied on a semantic divide between historical Spanish colonials and contemporary Mexican "foreigners." Moreover, racial, regional, and ethnic differences created by Mexicans themselves coexisted with American distinctions, resulting in overlapping hierarchies and forms of privilege and oppression.

Given the central role of mission history in the creation of California's regional identity, religion has provided one of the principal forums in which new configurations of civic life and racial/ethnic differences have been articulated. As demonstrated, shortly after the peak of mid-nineteenth-century anti-Catholicism, the emerging popularity of the colonial past fostered enthusiastic expressions of ecumenism among many American Protestants. However, this ecumenical spirit relied on logic that presumed an American recuperation of Spain's colonial project. The victory of the American Catholic Church in the Pious Fund Case deeply inculcated the idea of continuity between the original work of the missions' founders and American settlement. This historical bridge between colonial and postwar California went far in suppressing the history of American military conquest and bolstered the Americans' presentation of themselves as following in the "footsteps of the padres" in the far West.

2

Building a Region

"But Alessandro," cried Ramona, "why do you think it is not safe there, if Ysidro has the paper? I thought a paper made it all right."

"I don't know," replied Alessandro. "Perhaps it may be; but I have got the feeling now that nothing will be of any use against the Americans. I don't believe they will mind the paper."

"They didn't mind the papers that the Señora had for all that land of hers they took away," said Ramona, thoughtfully. "But Felipe said that was because Pio Pico was a bad man, and he gave away lands he had no right to give away."
—Helen Hunt Jackson, *Ramona*, Chapter XVI

It is not too boastful to say that we revere these venerable piles and would preserve them as landmarks reared by the brave pioneers of a new era of progress upon these shores. They represent an energy as forceful, a courage as unfaltering, a devotion as true as that manifested by the Puritan Fathers upon the bleak and unhospitable shores of New England; and here, now, at their shrine, do the forces of these two distinct civilizations meet and clasp hands in one common love of country. And we owe it to the past, to have the brave, heroic conquering force of these old padres that these missions be preserved. Their bells, calling to worship may be partially hushed, and the paths once trodden by thousands of the brown children of early days may become partially obliterated by orchards, towns, cities, railways and factories; but we shall never fail to reap the benefits arising from that mighty onslaught upon superstition, and the victory commemorated by the hoary walls of these crumbling missions. They tell a story of the past as nothing else can tell it today, and account for their restoration and preservation.
—Benjamin Truman, *The Missions of California*, 1903

"Isn't Semi-Tropical California a Wonderful Country?"

During the first decades after the Mexican-American War, California, the westernmost state in the American Union, remained isolated as an "Island on the Land."[1] Hundreds of miles of hostile deserts, mountain ranges, and "Indian Territory" separated it from the other states; the nation's bifurcated geography set the American East apart from its newly conquered West. The lure of the Gold Rush provided many Americans with a strong incentive to make the long journey to California by sea, or even more arduously by land across the continent, but large-scale American settlement in the state did not begin in earnest until after the Civil War.

Specifically, American migration to California began to accelerate with the completion of the transcontinental railroad in 1869. However, the Pacific Rail Acts of 1862 and 1864, which authorized its construction, specified that the rail's route was to run north of the Mason-Dixon line; California's first connection to the East would bypass the South.[2] This feature of the first coast-to-coast rail line had profound consequences for the demographic and cultural transformation of California, as Pullman cars brought northeasterners and European immigrants in greater and greater numbers to the West Coast.[3]

In the early 1870s, the Southern Pacific Railroad began to connect the terminus of the Central Pacific's cross-country rail line in Sacramento to settlements in Southern California, sparking a series of land booms; as the rail line made its way southward to Los Angeles, the price of property rose dramatically. Even the hint of rail access resulted in a boom; while the railroad did not arrive in Santa Barbara until 1887, promises that the town would have its own spur initially raised land prices as much as tenfold from 1870 to 1873.[4] Economic depressions during the 1870s and 1880s meant that boom times were quickly followed by cycles of busts, but selling California land nonetheless proved to be a lucrative enterprise. Overall, property values rose just as the ownership of most of the region's acreage changed hands from bankrupt Californio ranchers to American squatters, speculators, bankers, and rail companies.[5]

With the lure of the Gold Rush diminished, the marketability of California's real estate and attraction of tourists was dependent upon the state's image being carefully crafted as that of a desirable destination.

Beginning in the late 1860s, the Central and Southern Pacific rail companies mobilized considerable resources for the promotion of travel to and settlement in California. Agents were hired to write commercial literature, give lectures, and create exhibits, all advocating settlement and tourism. Life in California was portrayed as a cure-all for the woes of Americans and Europeans, be they related to ill health, financial misfortune, or crowded urban environments. Of the scores of railroad-financed promoters of California in the nineteenth century, by far the most prolific and influential were Charles Nordhoff and Benjamin Truman.[6]

Both writers began their employment with the Southern Pacific Railroad Company after garnering strong reputations as pro-Union newspaper journalists during and after the Civil War.[7] Nordhoff's *California for Health, Pleasure and Residence* (1872) and Truman's *California for Health, Pleasure and Profit* (1894) mark the beginning and end, respectively, of the genre of early California booster literature. The small but significant difference in the books' titles speaks to the success of promotional literature in transforming the state during the twenty years between their respective dates of publication; by the last decade of the nineteenth century, commerce and trade were flourishing in California as a result of the tide of migration that they and other promotional agents had helped to engender.

The greatest obstacle that boosters faced was the common preconception of California as a place of "big beets and pumpkins, of rough miners, of pistols and bowie-knives, abundant fruit, queer wines, high prices—full of discomforts, and abounding in dangers to the peaceful traveler."[8] They set about changing the region's coarse image by painting idyllic portraits of its agricultural fertility, scenic beauty, and colonial history. Principally, the natural feature most celebrated by early boosters was California's healthful climate.

Truman's first promotional monograph, *Semi-tropical California: Its Climate, Healthfulness, Productiveness, and Scenery* (1874), targeted health seekers from New England who sought warmer climes for the treatment of various respiratory diseases. He argued that California's moderate dry warmth made it a much more salubrious destination than the Caribbean or the South with their oppressive, humid heat. Lamenting easterners' hesitations to travel to California, he wrote,

If the eastern invalids—those who go to Cuba or Florida in the winter, to return to their homes in the spring, to die; or who make long and tedious journeys to the Mediterranean Sea, merely to coquette with death—could be made acquainted with the remarkable climate of Los Angeles, its charming equitability and rare healthfulness, how many hundreds of lives might be spared yearly, how many delicate constitutions might be made strong forever.[9]

The late nineteenth century saw the birth of an entire genre of popular medical literature dedicated to discussions of the benefits of California's "Mediterranean" or "semi-tropical" climes.[10] Even as Southern California's climate became one of its greatest selling points, boosters had to address the apprehensions of prospective tourists and settlers about the potential dangers of a "semi-tropical" climate. For northeasterners, residence in hot climates held connotations of savagery and a possible degeneration of American vitality into idle laziness. Boosters responded to New Englanders' climatological concerns by asserting that

California is our own; and it is the first tropical land which our race has thoroughly mastered and made itself at home in. There, and there only, on this planet, the traveler and resident may enjoy the delights of the tropics, without their penalties; a mild climate, not enervating, but healthful and health restoring; a wonderfully and variously productive soil, without tropical malaria; the greatest scenery, with perfect serenity and comfort in traveling arrangements; strange customs, but neither lawlessness nor semi-barbarism.[11]

Thus, the promotion of California's warmer climate as mild and beneficial often served to evoke images of the place as enticingly exotic but at the same time domesticated and safe.

While climate played a key role in promotion, boosters still had to work to address concerns about the character of society in the far West. Truman reprinted his 1875 jailhouse interview with Tiburcio Vasquez, thought to be the last of the Mexican social bandits in California, in *Occidental Sketches* (1881), a collection of vignettes about life in the West commissioned by rail baron Charles Crocker. The execution of Vasquez, "one of the bloodiest scoundrels of the century," was intended to reassure readers that the days of banditry in California had been dramatically ended.[12] Still, lurid accounts of frontier justice were not the most effective means of casting the state in a civilized light. Rather than call attention to crime in the West, a more successful strategy was found in the comparative assessment of life in California with city life in the East. The influx of impoverished immigrants in eastern cities provided western boosters with the opportunity to rhetorically invert the frontier, casting the East as a place of unassimilated barbarism and the West as a haven for true American civility. Nordhoff, for instance, advised his East Coast readership that California has "less of a frontier population than you in New York." He asked the eastern person

> to reflect for a moment upon the fact that New York receives a constant supply of the rudest, least civilized populations; that of the immigrants landed at Castle Garden, the neediest, least thrifty and energetic, and the most vicious remain in New York, while the ablest and most valuable fly rapidly westward; and that, besides this, New York has a necessarily large population of native adventurers; while on the other hand, California has a settled and permanent population of doubly picked men.[13]

Presaging the later arguments of eugenicists in California, Nordhoff cast migration to the West in Darwinian terms; natural selection ensured that the most able and intelligent from the Old World were drawn toward the opportunities of life in California. "Lighting out West" became testimony to an individual's vitality, ambition, and hardiness. In this influential scheme, "doubly picked" westerners became the most admirable of all Americans. Nordhoff, himself a Prussian immigrant, invited native-born and immigrant Americans "of the best sort" to live safely, healthfully, and happily among their kind in California.[14]

However, during the decade after the Civil War, lingering regional animosities meant that for northeasterners, some Americans were less desirable neighbors than others. As mentioned previously, the largest populations of Americans to migrate to Southern California after the Mexican-American War, but before the rails arrived there, were southeasterners. Nordhoff warned his audience in New England that "Los Angeles became, during and after the late war, a stronghold of Southern men; and it attracted a considerable number of a class known all over California as 'Pikes.' These are, in fact, the migratory Southern poor whites," but the rhetorical purpose of his warning was to invite assurances that the "Pikes" were on their way out.[15] While in actual fact southeasterners were not generally leaving California, Nordhoff portrayed the passing of the "Pikes" before the advance of Yankee civilization as "inevitable" as the earlier passing of the Indians and Mexicans. In the early 1870s, both Nordhoff and Truman celebrated the railroad as

> the great civilizer of the age. It not only quiets the Indians—it drives off the Pikes. They are selling out cheap and emigrating by scores to Arizona; and if you were here right now you might buy town lots and farms at very moderate prices, from men who "don't mean to live near no railroad—not if they know it."[16]

Southern cattlemen were described as indigent, "gypsy-like" wanderers moving "from place to place, as the humor seizes [them] . . . generally an injury to his neighbors. [They] will not work regularly . . . but [are] always ready for a lawsuit."[17]

Although Southern California's first railroad was financed in part by John S. Griffin, a wealthy southern secessionist in Los Angeles, Nordhoff nevertheless reported that

> the Pikes, poor and rich, are panic-struck. They are getting ready to leave [California] before the railroad shall utterly ruin it. And they are wise. Their empire is gone . . . all over the great plain south of Visalia, and in the foot-hills, and even down near the shores of the great Tulare Lake, you see little boxes of houses standing far apart, the signs of small farmers who have chosen each his one hundred and sixty acres, and who will no longer be worried and bullied by the [Pike] cattle owners.[18]

Thus, Southern California's transition from a cattle ranching economy to a settled and fenced agricultural one was presented as a reassuring sign of the exodus of undesirable southeasterners. Like many other promoters and developers during the 1870s, Nordhoff founded in Southern California his own agricultural colony that he named after himself. The growing presence of successful colonies of settled small family farms like his was taken as a sign of the end of the days of the free-ranging "Pikes" and evidence that California's rougher days lay behind it.

Depictions of the rise of small-scale farming also served as epitaphs for the cattle ranching Californios. In stark contrast to characterizations of southeasterners' poverty and hostility, rail boosters exaggerated the former wealth and hospitality of the Californios, giving Southern California a golden aristocratic past. Truman went so far as to claim that "the landed estates of European noblemen sink into insignificance, when compared with some of the ranchos of semi-tropical California."[19] But, the wealth attributed to the Californios was greater than the value of their lands or the gold from their trade in cattle—it was the inestimable wealth of happiness, luxury, and a life of ease. After his first visit to an "Old Californian Rancho," and hearing the nostalgic tales of its owner, "Señor M.," Nordhoff concluded that

> the old Californians were, so far as merely material existence is concerned, perhaps the happiest people who ever lived upon the face of the earth. They were few in number in a country of inexhaustible natural wealth; the climate enabled them to live out-of-doors all the year round, and made exercise a pleasure, for it is neither too warm [n]or too cold at any season. . . . Poverty was unknown, for he who was poor lived with his rich relations; their houses were always open to everyone. . . . Indians were their servants, and cheaply did their drudgery. Illness they did not know, nor doctor's bills.[20]

Imaginative re-tellings of life on the *ranchos*, like Nordhoff's, powerfully depicted life in the state as genteel and civilized. Boosters were determined that California not be seen as part of the wild western frontier but rather as a settled place with a history as long and romantic as that of New England or even Europe.

While a "semi-tropical" climate and great agricultural bounty provided the scenic backdrop, Indian labor was a key element in the romantic portrayals of the Californios' life of ease. Nordhoff reported that on the few remaining great *ranchos* near San Bernardino, "the farm laborers are chiefly Indians. These people, of whom California still has several thousand, are a very useful class. . . . I found that it was thought a great advantage for a man to 'have' Indians."[21] Lest his readers misunderstand his possessive description and think of the Indian workers as slaves, he added the caveat that "you must understand that in California parlance a man 'has' Indians, but he 'is in' sheep, or cattle, or horses."[22] Thus, the earliest American settlers continued racialized labor patterns in California emulating the "good life" of the Californios by also "having" a supply of "tolerably steady, and very useful, and indispensable laborers."[23]

Although California entered the Union in 1850 as a free state, "apprenticeship laws" passed the same year legalized a form of involuntary servitude for Indian children. Moreover, in 1860 the Act for the Government and Protection of Indians increased the duration of "apprentices'" servitude and allowed for the indenturing of adults. These laws were repealed in 1863, but by then as many as 10,000 Native American adults and children had already been forced to work in California's gold and agricultural fields. Although the Thirteenth Amendment had made slavery illegal in the United States in 1865, vagrancy laws, the perils of absolute homelessness, and routine kidnappings all ensured that a steady supply of Native American laborers continued to be available to California's landed classes, be they Americans or Californios, Republican Abolitionists or Democratic Secessionists.[24] An 1865 editorial in the *California Police Gazette* maintained, "Slavery exists in California in precisely the same condition that it did until lately in the southern States. There the blacks were slaves; here in almost every county Indians are unlawfully held as chattels." This claim was echoed a year later, in 1866, when California's Commissioner for Indian Affairs reported that the purchase of slaves, especially Indian children, was not uncommon in California.[25]

In spite of public discussions of the poor conditions of the Indigenous population, the occlusion of California's "peculiar institution" by boosters was largely accomplished by presenting their labor as the legacy of the benevolent missionizing efforts of the Franciscan padres. Although Nordhoff had written passionately as an abolitionist during the Civil War, in 1872 he told readers that the "California Indians were . . . a race pre-ordained to subjection, which [the padres] had aimed to make useful to the ruling race, and no doubt, as they piously thought, fit for heaven."[26] By portraying conversion as fair grounds for subjugation, Nordhoff could avoid direct equations of California's history of (religious) forced Indigenous labor with (economic) southern slavery.[27] By the mid-1870s, California's Indigenous population was in such drastic decline that boosters were able to portray them as sad relics of California's past that would not grow "to the stature of men of our century."[28]

Because the paternalistic Franciscan missions were seen as having ensured the well-being of the Indians, and the fall of the mission system was seen as a result of Mexican "misrule," blame for the poor contemporary condition of the Indigenous population could be placed squarely on the shoulders of ethnic Mexican elites. In spite of the common hyperbole of boosters' accounts of the aristocratic lives of the Californios, invariably their economic and political decline was still explained as a consequence of their tragic lack of "the energy and ingenuity of civilized life." Nordhoff told his readers, "It was a happy life they led—these old Californians. But it did not belong to the nineteenth century, and the railroad will, in a year or two, leave no vestige of it this side of the Mexican border."[29] In their place the rails brought Yankee settlers who were assured by boosters that their great "industry and zeal" would allow them to reap even greater rewards from California's natural bounty than their presumed-to-be-flawed Indigenous and Californio predecessors.[30]

As political and economic power shifted into the hands of the growing population of American settlers, the region's urban environments were quickly and dramatically re-defined. Old adobe buildings were torn down and more typically American wooden ones were put up, giving Southern California's towns a new appearance. Writing in 1874, Truman enthusiastically described this change, telling his readers that when he

> first visited Los Angeles in 1867, crooked, ungraded, unpaved streets; low, lean, rickety, adobe houses, with flat asphaltum roofs, and here and there an indolent native, hugging the inside of a blanket, or burying his head in a gigantic watermelon, were the, then, most notable features of this quondam Mexican town. But a wonderful change has come over the spirit of its dream, and Los Angeles is at present—at least to a great extent—an American city. Adobes have given way to elegant and

substantial dwellings and stores; the customs of well-regulated society have proved to be destructive elements in opposition to lawlessness and crime; industry and enterprise have now usurped the place of indolence and unproductiveness.[31]

Similarly, an 1875 essay in the *Santa Barbara Weekly* newspaper commended that community's complete metamorphosis, claiming that,

A year ago, the low, red-tiled adobes, the streets straying round in the most bewildering manner, the rough, wild-looking Mexicans galloping by, the strange sights which met me at every turn, all made me question whether I had not been transferred to Spain or Italy. Santa Barbara has now emerged from this transitional state[;] she is no longer a Spanish, but an American town.[32]

These transformations of California's urban environments were mirrored by architectural changes in the missions. The necessary restoration of decaying mission buildings offered a chance to add Americanizing features to some of the churches' façades, patterning them after New England churches. Priests at Mission San Juan Bautista hired newly arrived carpenters from the East Coast to modernize their church with a New England steeple and belfry in 1865.[33] Similar but more extensive renovations were begun at Mission San Luis Obispo in 1868, resulting in a complete makeover of the entire front of the church by 1880: A New England steeple was added, the red roof tiles were removed, and the structure was covered with wooden clapboard siding. Even more dramatically, when Mission San José was damaged in an earthquake in 1868, the original adobe structure was completely leveled and a wooden Gothic-style church was built over the colonial foundation.[34]

The Americanization of mission architecture did not reflect any dampening of enthusiasm for the Spanish Franciscans and the missions themselves. Rather, it was a concrete expression of the American appropriation of the Spanish colonial past. As we have seen, Americans on the Pacific coast began to claim a Franciscan heritage that they understood as comparable in many ways to that of the Atlantic coast Puritans. By the 1870s, Californians felt secure enough about the American-ness of the padres and their missions to employ them as romantic emblems of the far West. In 1876, the Los Angeles Chamber of Commerce sent Truman to the Centennial Celebration of the Declaration of Independence in Philadelphia to advertise Southern California. There, at this most American of celebrations, the California exhibit proudly represented the state's past through a collection of picturesque watercolors of the Catholic missions.[35]

Boosters also began to cast the Spanish Franciscans (generally solid monarchists) as great fans of the leaders of the American Revolution. Truman, for example, published a series of essays in the *Los Angeles Star* recounting early visits to the missions that attributed strong pro-American sentiments to the colonizing padres. He claimed to have met a very old woman at Mission Santa Clara who "told [him] that she distinctly remembered the time when the priests and soldiers of [her] young days unanimously espoused the cause of the [American] colonists, and that they prayed for the success of George Washington almost daily."[36] Similarly, he described a visit with Father Mut of Mission San Juan Capistrano in which the Spanish-born priest toasted to "the memory of a great man—Abraham Lincoln" and then showed Truman "an old record kept by Padre Gorgonio, dated San Juan Capistrano, May, 7, 1778, in which were these words: 'We prayed fervently last evening for the success of the colonists under one George Washington, because we believe their cause is just and that the Great Redeemer is on their side.'"[37]

In the late 1870s, Truman's writings about the padres began to mirror social changes occurring as a result of the end of southern Reconstruction (1865–77). As increasing numbers of southerners became customers for the western service provided by rail companies, Truman began to include prominent Confederates in his accounts of the padres' American heroes. Father Comapla, "a native of Vich, Spain" serving at Mission San Buenaventura, was credited with having engravings of George Washington, Stonewall Jackson, and Robert E. Lee on the walls of his study, "whom he looked upon, so he informed me, as great soldiers and good men."[38] However, in the context of the Southwest, Jackson and Lee were multivalent characters: They were more than just Confederate generals; they were also important figures in the "chivalrous" American occupation of Mexico City during the Mexican-American War. Thus, by portraying the padre as an admirer of the American conquerors of Mexico, Truman was able to do two things at once: to cast southeasterners as American heroes, while also reinforcing imagined historical connections between the Spanish and American conquerors of Mexico.

In Los Angeles, both during and after the Civil War, tensions between Unionists and Secessionists had regularly resulted in the cancellation of Fourth of July festivities. However, in 1876, the year that the Southern Pacific finally connected the city to the rest of the nation by rail, Los Angeles was largely under the political control of Republican northeasterners. These municipal leaders saw the nation's Centennial as an opportunity for a public celebration that would both unite the community and demonstrate loyalty to the nation.[39] The organizers of the celebration sought to turn attention away from the "late unpleasantness" of the Civil War, and like the Republicans who reestablished the Aztec Club, they did this by focusing on the triumph of the Mexican-American War, the war that had made California American.

Although the city was home to a fair number of Civil War veterans, the only veterans to march in the day's parade were those of the Mexican-American War. Following the performance of "Yankee Doodle Dandy," James G. Eastman, the official Orator of the Day, creatively followed the narrative conventions of the earlier war by connecting the history of the fall of the Aztec Empire with the day's celebration of the history of the United States. He began his address by telling his audience,

As the scepter was passing from the hands of the great Aztec monarch, it was given to him to see the future of this continent. The light of heaven's prophecy shone upon him, and, melting away the shackles of superstition, enabled him, through the vista of years, to see such a government as ours. He said: "The long, long cycles pass away; and age of battles intervenes and lo! There is a government whose motto is, 'Freedom and God!' Those words are dark to my understanding, but pass them down from generation to generation as a sacred tradition; for some time, with this motto, the people of this continent will take their place among the deathless nations of the earth." We are today celebrating the one-hundredth anniversary of the realization of Montezuma's prophecy.[40]

However, in a show of ethnic national pride, "Montezuma" was not the only Mexican forebear enlisted in the celebration of the American

Revolution. Californios themselves invoked the spirit of the late democratic reformer Mexican President Benito Juarez through the "fine display" presented by the carriages of the *Junta Patriotica de Juárez* in the parade. Significantly, Juarez was often presented in public functions by ethnic Mexicans as a Mexican analogue of Abraham Lincoln—as both had maintained the unity of their countries in the face of foreign invasion from France in Mexico and civil war in the United States. While Pio Pico, the last Mexican governor of California, was at best ambivalent about all things Yankee, his elegant hotel, the Pio Pico House, "led the van in the extent and elegance of adornment," most notably via a banner draped in front of the hotel displaying the sentiments of the organizers of the day. It read, "No North, No South, No East, No West. A Fourth of July for All."[41]

Ramonaland

On December 20, 1881, Helen Hunt Jackson made her way into the city of Los Angeles aboard a Southern Pacific Rail Pullman car. Local newspapers reported that the author was lodging at the Pio Pico House Hotel and had come to write a series of essays on the area for *The Century Magazine*.[42] But, in a relatively short span of time, Jackson's visit would result in much more. Her California writings would come to shape the way many Americans in Southern California understood and articulated their sense of place and region.

Prior to her arrival in the Los Angeles, Jackson was known for her poetry, children's stories, novels, and collections of European travel writings, but the year of her first trip to Los Angeles marked a significant turn in her literary career. That spring, she had published *A Century of Dishonor*, a historical work reprimanding Americans and the U.S. government for "a shameful record of broken treaties and unfulfilled promises" to Indian tribes. Her goal in writing the book was to appeal to the "heart and conscience of the American people" in order to redeem the country's name "from the stain of a century of dishonor."[43] The book did not achieve wide circulation, but Jackson took it upon herself to send every congressman a copy bound in blood-red cloth embossed with Benjamin Franklin's words to English Parliament, "Look upon your hands! They are stained with the blood of your relations."[44] In spite of her dramatic presentation, congressional response was muted and reviewers scolded the author for merely chronicling atrocities and offering no remedies to the "Indian problem."[45]

Having never publicly espoused any social issue, Jackson would have seemed an unlikely champion for Indian law reform. Nonetheless, in 1879, at the age of forty-nine, concern about American mistreatment of Native American tribes had become her obsession, and one that would last the rest of her life. Her passion for the issue was sparked at a rally in Boston for the cause of the Ponca tribe of Nebraska. Members of the tribe, described as having arrived in full "costume," recounted the ordeal of having had their lands wrongfully ceded to their enemies, the Sioux, by the U.S. government. They also told of their subsequent relocation to "Indian Territories" in present-day Oklahoma, where a third of their members had perished. When tribe members attempted to return to their original lands, they were arrested, and as the government weighed their case, they faced the prospect of homelessness and starvation in the harsh midwestern winter.[46] The Poncas' compelling story and the novelty of their physical appearance not only fired Jackson's moral indignation and curiosity, they also made their cause a popular one among a good number of reformers in New England; the Poncas' tour has been credited with greatly helping to expand the membership of fledgling women's home missionary groups such as the Indian Treaty-Keeping and Protective Association and the Connecticut Indian Association.[47]

Like these missionary reformers, Jackson saw conversion as the means to the Indians' spiritual as well as physical salvation. Most significantly, however, she strongly believed that "the great difficulty with the Indian Problem is not with the Indian, but with the Government and people of the United States."[48] As a result, her efforts at reform principally came in the form of moral critiques of the duplicity and cruelty of Americans, "made worse by murder, outrage and wrongs," that were typical of their dealings with Indians. She believed that until Americans and their government gave up the habit of "cheating, robbing, breaking promises" and refusing to legally defend "the Indian's rights of property, of life, liberty, and the pursuit of happiness . . . even Christianity can reap but small harvest."[49]

While Jackson had expressed little interest in California's Native American population during her previous visit to the state in 1872, by the time of the publication of *A Century of Dishonor* she was eager to investigate the condition of the Indians in the far West. *The Century's* commission for several illustrated articles on the state's old missions provided her with the perfect opportunity.[50] She did considerable research in the New York Public Library prior to her trip, immersing herself in writings about California and its history. Once in Los Angeles, she made use of letters of introduction collected from Catholic acquaintances in the East to meet the diocese's Bishop Mora. The bishop in turn introduced her to several aging Californios and priests at the missions who shaped her understanding of the state's past and its indigenous population.

At the time of her arrival, a distinct regional identity was just beginning to emerge there; a contemporary travel writer reported that residents of Los Angeles "call themselves, not Californians, but Southern Californians. The feeling is intense. I can only liken it to the overmastering love of the old Greek for the sunny shores that lay around the Aegean."[51] The "southern" designation spoke to cultural differences within the state and served to proudly bring Angelinos out from under the shadow of their more established San Franciscan counterparts. Quite significantly, Americans the state over had begun to claim the title of "Californian" that had previously been used to refer only to the native-born Mexican population.[52] It was this shift in ethnic ascription that finally marked those of Mexican decent as outsiders in American California. Los Angeles's ethnic Mexican population found itself outnumbered and segregated into "Sonora-town" (a common moniker for *barrios* that referred to Mexican miners arriving from Sonora during the Gold Rush). This appellation further reinforced the American understanding of the Mexican population as foreign to the region. Even native-born Californio elites such as former Governor Don Pio Pico were marginalized; while he was recognized as "a picturesque feature of the city," he lived in poverty, having lost title to the prominent hotel that still bore his name.[53]

Rail boosters in the 1870s attempted to lure settlers from the East to California with assurances about the region's transformation into a thoroughly American place. But, in counter to these marketing claims, in the 1880s Jackson found California's allure precisely in its pre-American past. In 1872, Nordhoff had praised Santa Barbara for having "the advantages of pleasant society. . . . [It is] a cozy nest of New England and Western New York people."[54] But, upon visiting in 1882, Jackson disliked the city for the very same features; she saw it as "too much like any one of a dozen New England towns—stodgy, smug, correct and uninteresting."[55] With the Americanization of the region well underway, and Californio political and economic power largely curbed, Jackson confidently led her readers to see Southern California's Spanish Catholic history as a fitting emblem for its developing regional character. Two of her *Century* essays in particular reflected this new attitude toward the past, one a description of Californios and Indians in Los Angeles, the other a history of California's Franciscans.

In 1883, *The Century* published Jackson's "Echoes in the City of the Angels," an essay that recounted the city's history and gave an "insider's" tour of the present-day remains of its Spanish and Mexican past. She wrote, "The city of the Angels is a prosperous city now . . . but it has not shaken off its past. A certain indefinable, delicious aroma from the old, ignorant, picturesque times lingers still, not only in its byways and corners, but in the very centres [*sic*] of its newest activities."[56]

"Echoes" was largely inspired by conversations with Antonio and Mariana Coronel, a Californio couple who provided a great deal of anecdotal material for Jackson's depictions of Southern California. She portrayed winning the couple's friendship as an entrée into the bygone world of the Californios, claiming that "Whoever has the fortune to pass as a friend the threshold of [the Coronels'] house finds himself transported, as [if] by a miracle, into the life of a half-century ago."[57] A great many American readers were intrigued by her display of those remnants of California's romantic past that still existed, hidden away behind closed doors. She claimed that a visitor could never

> know more of Los Angeles than its lovely outward semblances unless he have the good fortune to win past the barrier of proud, sensitive, tender reserve, behind which is hid the life of the few remaining survivors of the old Spanish and Mexican regime. Once past this, he gets glimpses of the same stintless hospitality and immeasurable courtesy which gave to the old Franciscan establishments a world-wide fame. . . . In houses whose doors seldom open to English speaking people, there are rooms full of relics of that fast-vanishing past,—strongholds also of a religious

faith, almost as obsolete, in its sort and degree, as are the garments of the aged creatures who are peacefully resting their last days on its support.[58]

Jackson seduced her readers with the implication that if they hurried out to California, they too might catch a glimpse of what remained of its exotic Latin Catholic past. In a very real sense, she showed that the pre-modern romance that had attracted American tourists to Catholic Europe could also be found in a domesticated form in America's far West.

The year 1883 also saw *The Century*'s publication of Jackson's "Father Junipero and His Work," a biographical essay about the life of Father Junipero Serra (1713–84), the Franciscan charged with the establishment of Alta California's chain of missions.[59] Hers was the first American hagiographic treatment of Serra to be read widely outside of California, and it soon became very influential; shortly after its publication, Little, Brown and Co. began reprinting the article for use in public schools and continued to do so until 1902.[60]

Jackson's own enthusiasm for California's Spanish Franciscan missionaries was, perhaps, surprising given that she had been brought up in a strict Congregationalist family in Amherst, Massachusetts, and her depictions of Catholic clergy in earlier European travel writings had often been negative.[61] However, in "Father Junipero and His Work" Jackson made a crucial distinction between Catholics in general and members of the Franciscan order in particular. Citing a Protestant biographer of St. Francis, she claimed that the Franciscans, like their order's patron saint, were motivated by a Christian selflessness so great that "Cardinals and Pope alike doubted its being within the possibility of human possibility."[62] By stressing the missionaries' Franciscan identity over their Catholic one, she made a distinction that helped to make them and their history broadly palatable to many Protestant Americans with less charitable attitudes toward Roman Catholicism.

Although Jackson drew most of her factual material from a translation of Francisco Palou's 1781 Spanish biography of Serra, her narrative portrayal of the missionary and his fellow Franciscans was a very American one as it condemned the Mexican secularization of the missions and bemoaned the churches' decayed condition. She called for efforts at restoration, remonstrating "both the Catholic Church and the state of California" for allowing Mission Carmel, the site of Father Serra's grave, to "be left to crumble away."[63] She denounced this neglect as a shameful lack of respect for the Franciscans' selfless spiritual conquest of California and their civilizing influence upon the Indians.

Most notably, Jackson went even further than most of her predecessors by favorably comparing California's past with that of the Atlantic seaboard. She told her national audience:

> There was a strange difference, fifty years ago, between the atmosphere of life on the east and west sides of the American continent: On the Atlantic shore, the descendants of the Puritans, weighed down by serious purpose, half grudging the time for their staid yearly Thanksgiving, and driving the Indians further and further into the wilderness every year, fighting and killing them; on the sunny Pacific shore, the merry people of Mexican and Spanish blood, troubling themselves about nothing, dancing away whole days and nights like children, while their priests were gathering the Indians by thousands into communities and feeding and teaching them.[64]

Thus, Jackson's idealized portrayal of the Franciscans greatly served her reformist cause; it provided her with the means to articulate a moral indictment of her fellow Americans for their treatment of the present-day Indian population. While earlier reformers in California had contrasted the image of the pious Franciscans with the absolute lawlessness of American prospectors and early settlers, Jackson was the first nationally read author to cast the Spanish Catholic missionaries as moral exemplars for all American "decedents of the Puritans." Citing historian John Dwinelle, she admonished her readers:

> If we ask where are now the thirty thousand Christianized Indians who once enjoyed the beneficence and created the wealth of the twenty-one Catholic missions of California, and then contemplate the most wretched of all want of systems which has surrounded them under our own government, we shall not withhold our admiration for those good and devoted men who, with such wisdom, sagacity, and self sacrifice,

reared these wonderful institutions in the wilderness of California. They at least would have preserved these Indian races if they had been left to pursue unmolested their work of pious beneficence.[65]

With her articles for the *The Century* completed, Jackson began a letter-writing campaign to Henry M. Teller, the U.S. Secretary of the Interior, resulting in her appointment as Special Agent to the Commissioner of Indian Affairs in Washington. She was asked "to visit the Mission Indians of California, and ascertain the location and conditions of the various bands . . . and what, if any, lands should be purchased for their use."[66] At the time of her appointment, she had made the acquaintance of Abbot Kinney, a wealthy real estate developer who shared her concern about the Indians in California. She requested that Kinney be commissioned as well, principally by citing his knowledge of California's land laws and his ability to serve as a Spanish language interpreter.

Their co-written "Report on the condition and needs of the Mission Indians of California" included a number of specific recommendations for governmental action for the betterment of the Indians' situation. However, Jackson and Kinney felt very ambivalently about the prospects for California's Indians. Like many Americans in California, they saw Indigenous peoples as doomed. They were convinced that those who had perished early from the predations of Mexicans and Americans were better off than the lost souls who were left alive to suffer. However, they also believed that their countrymen needed to make amends for the wrongs they had committed. They wrote:

> With every year of [American] neglect the difficulties have increased and the wrongs have been multiplied, until now it is, humanly speaking, impossible to render [the Indians a] full measure of justice. All that is left in our power is to make them some atonement. Fortunately for them, their numbers have greatly diminished. Suffering, hunger, disease, and vice have cut down more than half of their numbers in the last thirty years; but the remnant is worth saving.[67]

After fulfilling her assignment, Jackson concluded that her best recourse was to go beyond petitions to the government and appeal directly to the moral conscience of the American people. With the experience of the weak reception of *A Century of Dishonor*, she also knew that she needed to "sugar" her reformist "pill" for it to be at all effective. She decided to "write a novel, in which will be set forth some Indian experiences in a way to move peoples' hearts . . . [because] people will read a novel when they will not read serious books."[68] Jackson's immersion in Southern California's history and culture had provided her with a wealth of powerful material with which to appeal for reform. In December 1883, she returned to New York City, intent on writing "the *Uncle Tom's Cabin* of the Indians." She wrote to a friend, "If I can do one hundredth part for the Indian that Mrs. [Harriet Beecher] Stowe did for the Negro, I will be thankful the rest of my life."[69] In less than a year, she had produced *Ramona*, one of the most popular novels of its time.

The simplicity of *Ramona*'s narrative is its greatest strength. Ramona, a Cinderella-like character, is an adopted half-Indian, half-Scottish woman raised by a cold, pious stepmother, Señora Moreno. The Señora attempts to thwart Ramona's developing love affair with Alessandro, an Indian ranch hand, but the lovers escape and marry. As a result of Yankee prejudice against their Indian blood, Ramona and Alessandro face numerous trials and tragedies: Americans drive them from their home, their infant child dies, Alessandro goes insane and he is eventually shot and killed (following the same tragic narrative trajectory discussed previously). However, because the book became a romance, the tale has a rather abrupt happy ending: Ramona leaves California to the Americans and heads south to Mexico, where she creates a new life as a *Grande dame* in Mexico City.

Ramona's publishers advertised the novel as a plea for justice for Southern California's Indians, but the story's resolution largely blunted moral outrage over the passing of its tragic Indian and racially mixed characters. As a result, it was read as a romance rather than as a call for social action and reform. Like earlier American tales of the "tragic Californios," such as those of Ramon and Dolores or Joaquín Murieta, *Ramona* allowed American readers to feel the brief sting of guilt over the mistreatment of its characters, but ultimately the readers' discomfort was assuaged: Victimized protagonists driven to lawlessness by Americans were executed, Indians unattended by the Franciscans passed away, and California's ethnic Mexicans "returned" to Mexico. An otherwise positive review in *The Nation* admonished the author that if her goal was to inspire social reform, "the reader should be oppressed by the burden of their sorrows. So far from that are we, that though the murdered Alessandro is left dead on the lonely San Jacinto, Ramona disappears in a halo of prosperity."[70] Similarly, in the California-based *Overland Monthly*, a reviewer praised *Ramona* as being "Beyond comparison the best Californian novel that has yet been written" but also told its readers that the novel held "no burning appeal, no crushing arraignment" and was "no book such as *Uncle Tom's Cabin*."[71]

While *Ramona* largely failed as a reformist novel, it did instigate profound changes in Southern California, most obviously in the development of regional emblems that worked to create an attractive sense of place. Previously, boosters had attempted to domesticate perceptions of California by emphasizing its American future, but Jackson's writings turned back to the state's history, powerfully evoking a nostalgic feeling of an era just past, whose ghosts still lingered. *Ramona's Overland Monthly* reviewer denounced Jackson's portrayal of California, claiming that

> somehow, by some impalpable quality put in it or left out . . . [it] misses being *our* California. The truth is that it is probably no one's California; that while every description is true to nature, the story is really laid out in the poet's land, which can never be exactly the same as any region of the realistic earth.[72]

But early critiques of verisimilitude in *Ramona* aside, it was precisely this poetic portrayal of the state that came to shape its reality, sometimes quite literally. Just months after the novel's publication, one group of residents in San Diego County enthusiastically changed the name of their settlement from Nuevo to Ramona. Thus, Jackson's pastoral descriptions of the novel's setting and the engravings of Arcadian scenes that accompanied many of her California writings framed her readers' vision of the state, making Southern California's past tangible and attractive to Americans settling in the state as well as to readers in all parts of the country.

As the novel began to garner public acclaim, Jackson returned to California and its much-vaunted climate in hopes of mending a broken leg and to overcome a respiratory ailment. While she was gratified by *Ramona*'s popularity, she was chagrined by its failure to stimulate reform in Americans' treatment of Indians. As her health deteriorated, she prepared to write another "Indian story." Tragically, this second project was never begun. She died in San Francisco on August 12, 1885, never witnessing the profound effects her writings were to have on the future of Southern California.[73]

In November of the same year of her passing, the Santa Fe Rail established a southerly transcontinental rail line to California in direct competition with the Central and Southern Pacific rails. This challenge to the established rail monopoly over access to California resulted in a rate war between the companies. Fares to cross the continent were commonly reduced to only $25.00, and for a few days in 1887 a traveler could make the trip for a mere dollar.[74] The lowered fares resulted in a dramatic increase in Southern California's population: Los Angeles County grew from 33,381 inhabitants in 1880 to 101,454 in 1890, and similar or even greater gains were seen throughout the rest of the region.[75] In the words of Glenn Dumke, an authoritative historian of the era, "[T]he reduction of rates to unheard-of levels stimulated the migration of hordes of people who otherwise would have confined their interest in California to reading about it."[76]

Once they arrived in California, however, what those tourists and émigrés had read about the state was crucial to their understanding of the place. A great many of the growing numbers of Americans arriving in Southern California had read *Ramona*, and those who had not were made familiar with the basic elements of the story through other forms of popular culture. These newly arrived Californians would have disagreed with the *Overland* reviewer's assertion that the novel was not faithful to its subject; for many of them, the state was to be experienced *precisely* as *Ramona*'s California.

Jackson herself had posited a connection between the region's built environment and the romantic past portrayed in the pages of her novel. Southern California's numerous crumbling adobes, reviled just a few years earlier, would now serve as monuments to her nostalgic depiction of life on the *ranchos*. She described

Señora Moreno's house [as] one of the best specimens to be found in California of the representative house of the half barbaric, half elegant, wholly generous and free-handed life led there by Mexican men and women of degree in the early part of this century, under the rule of the Spanish and Mexican viceroys, when the laws of the Indies were still the law of the land, and its old name[,] "New Spain," was an ever-present link and stimulus to the warmest memories and deepest patriotisms of its people. It was a picturesque life, with more of sentiment and gayety in it, more also that was truly dramatic, more romance than will ever be seen again on those sunny shores. The aroma of it lingers there still; industries and inventions have not yet slain it; it will last out its century,—in fact it will never be quite lost as long as there is one such house as the Señora Moreno's.[77]

During Jackson's 1881 visit to Southern California, Antonio Coronel had recommended that she pay a visit to the home of the Del Valle family at Rancho Camulos, in Ventura. Coronel reputedly told her that this was the one place in California where she could still see ranch life as it had been before the coming of the Americans. When Jackson arrived at Camulos, the Del Valles were out, but the family's servants welcomed her and gave her a two-hour tour of the ranch. She was most keenly interested in artifacts rescued from the missions that were kept in the family's chapel, but in a letter to the Coronels she later lamented the fact that although she "saw some of the curious old relics . . . the greater part of them were locked up and Mrs. Del Valle had the keys with her."[78] In spite of the brevity of her visit, Jackson largely based her descriptions of the Moreno home and chapel in *Ramona* on what she had seen of Camulos.[79]

Although Camulos gained its prominence in popular culture as a typical example of the Californio *rancho*, its history was, in fact, a rather anomalous one. The Del Valles had lost the ranch in a legal dispute resolved in a Mexican court at the outbreak of the Mexican-American War. While many Californios had lost their lands after the war as a result of litigation, legal expenses, and the lengthy wait for the recognition of land grant titles, in the Del Valles' unique case, the U.S. government restored the lost ranch to them. Also unlike most Californios, the Del Valles were quick to embrace finance capitalism and were among the first cattle ranchers in Southern California to switch to less financially volatile forms of agriculture. By the late 1860s,

Rancho Camulos was a model American farm with crops of citrus and nuts as well as a vineyard and wine press, all products that could be easily shipped long distances to market by rail. Even the ranch house itself, greatly lauded as a testament to the past, was largely built after the American conquest. Sixteen of the house's twenty rooms were added after 1850.[80]

Nonetheless, Jackson's visit to Camulos set the stage for later curiosity seekers. As rumors began to circulate that the ranch was the inspiration for the Moreno home, it became a landmark for tourists. However, visitors' desire to see *Ramona*'s California blurred the distinction between inspiration and reality. Camulos quickly came to be known and marketed as the "true home of Ramona." Although Jackson never met the Del Valles, visitors came to wed the identities of the fictional characters of her novel to the actual family owning and inhabiting the ranch. Reginaldo Del Valle, an elder son and a state assemblyman, was quoted in the *San Francisco Chronicle* as lamenting that "many who come here do not believe that we are not the ones they wish to see."[81] The Del Valles were also greatly distressed that the beloved matriarch of their family, Ysabel Del Valle, was commonly seen as the model for the cold Señora Moreno.

Still, local promoters enthusiastically supported the superimposition of *Ramona*'s characters onto the Del Valle household. In *Santa Barbara and Around There* (1886), Edward Roberts invited his readers:

Come with me on a two days' visit to the Camulos ranch, where the heroine Ramona lived with the Señora Moreno and her foster-brother Felipe, and where she met Alessandro at the sheep-shearing season. We shall find a second Señora Moreno, calm and iron-willed, but kind and gentle, and not hating the Americans as did the first Señora we knew; and we shall find a second Ramona too, and another Felipe, and shall see Juan Can lounging about the sheep-corrals, and maids doing the week's washing at the creek, down by the artichoke-patch. Yes, and there will be coquettish Margarita, and old Marda the cook, and the chapel, and the olive-patch, and the verandas, with their vines and linnet's nests. The story will seem like reality to us as we wander about. We can visit the Señora's room, with its Saints and Madonnas, and see where good Father Salvierderra used to sleep, and where Baba was corralled, and the sheep that Capitan herded, and the crosses on the mountains, put there by the Señora to warn passers-by that they were on the property of a good Catholic. We will see Felipe's room, and the window through which Ramona tossed the note the night she ran away with Alessandro, and we will sit on the veranda and look out upon the flower-dotted courtyard, across which the children carry great smoking dishes from the kitchen to the Señora's dining-room. If we are fortunate, we shall be shown the altar-cloth, safely placed out of harm's way in the chapel, that Ramona mended the day that Father Salvierderra arrived. We shall have, in fact, the reality in place of fiction, a quaint, strange, utterly foreign reality, rarely found even in California, and now thanks to "H.H.," given a coloring and an interest that has already made it a place of pilgrimage for the many readers of the gifted writer.[82]

Just as Jackson herself had given Americans hope that they might still gain a voyeuristic entrée into the world of the Californios in her essay "Echoes in the City of the Angels," Roberts's promotional book assured visitors of the Del Valles' hospitality.

There being no hotels in the neighborhood, Camulos is regarded more or less as a hotel. . . . [I]f one brings her letters or is known, the calm, strong face is all smiles, and the private rooms of the house are opened; and in rare instances the Señora exhibits the treasures of her chests, and shows rare old laces, and embroidered clothes, and heavy silks, that were worn when she was a girl.[83]

Strikingly, Roberts demonstrated the remarkable degree to which a connection between the characters in the novel and the Del Valles could be insisted upon. He reported that Ysabel Del Valle had read *Ramona* approvingly and would guide visitors to the places described in the book. But he also disbelievingly quoted her as saying that "the real Señora and the real Ramona . . . are not here, although this is the house," noting how "strange [it is] that she would think she is not the real Señora."[84]

In time, however, the Del Valle family began to see tourists' demands at their door for "Ramony, Ramony, where is Ramony?" as a great opportunity rather than as a tiresome annoyance.[85] Charles F. Lummis, editor of the *Los Angeles Daily Times*, was invited to produce a book of photographs entitled *The Home of Ramona*, in 1887, that more modestly documented the parallels between Camulos and Jackson's description of the Moreno home. Unlike Roberts's efforts, Lummis's book included an essay that cautioned his readers, "None of the characters [in *Ramona*] were drawn [from individuals at Camulos]; and possibly outside of the quaint old servants, there are no parallels in this blue-blooded Spanish family—certainly none of the weak Felipe or the pitiless Señora."[86] Quite cleverly, lest the tie between *Ramona* and Camulos be weakened overmuch, Lummis ended his book with a picture of the Del Valles' close family friend Antonio Coronel, white-haired and dressed in period garb, dancing "a Spanish waltz of a hundred years ago" with a young *señorita* on the veranda at Camulos.[87]

Following the publication of Lummis's book, Reginaldo Del Valle decided to put the popularity of the familial *rancho* to use both politically and commercially. He worked to organize the "Ramona Parlor of the Native Sons of the Golden West," a fraternal organization for Southern California's leading citizens that would be dedicated to the "perpetuation of the romantic and patriotic past."[88] Perhaps most significantly, he appealed to rail baron Charles Crocker for the construction of a Southern Pacific stop at Camulos. Although Del Valle, a Democrat, and Crocker, a Republican, were longtime political rivals, they were both well aware of the potential benefits of drawing tourists and settlers to the region with "Ramonana." The rail stop was built quickly, but Del Valle and Crocker were not the only ones to realize the profitability of stoking tourists' desire to see the places they had read about in *Ramona*.

As early as 1888, a farmer named Cave Couts Jr. began to suggest that Jackson's visit to his ranch, Guajome, forty miles north of San Diego, had been the true inspiration for the Moreno *rancho*. His assertions were supported by the claim of Father Ubach of Mission San Diego that he had introduced Jackson to the "real" Ramona on a tour of local Indian villages.[89] In 1894, the Santa Fe Railroad added a competing spur to bring tourists to Guajome, giving the rail company its own "True Home of Ramona." Postcards and railroad souvenir picture books that interspersed images of the missions and scenes from *Ramona*'s California were eagerly bought, sold, and traded. Soon rivalries for tourist dollars between cities in Southern California resulted in a plethora of competing claims about the location of many of the places described in *Ramona*.[90] Rather than dampen visitors' enthusiasm for "Ramonana," the proliferation of "actual" or "hyper-real" locations for the events in the novel only created a hunger for more; the buzz of speculation merely fed visitors' desire to find the places that had inspired Jackson.

However, *Ramona*'s impact on Southern California went far beyond inspiring tourists' quests to find the landmarks of the novel. It fueled an already growing desire on the part of Americans to define Southern California as a unique place; *Ramona*'s readers' insistence on attaching romantic narratives to the built environment helped Americans begin to formalize their collective understanding of the region and its past. It wasn't long before Southern California's pre-American features (its crumbling adobe buildings and Spanish place names) came to be employed in the articulation of a distinctive and enduring sense of place.

Creating the Southern California Type

By the late 1880s, boosters' efforts to promote settlement in Southern California had borne fruit on an unprecedented scale. Between the 1884 publication of *Ramona* and the decline of the rail-line rate war in 1888, more than one hundred "boom towns" had sprung up in Los Angeles County alone.[91] This rapid development gave rise to a growing sense that the region was finally coming into its own and inspired optimistic speculation about its future, sentiments that were articulated in contemporary promotional literature. For example, *California of the South* (1888), a guidebook for settlers and health-seekers by Los Angeles physicians Walter Lindley and Joseph P. Widney, voiced popular local opinion that the time was ripe for political autonomy from Sacramento. They cited cultural distinctiveness born from contact with "Spanish civilization," a more healthful climate, and growth in population as evidence that "California of the South" should be disjoined from "California of the North" and become its own separate state.[92] Similarly, veteran booster Charles Nordhoff turned away from the North in his publication of *Peninsular California* (1888), a settlers' guide that advocated the American colonization and annexation of Baja California. Nordhoff argued that contiguities with Baja's climate, agricultural fertility, and scenic missions made the South a logical point of expansion for the region.[93] However, in spite of Southern Californian's growing estrangement from the North, the signature element of its regional identity, a new architectural style, was to be elaborated by visitors from Northern California.

During an economic slowdown in the North, the building rush in the southland attracted many young architects from San Francisco. The work of notables such as Willis Polk, John Galen Howard, William P. Moore, Ernest Coxhead, John C. Pelton, W. J. Cuthbertson, and Joseph Cather Newsom was deeply influenced by their exposure to Southern California's Latin American architecture. Most of these men arrived in Los Angeles and San Diego just as Jackson's romantic influence was in ascendance; it was a time when the popularity of *Ramona* was fanning Americans' interest in the missions into a heated passion. Much as did growing numbers of visitors to the old churches, these architects sketched and painted them, observing their forms and admiring elements of their design.[94]

The missions' "beauteous decay" was the source of much of their aesthetic appeal for Americans. As a result, many of the adobe churches had endured forty or more years without repairs and were nearing complete collapse. Early mission preservation efforts by Catholic priests had focused on maintaining the structural integrity of the buildings, usually with little concern for retaining their original appearances. However, as the missions assumed the role of regional emblems, Southern Californians began to take an active interest in the grooming of their "stately ruins" and insisting on historical authenticity in their repair and restoration. In 1889, Los Angeles City Librarian Tessa L. Kelso organized the Association for the Preservation of the Missions with the help of the Historical Society of Southern California, recently established by Pious Fund attorney John Doyle. Both groups organized educational tours of the missions that at once served to inculcate American versions of the missions' history and to raise funds for their preservation.[95]

Just at the time that mission preservation efforts were beginning to come into vogue, the speculative financing that had driven Southern California's building boom gave way to a bust. As construction dwindled, many boomtowns became ghost towns, and visiting architects returned to work in more economically stable San Francisco.[96] Nonetheless, their exposure to the growing romantic enthusiasm for the missions in Southern California would inspire their attempts to create a distinctive new architecture for the state.

The articulation of a Californian style of architecture had been attempted by Americans as early as 1883. That year, rail baron Leland Stanford commissioned landscape architect Frederick Law Olmstead and the architectural firm of Shepley, Rutan, and Coolidge of Boston to build his university in a manner that was "an adaptation of the adobe building of California." But this goal was beyond the vision of the Boston firm. The end result, Stanford University's brown sandstone buildings, more closely followed the pattern of Mediterranean Romanesque, a set of forms more familiar to the Boston architects than the style of the whitewashed adobes of California.[97]

Less than a decade later, in 1890, Bay Area architect Willis Polk, returning from his sojourn in the southern portion of the state, published sketches for "An Imaginary Mission Church of the Southern California Type" in the New York–based *Architecture and Building* magazine. In doing so, Polk presented the design of the adobe missions for serious consideration and imitation by the broader American community of architects. He made use of his Southern Californian sketches to assemble a building that drew architectural elements from several different missions, adding the novel feature of a tower over the nave. His imaginary church was remarkable in that for the first time, stylistic elements from the missions were divorced from specific church buildings and employed as an architectural vocabulary of forms, much in the same manner as other revival architectures.

This breakthrough coincided with early deliberations about the style to be employed in the construction of the California building representing the state at the 1893 World's Columbian Exposition in Chicago. Polk and other architects who had worked in Southern California published a number of essays in *Architectural News* and *California Architect and Building News* that carefully considered the best design elements of California's missions. Their stated hope was that "These papers will be both timely and useful in the proposition to represent this semi–Spanish Renaissance in the Architecture of California's buildings at the coming Columbian Exposition."[98]

The Californian World's Fair Commission held two successive contests to judge designs for the state's building. The first produced an eclectic mix of entries, none of which were deemed distinctly Californian enough. As a result, the California commissioners limited the second competition to designs in an as yet "unknown conglomerate style of . . . Moorish and Old Mission" that, it was hoped, would be more evocative of life on the Pacific coast.[99] Here "Moorish elements" referred to the more ornate architecture of southern Spain and "Old Mission" to the solid-feeling and relatively clean lines of colonial adobe buildings.

The winning entry was produced by A. Page Brown. His design for a large 144- by 435-foot building borrowed elements from Missions Santa Barbara, San Luis Rey, and San Luis Obispo and added a "Moorish" central tower. It was to be constructed out of metal and wood with a sheath of plaster of Paris molded around fibrous jute cloth, thereby quickly and economically providing the semblance of weighty adobe.

The *California Monthly World Fair's Magazine* enthusiastically claimed that Brown's building would take its visitors "face to face with the California of Yesteryear. . . . We will have a building whose architecture is all our own, which will take the beholder back to the days when the Fathers, with their old Missions, started the march of civilization in the Golden West."[100] Upon completion, the *Official Guide to the World's Columbian Exposition* described Brown's building as having

> carefully followed the old mission style in the design, but has interjected enough of the more ornate Moorish to relieve the somewhat somber effect of the old adobe church, while giving the required light and roominess. Outside, there is a clear story with a great flat central dome as the crowning feature, and a roof garden to heighten the semi-tropical appearance. . . . On the four corners and flanking the dome are towers designed after the mission belfries, and in them are swung some of the Old Spanish bells that have outlived the padres and their crumbling churches.[101]

An estimated 27 million visitors attended the Columbian Exposition, roughly equivalent to one-quarter of the nation's population at the time. Of all of the buildings representing the states, the California building was often seen as the biggest crowd pleaser, and its new architectural style was strongly endorsed. While it was a clear favorite, it was not the only state building at the Exposition built in the manner of a "semi–Spanish Renaissance." The missions at San Antonio reputedly inspired the look of the much smaller Texas building; but, apart from its

CALIFORNIA BUILDING, AT THE WORLD'S FAIR, CHICAGO, 1893.

Illustration of the Mission Revival California Building at the Columbian Exposition 1893 from the back of *The Land of Sunshine, Southern California: An Authentic Description Of Its Natural Features, Resources, and Prospects, Containing Reliable Information For The Homeseeker, Tourist and Invalid, Compiled For Southern California World's Fair Association*, compiled by Harry Ellington Brook, Los Angeles, World's Fair Association and Bureau of Information Print, 1893.

red-tiled roof, other features such as its narrow Romanesque windows, its two-story design, and its wooden siding recalled little of the Texas missions' architecture. While the Florida building was also modeled after Iberian architecture, it was a direct reproduction of the Spanish-built Fort Marion near Saint Augustine, not an attempt to articulate any new architectural style.[102]

In and among its monumental architecture and immense grounds, the Columbian Exposition showed visitors the world, the continent, the nation, and the states. It was designed to encourage reflection on America's past and future. Quite appropriately then, the 1893 annual meeting of the American Historical Association was held in conjunction with the Exposition. At this inspiring venue, on July 12, 1893, a young Frederick Jackson Turner presented his signature essay "The Significance of the Frontier in American History," stating,

What the Mediterranean Sea was to the Greeks, breaking the bond of custom, offering new experiences, calling out new institutions and activities, that, and more, the ever retreating frontier has been to the United States, and to the nations of Europe more remotely. And now, four centuries from the discovery of America, at the end of a hundred years of life under the Constitution, the frontier has gone and with its going has closed the first period of American history.[103]

In contrast with Turner's mournful interpretation of the end of westward expansion, Southern California boosters celebrated the passing of the frontier as evidence that, with America's westward expansion completed, a new phase of civilization was arising in the far West. In its Exposition literature, the Southern California World's Fair Association let "home seekers, tourists and invalids" who might visit the state know that

[t]hose who may have conceived the idea that society in Southern California partakes in any degree of the "wild and woolly West" character will find themselves most disagreeably disappointed on arriving here. . . . [Southern California] promises to become to the United States what Greece was to ancient Europe. Culture in the New World is finding its ultimate home in the same latitude that witnessed its greatest development in the Old.[104]

Like the Greeks, Southern Californians had developed an architecture that would connote their identity and reinforce their invented historical traditions, both for themselves and to outsiders. In short order, the architectural forms of the Mission Revival would become visual shorthand for Southern California itself. Just as Americans had claimed the right to the title Californian, marking ethnic Mexicans as foreigners, the American production of Mission Revival architecture celebrated the Franciscan colonial enterprise and the imagined affluent lifestyle of the Californios, marking them and the state's past as divorced from Mexico and now elements within American culture.

Coda

Immediately following the Mexican-American War the arrival of prospectors from all over the world to the newly acquired territories intensified American efforts to naturalize their ownership of place and mark non-Anglos as foreigners. The California Gold Rush and other western mineral rushes had a greater social impact through lasting demographic, geographic, and cultural transformations than they did through the creation of wealth for miners. As the rushes faded, the incorporation of the far West into the Union continued through attempts to convert contentious spaces into domesticated places.

As we have seen, the earliest ways in which Americans understood California's history had a profound effect on re-formations of space and place in the final decades of the nineteenth century. Postwar historiography that embraced the colonial Spanish Catholic past worked as a foundation for a new regional identity that was made manifest through commercial boosterism, popular literary culture, and architectural innovations. This occurred in a number of related ways: through the disenfranchisement of ethnic Mexicans and the denial of their claims of land ownership in favor of American squatters and speculators, through the subsequent transformation of the dominant economy from Mexican-era cattle ranching on the range to farm-based agriculture, and in the creation and transfiguration of urban spaces. However, overlapping sets of issues concerning Civil War–era rivalries, land speculation, and the contemporary situation of Native peoples in the region complicated these processes.

As a result of regional cultural differences and rivalries between American arrivistes, Americanization was a particularly complex proposition in the decades leading up to and subsequent to the American Civil War. The conquest and annexation of the far West is widely understood by historians as an exacerbating factor in the tensions that led to that later internecine conflict. It is unsurprising then that North–South rivalries had a significant effect on the ways in which far southwestern regionalism was constructed and codified. Following the Civil War, rhetoric on the part of railroad boosters claiming that California was witnessing the passing of the southern white "pike" echoed earlier language that assumed the inevitability of the passing of the Indigenous and ethnic Mexican populations. However, in actual practice on the ground, the increasing numbers of northerners and southerners were challenged to come to terms with each other as they became westerners. The patriotic commemoration of military victory over Mexico (of particular salience in the far West) often provided a neutral common ground for Americans who had been fiercely loyal to opposite sides during the Civil War.

This reconciliatory cultural moment encouraged romantic representations of the region's past most notably though the development of the genre of pastoral California literature and art. This new genre was greatly influenced by the postwar changes in the southern pastoral tradition that held a nostalgic view of the paternalism of plantation life. California pastoral served American writers seeking to resolve the tension between an imagined simpler pre-American past, suffused with exaggerated images of Franciscan piety, affluent Dons, and plentiful Indian labor and the experience of a living in a more complex contemporary situation.

Historically, the pastoral literary genre has typically flourished in times of cultural upheaval, such as that of the decades following the Mexican and Civil wars. Writers trying to make sense of a dislocation from the familiar have often turned to the tropic conventions of the pastoral to memorialize the past in forms that serve to make sense of the ills of the present. In pastoral literature the past becomes an idealized, mythic place much like Virgil's classical depiction of Arcadia; the past is imagined in such a way that the natural and social worlds exist in a joyous state that ultimately will be lost in a way that leads to present-day concerns. In the case of late-nineteenth-century southern and Californian pastoral depictions of the past, these genres emerged with a deeply problematic core in that both were predicated on nostalgia for paternalism and the exploitation of racialized pools of laborers.

Helen Hunt Jackson's *Ramona* was written in this genre, presenting a vision of the fall of an Arcadian past brought about in part by unjust land laws and the predations of Americans. While the novel was intended as a moral critique of the mistreatment of Indigenous peoples after the American conquest, the book also re-inculcates a tragic understanding of their fate and naturalizes the "return" to Mexico of ethnic Mexicans born in California. This wildly popular depiction of the declining fortunes of wealthy Californios and the Indigenous peoples who worked their lands distinguishes Jackson as the single most successful author of California pastoral literature. As a result of her success, her western oeuvre, consisting of *Ramona* as well as the prior work in *The*

Century Magazine, became foundational texts that helped articulate a broadly held sense of American Southern Californian regionalism.

The unique role Jackson's literary work played was a result of her use of extant narrative conventions that provided Americans with a palatable narrative past for California. Like the earliest American works on California, Jackson's critiqued the secularization of the missions under Mexican rule and portrayed the sale of former mission lands as a criminal product of Mexican greed. Just as John Rollin Ridge blamed the initial atrocities committed against Joaquin and other ethnic Mexicans on Americans who "failed to support the honor and dignity of that title," Jackson also made distinctions among violent American squatters, corruption in the decisions of the Land Commission, and the sympathetic actions of poor southern whites who behaved as true "Ummerikans." Most important, the novel follows the logic of Manifest Destiny by representing the decimation of the Indian population and the departure of the main protagonists from American California to Mexico as inevitable and paving the way for the completion of the American settlement of the state.

These elements were coupled with narrative innovations that helped to provide a sense of place for California in the larger Union in the years just following the era of Reconstruction. Jackson's favorable comparison of Franciscans to Puritans allowed the foundational mythology of the East to be mirrored in the West. In a radical departure from Puritan anti-Catholicism, Jackson's colonial mission past was depicted in effect as a chain of cities "on the hill" that modeled piety and industry, but without the stern dourness commonly associated with early New Englanders. Concurrently, the portrayal of the effects of secularization in the novel provided a western narrative of religious declension familiar to eastern Protestants. In this schema, Franciscans became Puritans, Mexicans became foreigners, Americans became heirs to an Arcadian past, and Indians were destined to pass away.

The use of these familiar conventions encouraged *Ramona's* readers to construct a hyper-reality in which they mapped the fictional settings and characters of the novel onto actual places and individuals. Through the course of this process, romantic representations of California's past became so detailed and commonly believed in that they re-defined the places and peoples Jackson intended to represent. Thus, through its enormous influence, the map provided by Jackson's writing became territory.

As a result of a number of interrelated factors, by the late 1800s attempts to bring California fully into the national fold were coalescing. The arrival of the transcontinental rail, the advent of the first generations of Americans to consider themselves Californians, the reception of Helen Hunt Jackson's writings, and the rise of large-scale speculation and development of land all contributed to the rapid transformation of space and place in the far West.

The period's construction boom cycles led to a search for a distinctive signature regional architectural style. This search, as we have seen, culminated in the enormously successful display of Mission Revival architecture at the Chicago Columbian Exposition, a venue from which it emerged as a central stylistic signifier in emerging ways of understanding of American California. Just as the imagery of *Ramona* popularized and reified a pastoral vision of California's history, Mission Revival aesthetics provided an accessible and enormously popular simulacrum of the missions that would come to define repetitively the built environment throughout Southern California. Though the style was never intended to be a direct copy of the actual mission churches, it became a shorthand sign for the region, a relaxed and affluent lifestyle, and domesticated exoticism. In part it took its meaning from the romance of the missions and in part it re-defined them as icons in popular culture. Moreover, as we shall see, the proliferation of the style served to divorce the regions' Catholic mission architecture from its denominational moorings.

Through the study of the emergence of an American Californian historical and cultural canon, it becomes clear that popular history is never merely the reconstructed past; it is structured by ongoing social realities. Changes in social reality are shaped dialogically and are determined by relations of power, but they are commonly experienced through the influence of individual cultural agents. Helen Hunt Jackson powerfully affected the Americanization of California, as did boosters, architects, and a great many individuals who came after her, expanding upon and responding critically to her influence.

3

The Spanish Heritage

Cold climes make thick fur and ferocity or thick blubber and
voracity.

Fruit and sunshine are good for body and brain and soul.
When the conquering New Englander has done exterminat-
ing the Indian and struggling for a living, let him come here
and live—calmly, wisely, nobly, healthfully and happily.
—Charles Lummis, "The Lion's Den" in *Land of Sunshine*,
June 1895

A missionary enterprise of a peculiar character has been in
existence for some time on the Pacific slope. Though strictly
Catholic in its aims and purposes, it was founded by Protestants and has been supported by them from the beginning.
This enterprise is known as the "Landmarks Club" of California, and has for its object primarily and principally the
preservation of the old Missions. Charles F. Lummis of Los
Angeles, the man who founded it, is not a Catholic. It would
be doing him, however, a great injustice to call him a Protestant in the strict sense of the term.
—Reverend J. T. Roche, "The Landmarks Club," *Extension
Magazine*, June 1907

The 125th anniversary of [the] La Purisima Mission
founding was a grand affair. . . . An organ was there and the
choir composed of Protestants and Father Aloysius sang an
easy Mass neatly. A huge cross of cement was blessed by the
bishop. A few Indians sang a hymn in Spanish to the cross.
Then we were taken to the banquet hall. There must have
been a thousand people on the hill, mostly Protestants.
There were a few Catholics. All went nicely. At the banquet
only Protestants spoke, also Rev. Raley and the bishop. It did
a lot of good and created a good impression. Women also

spoke. A Camino Real Bell was blessed near the cross by the
Bishop.
—Father Zephyrin Englehardt, *Franciscan Provincial
Annals*, December 6, 1912

With the march of the years, Santa Barbara came to be perhaps the chief town of the Pacific Coast in America. Not a
big town ever, but an important and enticing town.

Throughout the old Spanish and Mexican eras of
California it was a center of fashion and culture, as it is
indeed today. It was the scene of many colorful and romantic
episodes, and it is still of first importance concerning all that
remains of the old Spanish times.
—Steven McGroarty, *Santa Barbara*, 1925

Southern Californians: Easterners Graduated

In April 1894, Los Angeles's civic leaders organized the first annual
Fiesta de Los Angeles. The staging of the festival was motivated in large
part by the business community's desire to lure tourists south from San
Francisco's Midwinter International Exposition, which had opened just
as the Columbian Exposition in Chicago had closed.[1] In his promotion of the event, Max Meyberg, the president of the *Fiesta*, made use
of regionalist tropes by obliquely referencing the purported frugality of
California's Franciscans as well as the legendary wealth and generosity
of the old Spanish Dons. He wrote, "We Americans do not appreciate
that this incessant striving for gain is making us a selfish people. Is it
not time to stop and consider for what purpose we exist? This is the aim
of the Fiesta."[2] By celebrating the city's Iberian roots, the *Fiesta de Los
Angeles* could provide *American* tourists and residents with a haven for
existential reflection or at the very least a break from the demands of
the accumulation of capital. However, capitalist interests were, in fact,
central to the event. Meyberg congratulated the members of the Los
Angeles Merchants' Association for their integrity and commitment

to "public matters" as central organizers of the *Fiesta*. Although its president was billing the celebration as a reprieve from Americans' "incessant" economic drive, the cultural expression of the *Fiesta* was very much driven by economic design; the staging of the event provided a forum for the assertion of a nascent form of cultural hegemony that reinforced regional images of leisure as a mark of wealth, popular American views of the colonial historical record, and evolving but exclusionary conventions for civic engagement.

In form, the *Fiesta* was modeled on civic festivals and historic pageants that were becoming increasingly popular in the eastern United States but in this setting featured local Californian themes, including an odd amalgam of spectacles: a floral procession much like Santa Barbara's Flower Festival and Pasadena's Tournament of Roses, a Chinese pageant with a "wealth of Barbaric splendor and its 225-foot dragon," and a contingent of "mission Indians" processing in an "anthropological layout," some of them reputedly one hundred years old (demonstrating the benefits to health and longevity of the mild Mediterranean climate).[3] Sumner Hunt, the architect who had designed a Mission Revival "Southern California" building for the Midwinter International Exposition, also designed nineteen historical floats to be paraded in Los Angeles. These horse-drawn *tableaux vivants* provided spectators with a uniquely southwestern American history lesson. The common romantic portrayals of the Spanish conquest of the Americas and the Franciscan conquest of California were played out and celebrated at this inaugural American organized *Fiesta*.[4]

Unlike earlier citywide *Fiestas* held in Los Angeles by Californios, such as those celebrating Mexican independence, the American-organized *Fiesta de Los Angeles* commemorated no singular historical event. Rather, it was intended to promote the region through the power of spectacle. It was to be a drama wherein "the place [was] the hero and the development of the community [was] the plot."[5] An anonymous chronicler of the organization of this first *Fiesta* reminisced:

> It was designed to be not merely a season of merrymaking; but a specific and typical affair which should reflect the matchless romance of the Southwest and the Pacific Coast, instead of copying after New Orleans and Saint Louis and every other conventional carnival. The central theme

was the Romance of the Pacific—the Incas, the Aztecs, the Pueblos, the California Missions, and the details were carried out with unusual sincerity. . . . [T]he only way to succeed with a fiesta is never to let it subside to any suggestion of a fake.[6]

No organizer of the *Fiesta* was more insistent on authenticity in the portrayal of the romance of the Spanish conquest of the Pacific than Charles F. Lummis, a former editor of *the Los Angeles Times* and *Ramona* enthusiast who would become the best-known booster of the region's Spanish colonial past.

Lummis had left his newspaper post in 1888 after suffering a debilitating stroke. Although he was a great advocate of the health benefits of California's climate, he moved to New Mexico for several years to recover from the stress of his job as a Los Angeles promoter. During his convalescence in New Mexico he made the fast friendship of ethnologist Adolph Bandelier, a convert to Catholicism and great admirer of America's Spanish missionaries.[7] The two traveled throughout Peru, Mexico, and the American Southwest, and these travels greatly influenced Lummis's understanding and later promotion of Southern California and its history.

At a time when William G. Ritch, the Secretary of the Territory of New Mexico and president of the New Mexico Bureau of Immigration, was promoting that region to American tourists and settlers as Aztlán, "home of the tribes that settled Mexico City" and Santa Fe itself as the birthplace of "Montezuma," Bandelier (and subsequently Lummis) argued strongly against the American conflation of Indigenous southwestern and Mesoamerican peoples that had been inherited from the Mexican-American War.[8] Significantly, their insistence on the distinctiveness of Native American cultures of the Southwest commonly relied on the denigration of those of Mesoamerica. In his popular southwestern travel guide *Some Strange Corners of Our Country* (1892), Lummis condemned the wartime naming of Montezuma's Well by "the class that has pitted the Southwest with misnomers." He warned his readers:

There is a legend (of late invention) that Montezuma, after being conquered by Cortez, threw his incalculable treasure into this safest of hiding-places; but that is all a myth, since Montezuma had no treasures

Parade floats from the Los Angeles *Fiesta* depicting various fantastical images of the pre- and post-Columbian Americas, "*Glimpses of La Fiesta De Los Angeles, April 1895,*" *Land Of Sunshine*, V. 2, No. 6, May, 1885: cover interior supplement.

and in any event could hardly have brought the fabled tons of gold across two thousand miles of desert to this "Well," even if he had ever stirred outside the pueblo of Mexico after the Spaniards came—as he never did. But as one looks into the awesome abyss, it is almost easy to forget history and believe anything.[9]

Following Bandelier's example, Lummis insisted that the actual "Montezuma" was "the war-chief of an ancient league of Mexican Indians; and not 'Emperor of Mexico,' as ill-informed historians assert."[10] Moreover, Lummis believed that Mexicans themselves were to blame for providing this misinformation about the Southwest to gullible Americans. He later saw American congressional proposals "to admit Arizona and New Mexico as one State under the name of Montezuma" (in a manner reminiscent of but with different motives from earlier Mexican attempts to rename California *Moctezuma*) as indicating

that the brilliant intellects that selected it . . . do not know that this tinsel Montezuma myth as to New Mexico was invented by Mexican politicians just before the Mexican War, and by them seditiously promulgated among the Indians of New Mexico to get them to side wth Mexico in the impending struggle.[11]

Lummis credited the "seditious" Mexican authors of the "Montezuma myth" for providing "the Southwestern Indians . . . who absolutely never confide their real beliefs to the tenderfoot tourist [with] a handy and amusing story to put him off with."[12]

Lummis often lauded the Hopi, Pueblo, and Zuni peoples of the Southwest in his writings, generally praising their cultures and avidly collecting their artifacts, but he reserved his greatest admiration for the Spanish conquerors of the Americas, authors of "the largest and longest and most marvelous feat of manhood in all history."[13] In 1893, upon returning to live in Los Angeles after his southwestern and Latin American travels, Lummis published *The Spanish Pioneers*, a historical "guideboard to the true point of view" of the "romantic and gallant" Spanish conquest of the Americas. He introduced the book by claiming that he had written it because I believe that every other young Saxon-American loves fair play and admires heroism as much as I do. . . . That we have not done justice to the Spanish Pioneers is simply because we have been misled. They made a record unparalleled; but our textbooks have not recognized that fact, though they no longer dare dispute it. . . . [W]e are coming to the truth,—a truth which every manly American will be glad to know. In this country of free and brave men, race-prejudice, the most ignorant of all human ignorances, must die out.[14]

While Lummis sought to fight anti-Spanish prejudice, *Pioneers* was a celebration of the campaign to "civilize" "savage" Indigenous peoples. In a fitting gesture, the book was poignantly dedicated to Santa Barbara resident and longtime Lummis friend Elizabeth Bacon Custer, the widow of General George Armstrong Custer.

The Spanish Pioneers spoke to Americans' fascination with the Iberian conquest of the Americas and sold well, printing sixteen editions, including one published in Spanish in Madrid (1916) and a final expanded edition that also included a history of the California missions (1929). Though written in a popular form, *Pioneers* would influence later American historical texts, most notably Herbert E. Bolton's *The Spanish Borderlands*.[15] In time, the work of Lummis and Bolton (both Methodists) did much to stem the influence of the anti–Spanish/Catholic Black Legend in American popular culture and in professional American southwestern historiography.[16]

Lummis's enthusiasm for and knowledge of things Spanish made him an invaluable organizer of the *Fiesta de Los Angeles* with its reenactments of the fall of Tenochtitlán and Cuzco, dioramas of the cities of Cibola, and celebration of the Franciscan conquest of California. Consequently, the success of this historical production did not go unnoticed; friends in the Los Angeles Chamber of Commerce offered Lummis the position of editor of their new magazine, *Land of Sunshine*, a serial version of the pamphlet that was assembled to promote the region at the World's Columbian Exposition. This job would serve him well as a soapbox from which to promote, influence, and comment upon Southern California's maturing regionalism.

Under Lummis's stewardship, *Land of Sunshine* followed many of the conventions of earlier booster literature: It regularly included writings that celebrated *Ramona* and other romantic California fiction; it discussed the nature of society in Southern California and boasted that "the ignorant, hopelessly un-American type of foreigners which infests and largely controls Eastern cities is almost unknown here. Poverty and illiteracy do not exist as classes"; it also noted the beneficial effects of Southern California's climate on the Anglo-Saxon race (these articles were punctuated with images of cherubic white children at play outdoors with captions reading "This Climate Suits Me!" or "A Typical Winter Day in California"); and it provided illustrated commentary on Spanish, Italian, Moorish, and Mission architectural forms that could serve as models for builders in Southern California.

At times, Lummis's promotional writing in *Land of Sunshine* also took an explicitly political turn. For example, his editorial column "In the Lion's Den" often praised Mexican President Porfirio Díaz for his openness toward American financial investment in Mexico. In Lummis's eyes, Díaz was a "Mexican Wizard" who "created a truly great nation from more chaotic material than statesmen ever worked on before."[17] More locally, during the Spanish-American War (1898), Lummis defended California's Iberian heritage from the anti-Spanish sentiments of the time. He harshly ridiculed those who "desire to change the names of California, San Francisco, Los Angeles and the like, 'because they are Spanish.' . . . They should get out of America all together; for it was discovered by the Spanish."[18] While he praised the valor of American troops, he scolded Theodore Roosevelt (a former Harvard schoolmate) for the "unnecessary war" and questioned the wisdom of the colonizing of Cuba, Puerto Rico, Guam, and the Philippines.

Given a solid military victory and the acquisition of new colonial territories, American antipathy toward Spain ebbed quickly after the short war. In fact, just five years after leading his Rough Riders, President Theodore Roosevelt himself visited Southern California and congratulated its residents for

> the way in which you are perpetuating the memorials of that elder [Spanish] civilization. It is a fine thing in a new community to try and keep alive the continuity of historic interests; it is a fine thing to try and remember the background which even those of us who are most confident of the future may be pleased to see existed in the past; and I am

pleased to see how in your architecture, both in the architecture of new and great buildings going up, and in the architecture of the old buildings, and in many other ways, you are, by keeping the touch and flavor of the older civilization, giving a peculiar flavor to our own new civilization, and in an age when the tendency is a trifle toward too great uniformity.[19]

Here Roosevelt lauded the cause closest to Lummis's heart, that of "perpetuating the memorials of that elder civilization," but in doing so he relegated Spanish and Mexican influence and political power to the past.

Shortly after Lummis assumed the position of editor of *Land of Sunshine*, Tessa Kelso, the principal organizer for the Association for the Preservation of the Missions, retired from her post as City Librarian and left Los Angeles. At her suggestion and with the help of influential friends such as Reginaldo Del Valle, Harrison Gray Otis, and Phoebe Hearst (William Randolph Hearst's mother), in 1895 Lummis established a new preservation group, the Landmarks Club. Making use of the media available to him, he employed the pages of *Land of Sunshine* to remind Southern California business owners that they should "recall the material truth that the Missions are, next to our climate and its consequences, the best capital Southern California has" and, as such, should be cared for and preserved for posterity.[20]

However, in spite of the fact that he had inherited the membership rosters of the earlier association, Lummis initially found little popular support for his efforts to restore the most decayed of the missions. While Catholic priests had long worked to preserve those missions that continued to serve as churches, they had largely ignored other mission buildings that lay in ruins.[21] Because both Catholic and Protestant Americans' historical understanding of the Franciscan churches centered on their secularization and decay, any restoration threatened to undermine their role as crumbling monuments to Mexican misrule.[22] While many turn-of-the-century Southern Californian Protestants were willing to romanticize Spanish Franciscan missionaries in the past, bringing ruined Catholic churches back to life in the present was another matter altogether. Lummis wrote in his memoirs, years later, that

[i]t seems incredible to me now what uphill work it was to arouse any interest whatsoever in this [mission preservation] cause. In the first

place a tidal wave of the thrice-damned A.P.A. (Pre-cursor to the Klu Klux Klan) had swept over California and religious bigotry (on the one side) was intense. Absurd as it seems, it is a literal fact that thousands of otherwise sane business men and citizens in Los Angles firmly believed that the Catholics were drilling every night in the basement of the cathedral to rise and massacre the Protestants. The fact that the cathedral had no basement cut no figure at all.[23]

In order to assuage the common anti-Catholic sentiments of the time and court Protestant participation in the Landmarks Club, it was crucial that the promotion of mission restoration be cast as the preservation of *civic* historical monuments. The Landmarks Club ultimately gained the widespread favor of the region's Protestants, in part as a result of Lummis's repeated assertion in *Land of Sunshine* that "Those mighty piles belong not to the Catholic church but to you and me, and to our children and the world. They are monuments and beacons of Heroism and Faith and Zeal and Art. Let us save them—not for the Church but for Humanity."[24]

However, the missions' Catholic past was still central to their significance for Americans. A mission building divorced from its religious identity held little historical or cultural significance. This was something that Lummis came to realize during his acquisition of the chapel of the *asistencia* at Pala. He recounted:

A squatter named Veall "jumped" the Pala Mission and homesteaded most of the valley. His wife[,] Kanaka, was a good Catholic, but Veall was a rabid A.P.A. Somehow, however, he had liked me in the old days when I went down there hunting and photographing. . . . I suggested to him one day that maybe he should sell it to me. . . . So in a few weeks I was the happy possessor of the Pala Mission. What a beautiful thing if the Landmarks Club could have a mission of its very own, a public park, with all its value as a monument of tradition and romance and achievement, but without any other "strings" whatever. But at the next meeting of my associates when I wanted to expiate on this dream, my tongue went flat, and almost to my own surprise I said, "Damn it boys! Pala wasn't built for a landmark or a park, but for a temple! I think we would be fences with stolen goods to keep it!" To my delight there wasn't a hem or haw. Not one of us was a Catholic, but we all felt this certain fitness and reverence—as no one could help feeling who had worked so long in the presence of the work done by those great Apostles.[25]

For the Club to reduce a mission to a secular building would be to commit the much-criticized sin of California's Mexican regime. Ultimately, the chapel at Pala was sold to Catholic Archbishop Montgomery for the price that Lummis had originally paid for it and the promise of a ten-year lease on the chapel, during which time the Club would effect its restoration as a functioning church.

Thus, the promotion of mission preservation occurred within a tension between establishing the missions as civic monuments for Americans of all denominations and ultimately revitalizing them as living Catholic churches. However, this tension was a creative one. Restoring churches that had "fallen victim" to Mexican secularization became a progressive and patriotic civic act, one that allowed preservationists to reinforce Americans' understanding of their conquest of California as an echo of the Franciscans' earlier "spiritual conquest." Mission restoration legitimized the American "inheritance" of the state and thereby promoted an ecumenical base of support for the Landmarks Club's work from many of the region's religious leaders. Shortly after the restoration of the chapel at Pala began, an ad for the Landmarks Club in *Land of Sunshine* announced:

A course of lectures on behalf of the Club is now inaugurated. Rt. Rev. Geo. Montgomery, Bishop of Los Angeles and Monterey, opened the course December 28, with an extremely instructive lecture on the "Secularization of the Missions." It is notable that the work of preserving our historic landmarks is alike generously encouraged by this Roman Catholic bishop and by the Episcopal bishop of Los Angeles, Rt. Rev. Joseph H. Johnson, who shared the platform and prefaced the lecture with a cordial address. The old bigotries fall away before the joint interest of educated Americans to save the historic and the artistic.[26]

Though the leadership of the Landmarks Club was largely male, its foot soldiers and main organizers were primarily wealthy, white, Anglo-Saxon, Protestant women. One of the Club's most prominent female members, Eliza Otis, "California's Beloved Mission Poet" and wife of Harrison Grey Otis, perfectly captured the tone of the Club's civic-minded ecumenism in a recruitment ad in the *Los Angeles Times* (1905). She wrote:

> Catholicism and Protestantism are looked on generally as opposing forces, but here each had its work of preparation to accomplish, and each did it well, and today they stand face to face without a thought of conflict. Puritanism commends the work accomplished by those early Mission Fathers, and comes here to sow and to reap in the soil which they made ready for the larger and grander life of this later century. The work proposed by the Landmarks Club, "to conserve the missions and other historic landmarks of Southern California," is a most commendable one and should have the hearty support of every public-spirited citizen of the state.[27]

The largely Protestant members of the Landmarks Club reinforced narratives like Otis's linking colonial Catholic California to American Protestant California by expressing a deep and abiding admiration for the founder of the missions, Father Junipero Serra.

In an extension of their efforts in the promotion of the preservation of the Catholic missions, Landmarks Club members launched a campaign for the canonization of Junipero Serra. Lummis himself inquired of Father Zephyrin Englehardt, a Franciscan historian and caretaker of the mission archives at Santa Barbara, why the Church hadn't already declared Serra a saint and what the probability of its happening soon might be. Lummis wrote that he felt

> this man [Serra]—whom, as a historian, I count foremost among all missionary pioneers and administrators of the New World—should have the proper recognition. It isn't for me to meddle with the programme [*sic*] of the church; but I have a right to work as an American and a Protestant and a Californian in recognition of the hero whom not even the A.P.A. seems to hate.[28]

When Englehardt expressed his doubts about the likelihood of Serra's beatification, much less canonization, Lummis seemed all the more determined and enthusiastic about his cause. He responded to Englehardt:

> I am a good deal disappointed at the improbability that we can secure the canonization of Junipero Serra. . . . However, I am a somewhat obstinate person; and am going to keep at this until whipped off the circuit. We have vague whispers of miraculous affairs; and I am going to trace them down.[29]

Sadly for the Landmarks Club's cause, Lummis was unable to document any miracles attributable to Serra. Still, in good measure as a result of the Club's efforts, Serra's sainthood became a matter of public interest and regional pride for many Californians, regardless of their denomination. In time, a controversial movement for Serra's canonization would emerge within the Catholic Church, its deliberations relying, in part, on the testimony of Protestant historians of the missions, most notably Herbert Bolton himself.[30]

The endorsement of Serra as an American hero and the missions as public monuments not only worked to promote preservation efforts, it also reinforced the perception of Mission Revival as the rightful and definitive architecture for the region. In the first decades of the twentieth century, designers of Southern California's city halls, Carnegie libraries, public schools, and resort hotels relied heavily on mission stylings. Both the Southern Pacific and Santa Fe rail lines also rebuilt the region's rail depots exclusively in the Revival style. It became the regional norm that for each Southern California house "done in the New England style . . . there [were] a thousand of the 'Mission Architecture.'"[31]

Even missions that were restored by the Club were given a revival treatment; because of their advanced deterioration, their preservation and restoration often became a matter of imaginative reconstruction. Lummis recruited Sumner P. Hunt and Arthur B. Benton as the Landmark Club's architects "on account of their particular understanding [of] and sympathy with the Mission architecture." While Lummis had insisted on "authenticity" in the restoration of the missions, often entire sections of the church buildings provided little evidence of their original form and were redesigned by the Club's architects—blurring the line between the Franciscans' mission design and Mission Revival architecture.[32]

By far the most striking use of Mission Revival style, however, was its regular appearance in the design of Southern California's Protestant churches. Lummis rightly boasted that the Protestant acceptance of the style was due in fair measure to the ecumenical influence of the Landmarks Club's preservation work, noting:

> It is quite common in California to see a Methodist or Baptist church calmly adopting the identical lines of the old Franciscan Missions— which of course makes them better architecture than their denominational brethren. The world do move! The Mission architecture is as Catholic as the Pope himself. Yet when the Landmarks Club began its crusade, it is safe to say that not a Protestant church extant would have "stooped to Romish architecture."[33]

Preservationists' portrayal of "Old Mission Romance" as public history allowed the designers of Protestant churches to participate in the architectural vogue and integrate their houses of worship into the region's signature style, without troubling themselves overmuch about its Catholic inspiration. As Mission Revival buildings became ubiquitous in Southern California, Protestant churches built in the style became the most dramatic signs of Americans' reconciliation of the state's Latin American–Catholic past with its Anglo-Protestant present. There could be no stronger emblem for Americans' claim of historical continuity with the Franciscans' conquest of California than a Mission Revival Protestant church.

As even Protestant congregations became enthusiastic about Mission Revival, old mission romance came not only to define California's urban environments but also to shape the spaces between them, influencing the birth of another of Southern California's modern emblems—the highway. At the 1902 meeting of the General Federation of Women's Clubs in Los Angeles, a proposal was put forward to create a "California Road to be known as El Camino Real" that would link the missions, "the most important art treasures in the possession of the United States."[34] By 1904, the Los Angeles Chamber of Commerce had organized a Camino Real Association to raise funds and organize the road's construction.[35] Association delegates included David Starr Jordan (president of Stanford University), Reginaldo del Valle, Archbishop Montgomery, Father Ubach of San Diego (Helen Hunt Jackson's guide in San Diego), Charles Lummis, two California senators, and numerous Southern California business owners and society elites. Mrs. A.S.C. Forbes, a leading member of the Association and a great mission enthusiast, designed the Camino Real's distinctive eleven-foot-high "mission bell"–topped guideposts. These were to serve as mile markers along the newly paved roadway, "[linking] together Father Serra's rosary, the missions, about which lingers the memory of a saint and the scent of a rose." The first guidepost was installed in 1906, in Los Angeles, and by 1910, the year that Ford introduced the Model T, more than 400 Camino Real mile markers were in place along the roadway, the majority to be found south of Santa Barbara.[36]

From very early on, Southern California led the nation in per capita automobile ownership. The Camino Real allowed Americans to follow "in the footsteps of the padres," without the drudgery of actual walking by driving the scenic route of the state's presumed spiritual conquest with modern convenience. Promotional travel writers eager for tourist dollars claimed that the missions had been built "One Spanish Day Apart" and encouraged motorists to emulate the travels of the padres and spend a day at each of the missions while making their way up the entire chain.[37] Earlier American exaggerations of Franciscan and Californio hospitality were revived and used to lure automobile tourists to hotels, restaurants, and health resorts—travelers were assured that they would enjoy the same royal treatment that the guests of the hospitable padres and Dons had in old California. Notably, the first "motor hotel," or motel, in the nation was constructed alongside the Camino Real in San Luis Obispo, its main building and surrounding bungalows all built in the Mission Revival style.[38]

By the time of the appearance of the motel, however, Mission Revival–style hostelries were a common feature of Southern California. The genre's most elaborate expression was the Glenwood Mission Inn at Riverside, California. From 1902 to 1903, innkeeper Frank Miller undertook a $250,000 expansion of his Glenwood Inn with the financial backing of Henry E. Huntington and several local merchants. Riverside was to be developed as a new destination for Huntington's

Southern Pacific Railroad, and Miller's remodeled hotel-resort was to become a magnet for tourism. An active Landmarks Club member, Miller hired Arthur Benton, the Club's architect, to pattern his hotel after the missions. Just after the inn opened, Miller, a Congregationalist, explained that

> as to what led me to build in the Mission style: For many years I have been in favor of carrying out the ideas of the Mission Fathers in construction in Southern California,—First, because of the adaptation of this style to our climate (warm in winter and cool in summer). Second, because I believe in keeping alive the beautiful traditions of our early history,—in preserving the old Mission Land Marks, and building our buildings like them. Third, because of the simple strength and homelike comfort which the mission style represents.[39]

The massive 275-room Mission Inn took up nearly an entire city block, dominating Riverside's downtown.[40] Construction at the inn rarely ceased, as additions and renovations continued for more than thirty years after its opening—four-story "Choir" and "Spanish" wings were added within its first decade alone. Although Miller was perpetually in debt for expansions to his hotel, the venture proved to be a great financial success for its investors and the town of Riverside.

Its interminable balconies and arches look in on its large square central courtyard that is modeled after those of the missions, it featured original red roof tiles removed from the chapel at Pala during its restoration to lend a whiff of authenticity, its "Ramona dome" was lit through stained glass likenesses of the novel's characters, the rough brick wall of the main entrance was studded with weathered Spanish crests as well as "carved stone heads from pre-Aztec deities," and the entire structure was topped with a copper Saint Francis–shaped weather vane.[41] A promotional pamphlet circulated at the time of the inn's opening told potential visitors that "within as without Mission architecture prevails and is emphasized in decoration and quaint monastic furnishings."[42] The inn's Mission Revival architecture and Miller's choice of décor (largely plain oak "mission-style" furniture and displays of Catholic religious artwork) worked in concert to make the place a complete Spanish Franciscan–themed resort.

Visitors were even treated to an insider's view of the feature of Catholic churches that held the greatest power in Protestant Americans' imagination, the basement.[43] Subterranean passages that concealed the inn's modern amenities, such as steam heat, were called "the catacombs" and modified to provide gallery space for Miller's growing collection of Catholic paintings and plaster saints. For a significant number of years, the main catacomb attraction was a small, dimly lit room featuring life-sized wax figures of Pope Pius X and thirteen attendants. When the Congregationalist church to which Miller belonged moved to a new building (done in a complementary Spanish Revival style) across the street from the inn, he had the substructures expanded the length of a city block to provide steam heating for cold Sunday morning services, resulting in what was, probably, the first and only Congregationalist church building with a Catholic-themed basement.[44]

Shortly after opening the inn, Miller organized the purchase of local promontory Mount Roubidoux as a scenic overlook of the whole of Riverside and its orange groves. By 1908, the mountain featured a large wooden "Serra Cross" visible from the city and a paved roadway had been built to its summit for tourists' automobiles. The following year saw the beginning of a yearly tradition of an Easter morning procession up the mountain for "all people who believed in the cross as a symbol of Christianity, no matter whether they belonged to a denomination . . . to sing Easter hymns, spend a few moments in silent prayer and then to recite the Lord's Prayer."[45]

Religious pageantry greatly appealed to Miller, and he regularly dressed as Junipero Serra for the Mount Roubidoux Easter service as well as for the inn's Christmas Nativity play. During a tour of Europe in 1911, Miller saw "The Passion Play" at Oberammergau, Bavaria, and was inspired to organize a similar production in Southern California. Upon his return, he sought the advice of Henry Van Dyke, a Princeton University English professor whose poem "God of the Open Air" was a standard reading in the Roubidoux Easter program. Van Dyke was enthusiastic about Miller's idea and recommended that Miller seek the opinion of Landmarks Club member and Stanford University president David Starr Jordan about a suitable playwright. The ultimate result of Miller's consultations was the commission of Los Angeles Times writer

John Steven McGroarty to write a play with California's religious history as its theme.[46]

Miller housed McGroarty at the Mission Inn during his months of writing, and the inspiring surroundings helped him to produce "The Mission Play." A special theater for the play was built in close proximity to Mission San Gabriel, the closest mission to the Mission Inn. The theater was also furnished with the emblems of Old Mission Romance. Its foyer contained a model of the Camino Real with miniatures of the missions, and the stage itself was flanked by large reproductions of the Henry Sandham illustrations of the ruins of Mission San Luis Rey and the campanile at Pala that had appeared in Helen Hunt Jackson's "Father Junipero and His Work" and various editions of *Ramona*. On April 29, 1912, "The Mission Play" opened to a packed house filled with Southern California's high society, including Catholic Archbishop Conaty, the Del Valle family, and Harrison Gray Otis. Its successful opening proved auspicious—during the play's twenty-year run in San Gabriel, it sold a staggering two and a half million tickets, the profits from which were used to fund mission and landmark preservation throughout the state.[47]

Though he revised it several times, McGroarty structured his play with a prelude and three acts, each of which "symbolized a historic epoch." The prelude, performed entirely in pantomime, re-creates the discovery of America with three costumed figures representing "The Savage Sensing the Approach of his White Conquerors, the Spectre of the Faded Military Glory of the Spanish Conquest, and the Spirit of the Ever-Living Faith in the Cross of Christ." Act One establishes the strength of Father Serra's character and faith in the face of many obstacles that forestalled the settlement of San Diego, the first Alta California mission. Act Two takes place fifteen years later at Mission San Carlos at Carmel, where priests have gathered from all the missions to report to Serra on their great progress in the "harvesting of souls." The priests' marveling over the conversion of the Indians is interrupted by a Spanish *Commandante* chasing a Ramona-like "half-blood girl" whom he intends to debauch. The girl is ultimately saved by a wrathful Serra, who excommunicates the soldier and calls down "the curse of the church" upon him. Following the rescue of the girl, a *fiesta* erupts and a colorful crowd of dancers takes over the stage. As the festivities die down and sunset falls, Serra is left alone praying at a cross for "this dear land of

California, and all its people—now and in the centuries to come . . . [as I] must soon say farewell."[48]

The third and final act, set amid the ruins of Mission San Juan Capistrano, "is one of lamentation and sorrow. It depicts the decay of the Missions after the seizing of the Mission property by the Mexican government. The brave and glad days are no more. The work of the padres is undone and the Indian neophytes have been driven forth to starve and die."[49] A party of mission Indians mournfully crosses the stage on their way to bury their beloved Franciscan padre, who has starved to death in the wilderness. Ultimately two figures are left alone on the stage: Ubaldo, an aging Indian caretaker for the mission property, and Señora Yorba, a forceful Latin matriarch in the model of Señora Moreno. Their final lines are a strong appeal to the audience for support of the preservation of the missions.

> UBALDO: Perhaps the Americanos, who are so great and strong, even if they are always in such a damnable hurry, will restore these broken walls, Señora.
>
> SEÑORA YORBA: If they will but do so, God will bless them, Ubaldo. Surely, when the Americanos are building their great cities, and their tireless hands are making California the wonder of the world, so also will they think, sometime, of these holy places where the padres toiled and builded too—so well. Though we may not see it, Ubaldo—neither you nor I—maybe in God's good time the Mission bells will ring again their old, sweet music, even in Purisima and in lovely Soledad—and all the way from San Diego's sunny waters to Sonoma's moonlit hills. Maybe so, Ubaldo, maybe so. Oh, the Missions restored—and again a cross on every hill, on the green road to Monterey!
>
> UBALDO: Oh, cross of Christ!
>
> SEÑORA YORBA: Farewell, dear place. Farewell, San Juan, that lingers in ruin beside the sunset sea. Sleep well, ye who shall here abide until God's judgment day. Farewell, my countrymen, brown priests and all. Farewell, San Juan—farewell—farewell.[50]

In effect, this conclusion of "The Mission Play" wrote the work of the Landmarks Club into the history of the missions—naturalizing historical connections between the Franciscans and Americans, most especially those who preserved and valued the missions.

McGroarty took his play's appeal very seriously; not only did he become an energetic member of the Landmarks Club, he planned to use some of the proceeds from "The Mission Play" to build a new, twenty-second mission in the chain that would serve as an American capstone to Serra's efforts. The construction of a "Mission San Juan Evangelista at Verdugo Hills" (just northeast of Los Angeles) was remarkably to be a "non-sectarian project" and had "men and women of all creeds and faiths rallying to [McGroarty's] aid with offers of assistance." A local developer, N. V. Hartranft, went so far as to set aside an acre of land for the church's foundation. In the end, McGroarty's plans for Mission San Juan Evange-lista were eventually set aside as a result of his two-term election to the U.S. House of Representatives—a post he won largely because of support garnered from his fame as author of "The Mission Play."[51]

While McGroarty was the only mission booster who planned lit-erally to follow in Serra's mission-building footsteps, comparisons between the promoters of Old Mission Romance and the Franciscans were common. The strongest example can be found in Frank Miller's biography by Zola Gale. Gale claimed that because of his dedication to the history and romance of the missions, "in time, [people] may say that Frank Miller was one of the padres—Junipero Serra or even St. Francis—returned."[52] Similarly, Lummis biographer Gordon Dudley told readers:

Incomprehensible as it may seem at first, Father Serra and Charlie Lum-mis had much in common; despite their differences, which were con-siderable, they were much of the same ilk, as the following similarities will reveal: Both men started as sickly youngsters; they both knew pain, and both traveled incredible distances across deserts. They both survived physical danger, poor health, and great hardships with little means, yet went on to great achievements. Both were many-talented and had great enthusiasm, will power and endurance. Both were good business men, innovators, planners and administrators. Both loved scholarship and held the doctorate; both were linguists, musicians and diarists. Both were persuasive speakers who could enlist the support of others, and who won lifelong friendships among people of great accomplishment.

Both were at times crotchety and fought tenaciously for principles; yet each had a sense of humor and was unselfish. . . . With Serra as a builder of missions and Lummis as a preserver of those missions, California had an admirable team of great men to whom modern Californians owe an enormous debt.[53]

Beyond these flattering comparisons with the Franciscans, Charles Lummis, Frank Miller, John S. McGroarty, and Herbert Bolton were all knighted in the order of Queen Isabella by King Alfonso XIII of Spain for their commemoration of California's Spanish heritage. McGroarty, the only Catholic of the group, was also made a Knight of Saint George by Pope Pius XI for his positive portrayals of the missionary work of the church in California.

Comparative assessments of mission boosters and Franciscans were also employed in accounts of the lives of the padres; in his influential 1917 essay "The Mission as a Frontier Institution in the Spanish-American Colonies," Herbert Bolton anachronistically explained that "the missionaries served as most active promoters, one might even call them 'boosters' of the frontier."[54] The promotion of the romance of the missions' history served to encourage religious ecumenism in Southern California and integrate the region's Spanish heritage into the narrative of American history, again occluding any question of the legitimacy of the American conquest of the state. At base, however, the turn-of-the-century romantic presentation of the region's history gained its momentum from its ability to define Southern California as a unique and important place within the nation and promote economic growth, largely to the benefit of Southern California's wealthy business-owning elites, a fact clearly recognized by mission boosters. Charles Lummis, for instance, reminisced:

In 1916, at the Landmarks' [sic] Club "Candle Day," at San Fernando Mission (where we had re-roofed and saved the enormous monastery and church), after a Catholic Bishop and a Church of England Bishop, and a Methodist Bishop and a Jewish Rabbi and other men of many creeds had paid eloquent tribute to Junipero Serra and the Franciscan Missionaries, who founded Civilization on the Pacific Coast and left us these noble monuments of Faith and Architecture—then came the Apostle of Business, John S. Mitchell, President of the Los Angeles Chamber of Commerce. . . . He said, earnestly and emphatically, to the audience of 7,000 gathered there: "I have a confession to make that should have been made long ago. We businessmen, who like to think that we are shrewd and far-seeing, have long been blind. It took us a great while to realize that the Old Missions had anything but a sentimental interest. . . . We realize today that the Missions have not only a commercial value, but the greatest! WE REALIZE TODAY THAT THE OLD MISSIONS ARE WORTH MORE MONEY AND ARE A GREATER ASSEST TO SOUTHERN CALIFORNIA THAN OUR OIL, OUR ORANGES, EVEN OUR CLIMATE!"[55]

Significantly, religious leaders themselves seldom condemned the commercial interests of the mission boosters. Father Englehardt approvingly took note in his diary entry for June 7, 1915, that after being hosted at a Landmarks Club meeting at the Mission Inn by Charles Lummis, he thanked the owner, Frank Miller, by saying that "Saint Francis will repay," to which Miller replied, "Ah, he has already."[56]

"Lo Mexicano" en California

At the same time that Southern Californian boosters in the United States were inventing and adopting a Spanish heritage, revolutionaries in Mexico were beginning to renounce theirs. In September 1910, Mexican painter Gerardo Murillo (better known by his assumed Náhuatl name, Dr. Atl) organized an exhibition of *indigenista* Mexican art celebrating Mexico's pre-Columbian cultures. Atl's show was organized as a counter to a grand display of contemporary Spanish painting that had been sponsored by President Porfirio Díaz at the centennial celebration of the nation's independence from Spain. Though schooled in Italy and France, Atl was a fervent Mexican nationalist and anticolonialist who believed that rather than commemorate cultural connections to Europe, Mexicans should celebrate their national independence by giving voice to their uniquely hybrid culture. His exhibition was an attempt to do just that—to make use of *indigenismo* in the visual arts to create a sense of "*lo Mexicano*" (that which is Mexican).[57] Following his lead, many of the artists featured in his counter-exhibit employed the images of

Mexica and Mayan Indians as allegorical representations of the Mexican nation and depicted pre-Columbian cultures as the spiritual and moral roots of all that was distinctively Mexican.[58]

The timing of Atl's exhibition was prescient; the following month, Francisco Madero's declaration of *El Plan de San Luis Potosí* marked the beginning of a decade of civil war in Mexico, the end of the Díaz regime, and the flowering of Mexican nationalism. Whereas Díaz's government had been closely connected to Mexico's largest land-owners—a handful of wealthy Mexican families, American corporations, and the Catholic Church—the revolutionary factions that deposed him were populist, deeply nativist, and anticlerical. Two American military invasions of Mexico during the decade contributed to the rise of anti-American sentiments, most especially the occupation of the port of Veracruz by U.S. Marines in 1914; and although American "Blue Shirts" did not march on Mexico City as they had during the Mexican-American War, the presence of American troops greatly fueled Mexican nationalism.[59] Also, while conflict between church and state ran throughout Mexico's history, the revolutionary constitution of 1917 forbade religious education, denied priests the right to vote or wear cassocks in public, and gave the government the right to strip the church of property.

Changes in Mexico's political leadership during and after the Revolution also created changes in the nation's intellectual leadership. Díaz had surrounded himself with a group of positivist social scientists collectively known as *Los Científicos* (the Scientists) who served as advisers for his program of Mexican modernization. *Los Científicos* were largely influenced by European social materialism and social Darwinism. They believed that as Mexicans of European descent advanced in the modern world, the nation's "less able" *Mestizo-*, Indian-, African-, and Asian-descended populations were to necessarily bear the burden. In stark contrast, Mexico's postrevolutionary leaders brought philosophical idealists into national prominence as advisers and cabinet members. These intellectuals were largely critical of scientific materialism and positivism and were also deeply committed to employing and supporting the resources of the humanities to solve Mexico's social problems, most notably through campaigns for the education of the nation's largely rural indigenous and *Mestizo* populations.

As political tides turned, the popularity of the idea of a uniquely Mexican art grew. In 1914, President Carranza named Dr. Atl as Director of the National Art Academy, where he inspired, mentored, and sometimes clashed with many of Mexico's greatest painters, including David Alfaro Siqueiros, Jose Clementé Orozco, and Diego Rivera. In his autobiography, Orozco reminisces that at

> nightly sessions in the Academy, as we listened to the fervent voice of that agitator Dr. Atl, we began to suspect that the whole of the colonial situation was nothing but a swindle foisted on us by international traders. We [Mexicans] too had a character, which was quite the equal of any other. We would learn what the ancients and the foreigners could teach us, but we could do as much as they or more. It was not pride but self confidence that moved us to this belief, a sense of our own being and our destiny.[60]

Atl indoctrinated these already politicized young artists into the belief that "Architects, painters and sculptors should not work with an exhibition or a degree in mind, but rather to decorate a building [with instructive murals]. . . . Reform must come at the same time in the political, administrative, military, and artistic orders."[61] For Atl there was no better venue for the expression of a new self-aware Mexican art than through public art, an idea his students would take to heart in their own work.

The didactic power of muralism was quickly recognized by José Vasconcelos, Mexico's Secretary of Education from 1921 to 1924. Vasconcelos launched the most ambitious program of literacy campaigns that Mexico had seen to date, but he saw public murals as a way to make the idea of a new Mexican nation immediately accessible and visible to all its citizens. The first building for which Vasconcelos commissioned murals was the colonial chapel of San Pedro y San Pablo in Mexico City, a church that had been converted for military use during wartime and that was now to serve as a public lecture hall. Appropriately enough, Atl was among the first artists commissioned to paint the desecrated church; he was extremely critical of the abuses committed by the Catholic Church in Mexico. While painting in Italy as a young man Atl had co-written with Benito Mussolini an anticlerical tract and during the Mexican Revolution he had led the sacking of many churches by Carranza's troops.[62] Commissions from Vasconcelos for murals at the National Preparatory School, the Bolívar Amphitheater, the Colégio Chico, and the Education Ministry building itself all quickly followed, but these went to his students, "*Los Trés Grandes*," Siqueiros, Orozco, and Rivera, younger painters who would become synonymous with Mexican muralism and popularize the movement worldwide.

In making his commissions, Vasconcelos chose the building and selected the artist, but he left all matters of content and form to the artists themselves, allowing for considerable freedom of expression. However, some calls for uniformity of style came from the muralists themselves; Siqueiros, for example, wrote an influential essay making "Three Appeals of Timely Orientation to Painters and Sculptors of the New American Generation." He counseled his fellow artists:

> As regards ourselves, we must come closer to the works of the ancient settlers of our vales, Indian painters and sculptors (Mayan, Aztec, Inca, etc., etc.). . . . Let us borrow their synthetic energy, but let us avoid lamentable archeological reconstruction so fashionable among us "Indianism," "Primitivism," "Americanism."[63]

Most muralists agreed with Siqueiros; they did not attempt to simply reproduce Indigenous art in their new and distinctively Mexican art. Rather, the muralists sought to bring the nation's past into conversation with its present. Their artistic *indigenismo* was largely an attempt to give shape to a modern understanding of the Mexican nation.

Though the Mexican mural movement quickly gained international acclaim, in 1924 Vasconcelos's term as Secretary of Education ended with the election of President Calles, and with it too ended much of the Mexican government's support for muralists. Diego Rivera was retained to continue his work painting the Ministry of Education building, but most other muralists left Mexico in search of new commissions in Latin America, Europe, and the United States. Mexican muralism would largely mature abroad.

Faced with strong political adversaries, Vasconcelos himself left Mexico for Spain in 1925. During that exilic year he wrote and published his most influential essay, "*La Raza Cósmica*." Although he remained a

Mexican patriot, in exile Vasconcelos's nationalism was broadened by a concern with pan–Latin American unity. "*La Raza Cósmica*" argued for the substitution of race for the nation-state as the central organizing principle for humanity and saw the current age as a conflict between Latin America and Anglo-Saxon America, "a conflict of institutions, aims and ideals."[64] He predicted the eventual triumph of Latin America in this struggle, claiming that "We in [Latin] America shall arrive, before any other part of the world, at the creation of a new race fashioned out of the treasures of all the previous ones; the final race, the cosmic race."[65] Because Latin America led the world in race-mixture and Latinos were a people for whom "beauty is the main reason for everything," they would be at the vanguard of a spontaneous movement of "aesthetic eugenics" that would usher in a new age for humanity. As marriage and reproduction became "a work of art" wherein people selected partners based on their desirable qualities instead of their race, humanity itself would be improved. In contrast with the future harmony of a racially mixed Latin America, Vasconcelos predicted, "The Yankees will end up building the last great empire of a single race, the final empire of White supremacy."[66] This "White Empire" would eventually collapse from its own inbred weaknesses and white Americans would ultimately give up their false pride and join the new cosmic race in the tropics.

But Vasconcelos's hope for a final "cosmic" racial synthesis clearly contained a racism of its own; racial mixture would better humanity by extinguishing what he saw as the less desirable traits in the "Indian, Black and Asian" races.[67] Similarly, he accused the "Anglo-Saxon" of committing "*the sin of destroying [dissimilar] races, while we [Latin Americans] assimilated them,*"[68] ignoring the long and brutal history of racism, genocide, and slavery in Latin America.

Although "*La Raza Cósmica*" was his most ardent anti-American statement, Vasconcelos left Spain in 1926 to continue his exile in the United States and teach at the University of Chicago and then at Stanford University. Significantly, the essay would have greater continuing cultural influence in the United States among later generations of ethnic Mexicans than in Latin America.

While the rate of Mexican migration to the United States rose during the Mexican Revolution in the 1910s, it was not until the 1920s that it reached its peak. This postwar migration doubled the number of

Mexican-born residents of the United States in a single decade, from roughly 750,000 in 1920 to 1,450,000 by 1930. By 1928 Los Angeles had the largest Mexican-born population of any city outside of Mexico.[69] This northward migration of Mexican workers was motivated, in part, by the worsening of protracted economic hardships in Mexico and the lure of jobs in the rapidly developing American Southwest; these were jobs available to Mexicans in large part as a result of new immigration restrictions placed on Asian and European laborers.[70] At the time, as many as a thousand Mexican laborers a week were recruited by agents of the Southern Pacific and Santa Fe railroads along the U.S.-Mexico border as track hands and agricultural workers; the very same rail lines that had initially brought American settlers to Southern California eventually re-introduced a large ethnic Mexican population as well. Upon arrival in Southern California, these Mexican immigrants encountered Americans' appropriation of the Spanish colonial past.

Although a great many ethnic Mexicans in California came to share Americans' love of *Ramona* and its attendant romance, their enthusiasm was born from a different understanding of the novel from that of its American audience. Mexicans' reading of *Ramona* was directly shaped by José Martí, the celebrated hero of the Cuban revolution.[71] Martí read the novel just after it was first published in 1885, while living in exile in New York City, and was so deeply moved by it that he immediately embarked on a Spanish translation. He saw *Ramona* as a "very Mexican book," a genuinely *indigenista* novel that would be instructive to Latin Americans in their treatment of Indigenous peoples.[72] Martí placed the narrative of *Ramona* in Mexico by translating all references to Southern California as Baja California, resulting in a version of Jackson's story that occurs in an oddly liminal place that is at once Mexico *and* the United States. In 1888, after three years of work, Martí's translation was printed and distributed in Mexico City at his own expense, but his effort initially met with limited recognition and muted response. Porfirio Díaz was still in office and modern Mexican *indigenismo* had not yet come into its own.[73]

Nonetheless, in the 1910s and 1920s, Mexicans living in Southern California responded quite favorably to *Ramona*. Most migrants intended to return home to the South as soon as they were able, and Ramona's triumphal return to Mexico City as a rich woman expressed familiar aspirations. The novel's condemnation of American injustice toward those of mixed and Indian blood also resonated with their experience as *Mestizos* facing white racism in Southern California. Even the novel's nostalgic treatment of the passing of California's missions spoke to Mexican immigrants. Many of them had been first-hand witnesses to the lynching of priests and the sacking of churches in the anticlerical violence of the Revolution and the *Cristero* Rebellion of the late 1920s.[74] Thus, the novel's lamentations about secularized Catholic churches and absent priests proved to be powerful imagery for Catholic Mexican immigrants in Southern California.

The first cinematic rendition of *Ramona* was directed by D. W. Griffith in 1910 and starred Mary Pickford. A longer and more popular version was released in 1927 starring Dolores Del Río, a Mexican actress who had only just emigrated to Hollywood two years earlier. Adoring ethnic Mexican audiences enthusiastically packed movie houses to see their favorite new actress as the heroic Ramona.

Although a great number of Mexico's Catholic clergy also came to Southern California during the 1910s and 1920s, their travels northward were largely a result of involuntary exile, and their principal concern was in returning to Mexico as soon as possible. As a result, they were not always able to tend to the spiritual well-being of Mexican Catholics in the United States. With the exception of limited Americanization campaigns and the funding of Sunday schools for Mexican children, Mexican and Mexican-American communities were largely neglected by the American Catholic clergy well into the 1940s. However, the neglect often went both ways. Though most Mexican immigrants were still nominally Catholic, the anticlerical violence of the war had left many of them unaccustomed to regular church attendance, and others were themselves staunchly anticlerical.[75]

The arrival of great numbers of Mexicans to Southern California did not, however, go unnoticed by Southern California's Protestants.[76] At the 1922 annual conference of Southern California Congregational Churches in San Bernardino, for example, ministers attempted to inspire interest in missionary work in the region's Mexican communities, reminding church members that

[t]he greatest mission appeal to the churches of Southern California is our Mexican mission—a work in the interest of a people who first settled

here and who have added their charms to our beautiful state with their musical names for our cities, mountains, rivers and canyons. The old missions have been the point of interest to adventurous settlers and tourists. Our State is beautiful because we have copied their mission architecture. We are too often interested in the poor heathen under the palm tree in Africa, but do not forget the man under the citrus and walnut trees on your own premises. . . . It is cheaper to convert the Mexican here than in Old Mexico and when converted, he makes a good church member and a good citizen.[77]

Still, in spite of Protestant efforts and relative neglect by the Catholic clergy, at the time the rate of conversion among Mexican Catholics in Southern California never exceeded 10 percent.[78]

Although Mexican participation in American Catholic services was low, domestic piety in the form of home altars and prayer groups maintained connections to the Catholic faith, much as it had for earlier Catholic immigrant groups. The proximity of the Mexican border and the speed of rail travel further limited incentives to actively assimilate or convert. These factors, combined with racism and segregation, resulted in relatively insular Mexican and Mexican-American communities in California in the early twentieth century; from 1910 to 1930, only 5 to 13 percent of Mexican nationals in the United States applied for permanent residency or citizenship.[79]

When José Vasconcelos set foot in California in 1928, nearly one in ten Mexican citizens lived in the United States as residents of *Mexico de afuera* or "greater Mexico."[80] However, less than a century before his arrival, California had still been part of Mexico, and some descendants of the Californios and the more established nineteenth-century Mexican immigrants *had* made a place for themselves in American society and its racial hierarchies, largely by charting their ancestry to Spain rather than to Mexico.

Upon his arrival at Stanford University, and much to his amazement, Vasconcelos witnessed a Californian "Spanish Fiesta." He described his reaction to the event in an essay entitled "*Noche Californiana*" in *La Opinion*, Los Angeles's Spanish-language newspaper. Vasconcelos reported that the featured performer of the event was Luisa Espinel, a California-born ethnic Mexican who had studied Spanish folklore. He was taken by her dark skin and beautiful brown eyes that were "deep like the millenniums of Indigenous America." When he heard her speak perfect English he expected her to "destroy" the Spanish language with "one of those English accents that are so inappropriate for one of the Hispanic race." To his great surprise, her Spanish was flawless and her singing was enchanting. He recounts,

> "Our motherland," said the Californian completely in English to her Anglo-Saxon audience, "our motherland is Spain." "And Mexico?" a compatriot of mine who was in attendance asked me. "Why hasn't she remembered Mexico given that she looks more Mexican than Spanish?" I did not know how to respond to his question, but later, in regards to another matter[,] a Californian told me: "My Spanish relatives came some from New Orleans, others through Mexico; others are Indians from Colorado or New Mexico who were influenced generations ago by Spanish culture that came from Mexico"; but that which is Mexican does not exist for these Californians who call themselves Latinos in order to differentiate themselves from their Anglo-Saxon compatriots. I thought to myself with a certain bitterness: What reason would they have to be devoted to Mexico if not for the common bond of Spanish traditions? . . . What else did Mexico give these regions in its half century of militaristic dominion? . . . Have we ever sent these brothers of ours a tool, an idea, or even a song? Almost nothing of the sort came here, not when we were Aztecs nor when we finished being Spaniards. We sent them nothing but armies that administered brutal punishments. . . . How then are we to have a right to be offended when the Californians don't celebrate their extinguished Mexicanness, but do patriotically embrace all things Spanish? If all the good that came to them from Mexico was Spanish? It is natural[,] then, for these reasons, that in their time of anguish, the Californians had turned with their entire hearts, not to Mexico because of whom they lost their country and destiny, but to Spain because of whom they possess and retain their soul.[81]

Spanish blood had long been an asset in Mexico's racial hierarchies, and thanks to American hispanophilia, so too in the United States. Spanish ancestry implied whiteness whereas Mexican ancestry did not. In California, ethnic Mexicans claiming Spanish ancestry did so, in part, within the racial and historical framework established by Americans. However, in Mexico, many postrevolutionary expressions of *indigenismo* championed the idea that Indigenous culture, not race, made one authentically Mexican, providing a more inclusive, though problematic, understanding of Mexican identity, one that would have a profound impact on subsequent generations of ethnic Mexicans in the United States.[82]

"More Spanish Than Any Hotel-de-Ville in Spain"

By the mid-1910s, Mission Revival had been Southern California's signature architectural style for nearly twenty years. It was a time when interest in the missions and mission preservation was growing. The ruins of Mission San Juan Capistrano alone were attracting between 500 and 2,000 visitors daily.[83] Even so, there was a demand for evolution in style. As hastily built Mission Revival bungalows became common in Southern California's mushrooming communities, critics began to see them as "cheap contraptions" that were "paperlike" and "flimsy."[84] Even Charles Lummis, perhaps the style's greatest proponent, came to believe that "most of the so-called 'Mission Style' now going up all over California isn't Mission at all, nor architecture, but an obvious, awkward and detestable FAKE."[85] Originally suggestive of romantic history and affluence, Mission Revival began to lose its appeal when poorly mass-produced; as a result, architects began to search for architectural alternatives that would still be appropriate to the region's style.

Among the most notable attempts were arts and crafts designs that sought to exemplify "the three essentials of good building, strength, simplicity and honesty," most typically in the form of the California bungalow[86] as well as a brief Mayan Revival that was inaugurated by Frank Lloyd Wright's Hollyhock House (1920) and continued in the fanciful creations of Robert Stacy-Judd. Though the Mayan Revival employed Mesoamerican as opposed to Spanish forms, Wright saw them as an expression of the "elemental landscape of Southern California," and Stacy-Judd problematically saw them as being true to the region's pre-history.[87] While these, and other, architectural trends made their mark on Southern California's built environment, by far the most popular new style to emerge was one that evolved directly from Mission Revival, and that was Spanish Revival.

In 1915, Californians celebrated the opening of the Panama Canal with two competing expositions, the Panama-Pacific International Exhibition in San Francisco and the Panama-California Exposition in San Diego. Although San Francisco put on the larger fair, it was San Diego's Exposition that would have a more enduring legacy in California, as it was here that Spanish Revival was truly popularized. Organizers in San Diego were not content to commission local Mission Revival architects for their Exposition and instead sought nationally recognized designers to raise the profile of their fair. John C. Olmstead (a son of Frederick Law Olmstead) was hired to plan the grounds in City Park, which was renamed Balboa Park after Vasco Núñez de Balboa, the Spanish explorer who crossed the Isthmus of Panama and was the first European to see the Pacific Ocean from the Americas. Bertram Goodhue was hired to plan the Exposition's grand buildings. Goodhue was one of the nation's leading Gothic Revival architects, but he saw the San Diego Exposition as a great opportunity to give light to his recent interest in baroque and colonial Spanish architecture.[88]

The result was a powerfully ornate architecture. In contrast to the simplicity of the lines of Mission Revival, Spanish Revival allowed architects to incorporate a wider and more elaborate range of forms. The imitation of all Spanish architecture became fair game, including even the flamboyant Churrigueresque, creating a feeling of exoticism and grandeur, while the retention of simple white plaster walls and red-tiled roofs maintained a continuity with the region's mission style and history.[89]

Following San Diego's Exposition, the residents of Nordhoff, California, changed their town's name to Ojai (after the original Indigenous name of the valley in which it was located) and rebuilt many of its principal buildings in the Spanish Revival style in an attempt to beautify and promote the place. Ojai's adoption of Spanish Revival was soon followed by the birth of the planned suburban communities of Palos Verdes and Rancho Santa Fe near Los Angeles and San Diego, respectively. Both of these developments employed the Spanish Revival style, and unlike earlier Mission Revival tracts, these communities were promoted as exclusive enclaves with "rigid, yet highly desirable restrictions

[that] protect your investment" and homes that were built with care and priced to match.[90]

However, the most successful citywide installation of Spanish Revival architecture was effected in Santa Barbara. Following the Panama-California Exposition, Bertram Goodhue had begun to winter in Santa Barbara, and he took an active interest in the city's architecture. The city still looked much as it had thirty-five years earlier when Helen Hunt Jackson dismissed it as a "New England town," and Goodhue convincingly advocated the introduction of the Spanish Revival style. Beginning in 1919 with a competition for a Spanish design for the city's new courthouse, Santa Barbara began to re-create itself in the Spanish mold.

In 1920, Bernard Hoffman, a wealthy New York transplant, purchased the former home of José de la Guerra y Noriega, known to locals as "the de la Guerra adobe" that sat in the center of town. Along with other city leaders, he sponsored the construction of "El Paseo de la Guerra," which was billed as a typical "Street in Spain" and adjoined the de la Guerra property with the intent of developing the downtown district for tourism.[91] However, not all residents were convinced of the desirability or equity of the economic benefits of the turn toward Spanish Revival. One concerned citizen, writing in 1922, cajoled the editor of the local newspaper not to support the creation of an upscale "Street in Spain" but instead fight to make Santa Barbara

> a city where any good square American citizen who has to work for a living can live and do as well as he can anywhere else and boost for some good stable industries so that Santa Barbara will be a truly American City, self-supporting, not living off the largess of the rich, but a producer that will be a credit to our great State of California and not an imitation of Greenwich Village. Why not in all fairness[,] Mr. Editor, does not the Chamber of Commerce put a big sign at each of the entrances to the city,
> "Millionaires Welcome"
> "Plain Americans, Abandon Hope All Ye Who Enter Here."[92]

However, the powerful economic incentives and popularity of the idea of re-creating Santa Barbara as "A City in Spain" were simply too great for the organization of any successful resistance. Shortly, nature itself would conspire to transform the place.

On June 29, 1925, a major earthquake destroyed most of Santa Barbara's downtown. Although the tremor claimed many victims—nine people were killed, hundreds were injured, and many thousands of dollars were lost in property damage—many of Santa Barbara's leading residents saw the quake as a blessing rather than a tragedy. It made the much-desired changes in the city's architectural landscape necessary. To their minds, Santa Barbara could "now make itself the most beautiful city in America."[93] Just two weeks after the Santa Barbara earthquake, a visiting banker, Dr. L. R. Sevier, predicted, "Just as sure as I am alive, it will only be a matter of time until real estate value in the present wrecked city will stand at a figure of twice what [it was] before the disaster."[94] He was soon proven right.

The nation's first Architectural Board of Review was assembled in Santa Barbara to maintain uniformity of design during the post-earthquake building rush.[95] All new structures were made to conform legally to the city's Spanish theme as even mailboxes and public trash receptacles were given a "Spanish" design. In the words of architectural historian David Gebhard, "The new Santa Barbara was to carry forth the Hispanic traditions as it [sic] might have evolved if California had remained a Spanish colony."[96] In 1926, more than 2,000 construction proposals were processed by the Review Board. By the year's end, tourists and residents encountered a uniformly "Spanish flavored" city whose architecture was tightly integrated.[97]

One Santa Barbara businessman was quoted in the *Santa Barbara Morning Press* as fairly gushing that if you

> add our historical charm, as represented in the Queen of the Missions, to the charm of a typically Spanish city and its wonderful setting of mountain and sea you have a lure that the tourist cannot resist. And there is no better "business" than the tourist business.[98]

As they remodeled their city, Santa Barbarans maintained a great awareness of what might be done to bring tourist dollars into the local economy, including being conscious of who the tourists were. A month after the earthquake, one editorial in the *Santa Barbara Morning Press*

highlighted the considerations of gender that had to be made in promoting tourism. The editor wrote that

> [i]n rebuilding our city, I wonder if we remember how many of our tour-
> ists are women? . . . It is largely the women who decide where the family
> shall spend its vacation and how long shall be the stay. . . . Through their
> clubs and various organizations women are becoming interested in civic
> betterment. We must win their approval of the way we rebuild our city.[99]

The upper-class women who formed the bulk of preservation and
historical societies, such as the Landmarks Club and the Camino Real
Association, were often the same ones who toured the missions with
their families on holiday. Santa Barbara captured these tourists' hearts
with an architecture that was well coordinated with its mission.[100]

Santa Barbara's Spanish transformation was not only cast in the static
shapes of the city's buildings, it was (and is still) also performed in the
city's "Old Spanish Days *Fiesta*." With Spanish Revival buildings serving as the sets, the pageantry of the Old Spanish Days festival acted out
the city's connection to Spain. Unlike previous historical parades such
as that of the Los Angeles *Fiestas* or even those held at the Panama-
California Exposition, the Old Spanish Days parade portrayed a specifically local history. This was the first American *Fiesta* to largely omit the
Spanish conquest of Latin America from its historical parade—no references were made to the Aztecs, Incas, or Pueblos. Instead, the Santa
Barbara "Historical Pageant Parade" presented

> [t]he history of Santa Barbara from the time the Chumach [*sic*] Indians
> made their way to the head of the lagoon to the raising of the American
> Flag by General Fremont portrayed in 14 episodes, each as exact a repro-
> duction of the time it represents as exhaustive research can make it.[101]

Every "episode" was portrayed by members of a different community group, each with a national flag appropriate to its time—ultimately
revealing the historical lesson of the "Old Spanish Days *Fiesta*."

- EPISODE ONE, Chumach [*sic*] Indians (Represented initially by the Rotary
  Club and at later *Fiestas* by "Mission Indians"), *Spanish Flag*.

- EPISODE TWO, Cabrillo with his Soldiers and Sailors (Represented by the Kiwanis Club), *Spanish Flag.*
- EPISODE THREE, Francis Drake and His Soldiers and Sailors (Represented by the Rotary Club), *English Flag.*
- EPISODE FOUR, Sebastian Viscaino with His Soldiers and Sailors (Represented by the Exchange Club), *Spanish Flag.*
- EPISODE FIVE, Gaspar de Portola and His Followers (Represented by Club La Iberica), *Spanish Flag.*
- EPISODE SIX, José Ortega, Filipe [*sic*] de Neve, Father Serra and Followers (Represented by Mission Fathers and Knights of Columbus), *Spanish Flag.*
- EPISODE SEVEN, José Francisco Ortega and Followers (Represented by Elks and Antlers), *Spanish Flag.*
- EPISODE EIGHT, Padre Fermin de Lasuen and Bretheren (Represented by Mission Fathers and Knights of Columbus), *Spanish Flag.*
- EPISODE NINE, Wedding Party [this is modeled after Richard Henry Dana's description of the wedding he attended at the de la Guerra house] (Represented by Direct Descendants of the Spanish Pioneers), *Spanish Flag.*
- EPISODE TEN, Hipolite Bouchard and Crew of Freebooters [pirates who had attacked Santa Barbara in the nineteenth century] (Represented by the Lions Club), *Spanish Flag.*
- EPISODE ELEVEN, Lieut. Luis Antonio Arguello and Soldiers (Represented by the 20-30 Club), *Mexican Flag.*
- EPISODE TWELVE, Bear Flag Party (Represented by the Native Sons of the Golden West), *Bear Flag.*
- EPISODE THIRTEEN, The Early Californians (Represented by Comision Honorifica Mexicana), *Bear Flag.*
- EPISODE FOURTEEN, Fremont in Santa Barbara (Represented by Members of the Eagles Aeire), *American Flag.*[102]

Curiously, the Mexican flag was carried by Anglo re-enactors and the Bear Flag was carried by ethnic *mutualistas.* Still, the message was clear: California's past was Spanish, with little connection to Mexico and Mexicans; the brief day-long landing of Sir Francis Drake on the California coast in 1574 was given as much play in the parade as the thirty years of Mexican rule in the nineteenth century that ended with an American military conquest.

Following the historical pageant, revelers were treated to a dramatic production entitled "*La Entrada de los Americanos*" that triumphantly portrayed the American conquest of the region. The climax of the play occurs when at "The Presidio Santa Barbara, [on] A Sunday Morning, December 28, 1846, while the good people of the pueblo were at church, Fremont was able to take the territory without resistance, adding California to the United States."[103] While this quick resolution made for less than stirring drama, it did allow the conquest of California to be presented as bloodless and unproblematic.

Because of the relatively small and intimate scale of the Santa Barbara *Fiesta*, organizers encouraged the entire population to dress up in stylized Spanish colonial costumes, not only during the historical parade but also during the entire three days of the fair.[104] One announcement advised revelers that "Spanish costume is worn generally through the Fiesta and is considered correct for all social occasions."[105]

Not only did the city's Anglo-American residents and tourists dress as Spaniards, its ethnic Mexican community that identified as "Spanish" did so as well. The descendants of Santa Barbara's Californios, most notably the de la Guerra family, became central, costumed participants in the "Old Spanish Days *Fiesta*," lending it a mantle of "authenticity," and they in turn received adulation from *Fiesta* organizers. At the first Santa Barbara *Fiesta*, Charles Lummis himself raised a toast to the de la Guerras, saying,

> As the blood of Castile represented the highest culture of Old Spain, so the blood of early Santa Barbara and Ventura families represents the highest aristocracy of California. I mean aristocracy not in the sense of snobbery, but in the old Greek sense—as representing the best, by right of effort, intellect and achievement.[106]

Social clubs and mutual aid societies such as La Iberica and Comision Honorifica Mexicana from Santa Barbara's growing Mexican-American community became regular participants in the parade and had prominent parts in the *Fiesta*, but (with the exception shown above) they typically portrayed only Spaniards or aristocratic Californios. California's Mexican history was to be denied even by some ethnic Mexicans in the presentation of the city's history. Still, Mexican culture *was* incorporated into the event by *Fiesta* organizers, but it was contained in a small "Mexican Village" where revelers could purchase curios and eat Mexican food while being entertained by hired Mexican performers.

Although the "Mexican Village" was initially a sideshow, its growing yearly presence at the *Fiesta* was significant as a marker of the rise of Americans' interest in Mexico. The 1920s had inaugurated the "good-neighbor" era in U.S.-Mexican political relations. American political and business leaders began a program of cultural exchange, sparking an "American re-discovery of Mexico" in order to promote the return of American financial investment to Mexico after the upheaval of the Mexican Revolution. At a time when Americans became increasingly interested in the folk art and culture of their own country, the Carnegie and Rockefeller corporations brought touring exhibitions of Mexican folk art to the United States, creating an "enormous vogue of things Mexican."[107]

By 1930, even Santa Barbara's "Old Spanish Days *Fiesta*" organizers were interested in hosting an "Exhibition of Mexican Popular Arts and Crafts" financed by the Carnegie Corporation. Strikingly, the exhibition was to be accompanied by no less a personage than Dr. Atl, who was to "be present at the time of the Old Spanish Days *Fiesta* as a representative of our neighbors in Mexico." Remarkably, *Fiesta* organizers had the temerity to ask Dr. Atl, a great Mexican *indigenista* and nationalist, to "bring a [Spanish] costume which would make it possible for him to participate in certain official projects."[108] Ultimately the exhibition fell through because of "a change of administration," and perhaps as a result of Atl's doubtless negative reaction at being asked to masquerade as a Spaniard.[109]

American hispanophilia and interest in Mexican folk art reached a strange synthesis that same year, with the opening of Olvera Street, a "picturesque Mexican Market" in Los Angeles's old Plaza, the heart of the city's Mexican-American community. Olvera Street was "restored" as a tourist attraction that would feature costumed attendants and Mexican curio shops, providing Los Angeles with a fixed and year-long *Fiesta*, largely through the efforts of entrepreneur Christine Sterling, with the political backing of Harry Chandler of the *Los Angeles Times*.[110]

Shortly after the opening of Olvera Street, F. K. Krenz of the Plaza Art Center commissioned David Alfaro Siqueiros to paint an eighty-foot mural that would be visible to patrons of the new marketplace. Unlike his colleagues Rivera and Orozco, who were also painting in the state at the time but whose California murals were largely uncontroversial, Siqueiros took the opportunity presented by his commission to express a strong ideological critique of the United States above the shops selling Mexican curios. During the entire five months he worked on the mural, it was invisible to the public under screened scaffolding, and when it was finally unveiled in October 1932, much of his American audience was scandalized.[111] In Siqueiros's own words, the mural *Tropical America* depicted

> our land of America, of undernourished natives, of enslaved Indians and Negroes, that nevertheless inhabit the most fertile land in which the richest and most ferocious people on earth lie. And as a symbol of the United States' imperialism, the principal capitalist oppressor, I used an Indian crucified on a double cross, on top of which stood the Yankee eagle of American finance.[112]

Leading Angelenos denounced the work as everything from communist to simply ugly, and the mural was soon whitewashed and forgotten. Nearly forty years would lapse before *Tropical America* would be rediscovered and celebrated in Los Angeles.

Shortly after he finished the mural and in part because of the controversy surrounding its reception, American immigration officials refused Siqueiros a routine extension of his visa, effectively deporting him. But he was not alone; by the 1930s the "Yankee eagle of American finance" was beginning to feel the effects of the Great Depression, and Mexicans became the targets of large-scale repatriation campaigns intended to divest the state of once-needed Mexican laborers.

Coda

During the first three decades of the twentieth century, more than 1 million Mexicans crossed the border into the United States and created a home away from home in a *Mexico de afuera*. In the context of Southern California, ethnic Mexicans became both consumers of American regional culture and agents that transformed it, defying exclusive definitions of space, place, and history. In doing so they created hybrid border cultures and *barrio* spaces that existed in direct relation (and often in opposition) to American cultural hegemony as well as to the cultural and political revolutions occurring in their homeland.

Immigrants' revitalization of Mexican culture in California during the 1910s and 1920s happened at a time when Mexico was redefining itself as a nation. The aesthetics of this nationalist project were carried out in large part through the celebration and reimagining of the nation's connections to its Indigenous past. In the far American West, this resulted in a paradoxical opportunity for cultural exchange; nationalist *indigenista* arts flowering in Mexico during and after the revolution were generally well received as foreign folk art by Americans deeply invested in their own regional hispanophilia. The cultural production of space and place through the use of Mission and Spanish Revival styles and widespread appropriation of California pastoral history served as a means to define what was American and what was not. Thus, this contradictory but functional divide allowed Americans to admire Mexican arts portraying Indigenous themes even as they claimed Spanish colonial aesthetics as their own. The fact that the popularity of Mission and Spanish Revival architecture intensified at the very moment that in-migration from Mexico was rapidly increasing suggests that the popularity of these architectural vocabularies was accelerated because of these contemporary social transformations.[113]

The firm inculcation of regional aesthetics promoted a form of ecumenism in California in which both Protestants and Catholics embraced romantic nineteenth-century narratives of California's Mission history. Moreover, this ecumenical culture encouraged the recognition of the significance of the missions as more than simply churches but also as local civic monuments. This complex but common uncoupling of mission architecture from Catholicism, in turn, encouraged congregations of many denominations to build their churches in the Mission Revival style.

While a great number of Mexican Catholic clergy lived in exile in the United States during the Mexican Revolution, their stay did not dampen American enthusiasm for mission preservation or change critical attitudes surrounding the issue of secularization during California's Mexican period. Instead, the issue of anticlerical violence in Mexico provided a further impetus for the popularization of attempts to preserve and reconstruct the missions.

Preservation efforts began in part through the influence of attorney John Doyle's Historical Society of Southern California and grew in popularity among civic-minded citizens. The most successful preservationists, members of the Landmarks Club headed by Charles Lummis, portrayed their work as a crucially important recuperation of the region's unique but rapidly fading history. Preservation provided Californians with a concrete way to morally and materially correct the consequences of the perceived crime of secularization. Predictably, the declension narratives that fueled preservation efforts followed the conventions that had been established decades earlier, given the imprimatur of validity through the Pious Fund Case and brought to life through the narrative of *Ramona*.

Thus, preservation was more than the simple reconstruction of ruined or damaged buildings. It actively created public history and in doing so gained considerable popular support in the early twentieth century as religious, commercial, and civic interests that benefited from it worked together to see its dissemination through a variety of means—from school curricula, to architecture, to the public spectacle of pageantry and theater.

At its peak in popularity in California in the 1910s and 1920s, pageantry used historical narration and theatrical performance in the service of regional boosterism and the promotion of local tourism. Moreover, embedded within these regional pageants were reinscriptions of social and spatial relationships between Anglos and Mexicans. As shown previously, American articulations of Southern California's regionalism delegitimized the presence of ethnic Mexicans and defined them as foreigners in places that retained their original place names (of colonial and Mexican origin) or had been given newly fashioned (and sometimes quite awkward) ones in anglicized Spanish.

The American hispanicization of space and place reached its apex in the rapid and wholesale architectural transformation of Santa Barbara from a city originally modeled on small New England towns into an exclusive and affluent community re-created in a legally enforced uniform Spanish Revival style. The nearly century-long annual performance of the pageantry of Santa Barbara's "Old Spanish Days" speaks to the success with which an Arcadian regionalist understanding of history and place has been deeply inculcated in this part of Southern California.

The transformations of space, place, and history that occurred in Southern California show us that architecture provides a monumental physical corpus for communal or cultural memories. The topography of the built environment comes to signify particular cultural assumptions and historical tropes. Thus, the mnemic traces that become attached to architecture reinforce particular historical conventions. They become the landmarks that unify a vision of community and establish its boundaries.

Cultural hegemonies would stand little chance of enduring without geographical and architectural landmarks as ever-present reinforcements of their social visions. By the same token, as we shall see, the creation of counter-hegemonies can make similar use of space, place, and public history as markers for resistance to dominant ideologies and nationalist assertions of subaltern cultures.

4

Making Aztlán

Mexicans who live in the region are doubtless more bewil-
dered by these annual Spanish Hijinks than any other group
in the community. Only Mexicans willing and able to pass
as Spaniards and Californios, denying their Mexican heritage[,] could hope to participate in southwestern civic life.
—Carey McWilliams, *Southern California Country: An
Island on the Land*, 1946

The capacity for dissociating the Indian of yesterday from
the Indian of today is a mental alchemy that endures to the
present.
—Bonfil Batalla, *Mexico Profundo*, 1996

A People In-Between

In the 1930s, Los Angeles (the American city with the largest Mexican-born population) became a focal point for Mexican repatriation
efforts. Roughly 50,000, or about a third, of the city's Mexican residents
returned to Mexico from 1930 to 1939, many forcibly, some voluntarily.[1]
Although repatriation campaigns were supported in the United States
by racist rhetoric and nativist legislation, in the initial portion of the
decade the American Immigration Service was aided by Mexican con-
sular officials in carrying out the campaigns. The Mexican government
was eager to facilitate the homecoming of its citizens; the return of
those who had left in the aftermath of the Mexican Revolution would
not only increase the ranks of Mexico's skilled and modernized laborers, it would also ease the embarrassment of the Mexican government
at having such a large émigré community in the United States.[2]

By the mid-1930s, Mexicans wishing to repatriate had largely done so, but those who chose to stay continued to face the risk of forced repatriation as well as a steady increase in anti-Mexican sentiment. With the arrival in California of destitute "Okies" from the Dust Bowl states, Mexican agricultural workers faced greater competition for precious jobs. Although these latter-day "Pikes" were often reviled by more affluent Anglo Californians, "Okies" were, nonetheless, usually, hired over Mexicans.[3] Beyond these adversities, Mexicans attempting to create more settled lives for themselves in the United States and no longer intending to return to Mexico were faced with serious issues around their identity. They were now more "*de afuera*" than Mexican, and yet they faced considerable challenges to their integration into American society as they were ostracized by established and poor migratory whites alike. This in-between condition as it was experienced during World War II was poignantly described by sociologist Emory Bogardus in his 1940 essay "Current Problems of Mexican Immigrants":

> When the Mexican has become a citizen of the United States and sought to improve the living environment for his family, he has been rebuffed. He has selected a home in a better neighborhood only to find that the "neighbors" in this area are opposed to him and that they even threaten him if he moves in. Under these circumstances he cannot help but wonder of what value is citizenship in our country. If you become a citizen but are treated as a foreigner, what have you gained? After he becomes a citizen he sometimes finds it difficult to find redress in the courts for any wrongs that he feels have been done him. When he could go to the Mexican consul he could get help, but as a citizen this aid is no longer available to him. He wonders about the values of citizenship, but today he faces the choice between naturalization or deportation (or possible concentration camps).[4]

The bleak picture that Bogardus paints of the condition of Mexicans in the United States would be further complicated by the institution of guest worker programs that greatly increased the ethnic Mexican population of the United States but left these newcomers with little in the way of protection of their basic civil rights.

With the labor shortages resulting from World War II and the end of the Great Depression, Mexican labor was sorely needed in the United States. Beginning in 1942, just three years after the end of the repatriation campaigns, the U.S. government initiated a bi-lateral labor agreement with the Mexican government to recruit Mexican men, largely as agricultural workers. This agreement, known as the *Bracero* program, was intended to end in 1947 but ran in various forms until 1964 and awarded nearly 5 million work contracts to Mexican laborers in the United States during its course, a very substantial portion of which were for jobs in California. Although most *Braceros* would return to Mexico, many secured residency in the United States, establishing themselves as another important generation of Mexican immigrants. Most importantly, however, the *Bracero* program firmly established a circular pattern for Mexican immigration to the United States that would last into the twenty-first century. Mexican laborers would cross the border to work seasonally, and off-season, they would return or be forced back to Mexico by draconian deportation efforts (such as the infamous Operation Wetback in 1954), resulting in periods of prolonged cultural exchanges between Mexican and nascent Mexican-American cultures.[5]

The initial influx of *Braceros* also coincided with the coming of age of the American-born children of Mexicans who had stayed in California through the repatriation campaigns of the 1930s. The condition of cultural "in-between-ness" was felt even more acutely by a young generation of self-styled Pachuca/os who developed a youth subculture that was greatly influenced by cultures of jazz; unlike their parents, and the more recently arrived *Braceros*, many in this this generation had few first-hand experiences of Mexico but were still considered a foreign minority within American society. Negative attitudes toward this generation of Mexican-Americans in Los Angeles were exemplified by the proceedings of the Sleepy Lagoon murder case (1942) and the Zoot Suit Riots (1943), during which American prosecutors, in court, blamed clashes between Pachuca/os and Anglos on the Pachuca/os' "bloodlust" derived from their presumed Aztec heritage.[6] These characterizations of Pachuco youths as the violent descendants of the Aztecs fit them neatly into the region's dominant structuring of history. Pachuca/os were seen as members of a race ever in conflict with Spanish and

American civility; to be seen as an Aztec was to be seen as the opposite of American.

By midcentury, the emblems of Southern Californian regionalism had been broadly assimilated into American popular culture. Mission and Spanish Revival architectural–style buildings and houses appeared throughout the country; their direct appeal was their ability to connote affluence and California's Mediterranean lifestyle. Even the American military culture made reference to California's iconic buildings. During World War II, a fleet of Mission Buenaventura Class Tankers ships were commissioned and individually named after many of the California missions. These ships served in the Pacific theater alongside the Liberty ship U.S.S. *Pio Pico*. Years later, the U.S.S. *General Vallejo*, a ballistic nuclear submarine, was commissioned in 1966 to protect the United States during the Cold War.

Similarly, the tragic narratives of Mexican social bandits were refigured and came to loom large in American popular culture. As early as 1919 Joaquín Murieta, the famed Mexican *bandido*, had been transformed into the popular figure of Zorro, a masked Spanish nobleman, protector of the missions from corrupt secular authorities and great crowd-pleaser in the nation's movie theaters. Thanks to the popularity of the Walt Disney–produced television show *Zorro*, costumes worn by the eponymous character were the single bestselling Halloween costume for American children in the late 1950s.[7] Similarly, O. Henry's Cisco Kid (from his short story "The Caballero's Way," 1907) was transformed from a murderous outlaw named Goodall into a heroic Californio Robin Hood accompanied by a heavily accented comedic sidekick named Pancho, played by Leo Carrillo, a descendant of Californios. The duo appeared in comic books and a long-running television series that remained in syndication until the 1970s.

Following this comedic mode, Metro-Goldwyn-Mayer studios produced in 1935 a short entitled *La Fiesta de Santa Barbara* that featured a long list of celebrities, from Buster Keaton, to Leo Carrillo, to a very young Judy Garland, to Gary Cooper, all participating in what was claimed to be "one of America's most famous historical celebrations."[8] Though the film showcased the Spanish costumed play of Santa Barbara's *Fiesta*, it nonetheless demonstrated the historical slippage central to the event by having costumed American cowboys and cowgirls perform alongside Anglos attired as Spanish *caballeros* and *señoritas* eliding the problematic historical relationship between the two groups. Moreover, Judy Garland's performance of "La Cucaracha" (an old *corrido* popularized during the Mexican Revolution) introduced nearly contemporary Mexican elements into the performative mix, confusing and conflating cultures and historical contexts even further.

In contrast to the bravado and humor portrayed in the adventure tales of horsemen and the theatrics of revelers, Alfred Hitchcock's classic film *Vertigo* (1958) made chilling use of fragments of California's past through its depiction of the ghostly and beguiling Carlotta Valdes and a reimagined Mission San Juan Bautista. Thanks to special effects and scale modeling, the place where the mission's odd New England–style steeple had stood was transformed into the film's signature oversized and deadly bell tower. Shots filmed in the graveyard at San Francisco's Mission Dolores further brought the film's audience into an uncanny relation to the region's pre-American past. Again, in the common slippage, the fair-skinned Carlotta is referred to as Spanish in the film while her fictional gravestone dates her as at least having been born a Mexican citizen (December 3, 1831–March 5, 1857).[9]

Although Southern California regionalism was firmly inculcated in American culture by midcentury, it was also in this postwar period that Carey McWilliams, the well-known progressive journalist and historian who helped to overturn the conviction of the Sleepy Lagoon defendants, articulated the first sustained critique of Americans' romantic understanding of Southern California's history and its relationship to ethnic Mexicans. Both in *Southern California Country: An Island on the Land* (1946) and in *North from Mexico: The Spanish Speaking Peoples of the United States* (1948), McWilliams sought to expose what he termed Americans' southwestern "Fantasy Heritage" and the violence that it occluded.

He portrayed Southern California's history as having been bifurcated by Americans into a mythic and romanticized "sacred" past that they embraced, and a "profane" past that they largely ignored, even though it was the "substratum of fact." While *Ramona*, the pious padres, and the wealthy Dons formed the "sacred" elements of the region's history, "The Padres' [elimination] of Indians with the effectiveness of Nazis operating concentration camps," the pretense of Californios' claiming "pure Spanish blood," and the legacy of American violence against impoverished "Mexican *paisanos*" were the constitutive features of its true or "profane" history.[10] McWilliams reserved particular venom for the Santa Barbara *Fiesta* pageant, seeing it as a premier example of the revival of "Spanish folkways in Southern California . . . a part of the sacred rather than the profane life of the region." He characterized it as a "spectacle of . . . frustrated business men cantering back and forth in search of some ersatz week-end romance, evoking a past that never existed to cast some glamour on an equally unreal today."[11]

The heart of McWilliams's moral, cultural, and historical critique was that "the dichotomy which exists in the borderlands between what is 'Spanish' and what is 'Mexican' is a functional, not ornamental[,] arrangement. Its function is to deprive the Mexicans of their heritage and to keep them in their place."[12] He believed that because Americans had

emphasiz[ed] the Spanish side of the [southwestern] tradition and consciously repudiat[ed] the Mexican-Indian side, it has long been possible [for Americans] to rob the Spanish-speaking minority of a heritage which is rightfully theirs. . . . [T]he constant operation of this strategy has made it difficult for the Spanish-speaking people to organize and it has retarded their advancement.[13]

Moreover, he idealized the notion that the first step toward bettering "Anglo-Hispano relations in the Southwest . . . is to get rid of the fantasy heritage. . . . [O]nce this veil of fantasy has been lifted, it should be possible for both groups to recognize the reality of cultural fusion in the Southwest."[14] But by the time McWilliams voiced his critique, Americans' deep investment in positing regional historical and cultural connections to the Spanish past, while deriding the Mexican past, was roughly one hundred years old, a period longer than the colonial Spanish and Mexican mission eras in Alta California combined. The heavy veil of the "Fantasy Heritage" in American national and regional culture would not be lifted easily. Instead, in time, young politicized ethnic Mexicans would create a countering heritage employing the racial logic and vocabulary of *indigenismo*, religious emblems of cultural hybridity, as well as strategies gained from the experience of subaltern life in the United States. In concert, these would ultimately provide a means for the political mobilization and ownership of a history that McWilliams argued the "Fantasy Heritage" had denied them.

As we shall see, the creation of this new form of *indigenismo* in the United States was not only born in response to American formations of regional history and racist practices but also was in part a response to Mexican nationals' derogatory characterization of ethnic Mexicans living in the United States as *Pochos* (an epithet stemming from its original use as a descriptor for discolored or rotten fruit) who were purportedly losing their language, culture, and connection to the motherland. In August 1944 conservative Mexican intellectuals went so far as to hold a national anti-*Pocho* week in protest of what they perceived to be a corruption of Mexican culture and language among ethnic Mexicans as a result of the influence of American culture.[15]

Just a few years after McWilliams penned his critiques of the "Fantasy Heritage," Nobel Laureate Octavio Paz, a figure recognized throughout his life as the leading Mexican intellectual concerned with defining "Mexican-ness," condescendingly described Los Angeles and its young ethnic Mexican population in his most famous collection of essays, *The Labyrinth of Solitude* (1950). Paz wrote,

When I arrived in the United States, I lived for a while in Los Angeles, a city inhabited by over a million persons of Mexican origin. At first sight, the visitor is surprised not only by the purity of the sky and the ugliness of the dispersed and ostentatious buildings, but also by the city's vaguely Mexican atmosphere, which cannot be captured in words or concepts. This Mexicanism—delight in decoration, carelessness and pomp, negligence, passion and reserve—floats in the air. . . . It floats, without offering any opposition; it hovers, blown here and there by the wind, sometimes breaking up like a cloud, sometimes standing erect like a rising skyrocket. It creeps, it wrinkles, expands and contracts; it sleeps or dreams; it is ragged or beautiful. It floats, never quite existing, never quite vanishing. Something of the same sort characterizes the Mexicans you see in the streets. They have lived in the city for many years wearing the same clothes as the other inhabitants, and they feel ashamed of their origin. . . . [T]hey act like persons who are wearing disguises, who are afraid of a stranger's look because it could strip them and leave them stark naked. . . . This spiritual condition, or lack of a spirit[,] has given birth to a type known as the Pachuco. . . . The Pachuco does not want to become a Mexican again; at the same time he does not want to blend into the life of North America. His whole being is a tangle of contradictions, an enigma. . . . The Pachuco has lost his whole inheritance: language, religion, customs, beliefs.[16]

Yet, contrary to Paz's pessimistic assessment of the anomie and *Pochismo* of young Pachucos, Mexican culture in the United States enjoyed regular renewals from the peregrinations of those who participated in circular migration, bringing with them reminders of Mexico and contemporary innovations in Mexican culture. Most commonly, migrants' nostalgia for the motherland was articulated through portable emblems of Mexican-ness such as the *indigenista* art common in Mexican cultural ephemera. In the context of the Southwest these images and emblems of Mexican-ness would inspire ethnic Mexicans to articulate an exilic nationalism of their own. This would become a hybrid ethnic nationalism, neither entirely Mexican nor entirely American, but one that spoke to the condition of people living in the borderlands, one that Paz himself would ultimately come to view in a positive light.

During the 1950s, many ethnic Mexicans in the United States were encouraged by the rise of the civil rights movement. As they witnessed African Americans' successes through demonstrations, picketing, and direct confrontations with racism, they began to emulate these tactics in overlapping political and religious spheres. Beginning in 1958, Reies Lopez Tijerina, a Pentecostal minister, radicalized questions of land ownership in New Mexico. Citing the often broken or neglected provisions of the Treaty of Guadalupe Hidalgo, which guaranteed the retention of lands by Mexican citizens remaining in the annexed territories, Tijerina called for the return of property that had been taken through American deception and fraud, including large tracts that were now under the management of the U.S. Forestry Service. In 1965, César Chávez headed early attempts by Mexican agricultural workers in California to unionize under the banner of the United Farm Workers. During Lent of 1966, members of the new union undertook a 300-mile march of "Pilgrimage, Penitence and Revolution" from Delano to Sacramento bearing a large image of the Virgin of Guadalupe at the front of their procession, followed by Mexican, American, and U.F.W. flags. Calling themselves "sons of the Mexican Revolution," the marchers articulated their grievances in "The Plan of Delano," a document modeled on Emiliano Zapata's call for agrarian reform in the *Plan de Ayala* (1911), penned during Mexico's Revolutionary War.[17]

Agricultural workers' camps had long enjoyed improvisational traveling theater as entertainment, and in the late 1960s Luis Valdez founded the *Teatro Campesino* and offered regular showings of "Historical Happenings" at the *Teatro*'s Cultural Center in Del Rey, California. These vignettes portrayed various events in Mexican history and the history of ethnic Mexicans in the United States, and in doing so they articulated a burgeoning sense of cultural coherence and solidarity. A 1968 issue of *El Malcriado* (The Brat), a pulp magazine circulated among agricultural workers by the United Farm Workers, encouraged its readership to attend the "Happenings" performed at the *Teatro*, which included reenactments of

> the reform of Benito Juarez; Porfirio Díaz and the Mexican Revolution; the Revolution and the Mexican-American; Mexican Immigration to the United States; Mexicans and WW II; Braceros and the Undocumented Workers; the Pachuco and Urban Life; the Korean War, 1950's; the strike in Delano; César Chávez and the farmworkers; the Alianza Federal de Pueblos Libres and Reies Lopez Tijerina.[18]

By the early 1970s the *Teatro* was also performing the miracle play of the apparition of *La Virgen del Tepeyac* (Guadalupe) as well as seasonal *Pastorela* nativity plays. Just as the historical pageantry of the *Fiestas* had inculcated American ways of understanding the history of the Southwest, the *Teatro Campesino*, and other improvisational theater groups like it, performed coherent communal visions of history and culture for many ethnic Mexicans leading lives in the United States.

Beyond simply creating a narrative history for themselves, politicized ethnic Mexicans in the United States began to establish a *heritage* outside of the national boundaries of Mexico by laying claim to the places they inhabited in the United States, reconfiguring regional histories and inventing attendant traditions. These early expressions of nationalism put to use the vocabulary of Mexican national *indigenismo* that celebrated connections to the pre-Columbian past while refiguring American conceptions of the Southwest as an extension of Mesoamerica. In doing so they asserted continuity between themselves and those who had previously been assumed by many Americans to be the region's first inhabitants: the Aztecs. The first published civil rights–era statement claiming this connection was made in 1962 in a mimeographed essay entitled "The Mexican Heritage of Aztlán" by Jack D. Forbes.[19] The tract draws a direct relationship between cultures of the Aztec/Mexica and the contemporary cultures of the Southwest, echoing, but politically transforming, nineteenth-century visions of the region.

The circulation of these new ways of understanding the past coincided with a number of political/social events with both great symbolic importance and considerable material consequences. On August 1, 1967, Mexico and the United States reached an agreement under which the obligation to pay interest on the Pious Fund would end, more than a century after the missions had been taken by Americans. Mexico agreed to pay more than 8 million pesos to discharge the previous debt of unpaid annuities and an additional 717,513.03 pesos as capital that would be used to provide the original annual penalty set by the tribunal, finally marking a conclusive end to the case. In a remarkable demonstration of the obfuscatory power of political speech, a spokesperson for the U.S. State Department characterized the payment and agreement as "a further demonstration of the close and friendly ties which characterize the relationship between the United States and Mexico."[20]

The nearly contemporaneous passage by Congress of the Hart-Celler Immigration and Nationality Act, signed into law by President Lyndon B. Johnson, phased out the national origins quota system that favored European immigration. With a pen stroke, a new era of mass migration from Mexico began. This new generation of immigrants brought with them contemporary expressions of Mexican *indigenismo* that had become extremely popular as a result of national pride in Mexico's hosting of the Summer Olympic Games in 1968. Though these nationalist expressions were sponsored by government cultural agencies, they were also employed by oppositional student groups to promote unity and a strong sense of identity. The unifying power of this centuries-old form of nationalism found fertile ground among ethnic Mexicans in the United States during the civil rights era and beyond.[21]

In 1968, Antonio Bernal painted two remarkable murals on the exterior walls at the entrance to the *Teatro Campesino*'s Cultural Center that were among the very first to explicitly make the connection between the Aztec/Mexica past and the emerging countercultural present. On one wall, Bernal painted eight members of the Aztec and Mayan elites led by an Aztec woman (possibly Malinche), and on the other, he painted eight revolutionary and contemporary civil rights figures, beginning with "La Adelita," the legendary archetype of the female Mexican Revolutionary; Pancho Villa; Emiliano Zapata; Joaquín Murieta; César Chávez; Reies Tijerina; a Black Panther (interpreted by some as depicting Malcolm X); and Martin Luther King Jr. These murals served to creatively bridge pre-Columbian, historical, and revolutionary figures with the political struggles of the present. Most importantly, they articulated a sense of heritage. This sense of historical connection and legitimate belonging within the political boundaries of the United States served to give many ethnic Mexican in the United States a new view of themselves not as Mexicans and not as Americans but as "Chicana/os"—a term that had been used disparagingly in Mexico to refer to individuals of low social standing perceived to be culturally crude (i.e., too "Indian") but now re-defined, politicized, and employed as an appellation that affirmed the identity of those who understood themselves as living between national cultures.

Activist, organizer, and writer Rodolfo "Corky" Gonzales articulated the tensions and liminality of this emergent neither/nor both/and identity in his widely influential bilingual poem "*Yo Soy Joaquín*/I am Joaquín: an Epic Poem" (1967). The titular homage to the famous postwar Mexican social bandit and the recurring identification with this figure throughout the poem underscores the centrality of political resistance to Anglo cultural, political, and spatial dominance in Gonzales's poetic expression of the identity of Chicana/os.

The poem powerfully interweaves many conflicting cultural, historical, and spiritual elements and celebrates a rejection of assimilation, embracing the often painful but also creative tensions within Chicana/o identity. Gonzales's inversion of the tragic view of Joaquín Murieta quickly became a canonical expression of the lived experience of cultural hybridity within the early Chicana/o movement; it has been reprinted innumerable times, read aloud at Chicana/o rallies and events for decades as well as performed by the *Teatro Campesino*, and made into a film by Luis Valdez.[22] The poem reads in the first person as Joaquín Murieta; however, this Joaquín embodies a complex multiplicity of identities that mirror the inherent contradictions experienced by those living betwixt and between Mexican and American cultures.

Although the narrating voice of the poem briefly identifies with pious "black shawled women," the Virgin of Guadalupe, and *Tonantzín* the Aztec goddess, the poem has also long been criticized for its masculinist perspective that does not directly address the unique experiences and historical subjectivity of Chicanas.

Originally written in English and subsequently translated into Spanish, "*Yo Soy Joaquín*/I am Joaquín" is now most frequently presented in bilingual form that switches from one language to the other. It begins with a statement of both lament and defiance:

> I am Joaquín,
> Lost in a world of confusion,
> Caught up in a whirl of a
> gringo society,
> Confused by the rules,
> Scorned by attitudes,
> Suppressed by manipulations,
> And destroyed by modern society.
> My fathers
> have lost the economic battle
> and won
> the struggle of cultural survival.
> And now!
> I must choose
> Between the paradox of
> Victory of the spirit,
> despite physical hunger
> Or
> to exist in the grasp
> of American social neurosis,
> sterilization of the soul
> and a full stomach.

The poem not only expresses the tensions common to the experience of being caught between the cultures of the United States and Mexico, it also shows how this tension exists in relation to the antecedent paradoxes central to nationalist Mexican conceptions of *mestizaje*.

> I owned the land as far as the eye
> could see under the Crown of Spain,
> and I toiled on my earth
> and gave my Indian sweat and blood
> for the Spanish master,
> who ruled with tyranny over man and
> beast and all that he could trample
> But . . .
> THE GROUND WAS MINE.
> I was both tyrant and slave.

This emphasis on ownership of land then relates the physical and cultural displacement caused by the war to contemporary social conditions faced by many Chicana/os, as well as to the arrogation of history engendered by the transformation of Mexico's northern frontier into the southwestern United States. The poem mourns that:

> The Treaty of Hidalgo has been broken
> And is but another treacherous promise.
> My land is lost
> And stolen,
> My culture has been raped.
> I lengthen the line at the welfare door
> And fill the jails with crime.
> These then are the rewards
> This society has
> For sons of chiefs
> And kings
> And bloody revolutionists,
> Who gave a foreign people
> All their skills and ingenuity
> To pave the way with brains and blood

For those hordes of gold-starved strangers,
Who
Changed our language
And plagiarized our deeds
As feats of valor
Of their own.

The powerful imagery and immense popularity of "*Yo Soy Joaquín*/I am Joaquín" provided a vehicle that would help to constitute an imagined community of Chicana/os with a shared understanding of the past and present.[23] It does so in part by concluding powerfully with an expression of hope offered by the very cultural contradictions and tensions that make up Chicana/o identity and serve to resist social death and assimilation:

. . . I am the masses of my people and
I refuse to be absorbed.
I am Joaquín.
The odds are great
But my spirit is strong,
My faith unbreakable,
My blood is pure.
I am Aztec prince and Christian Christ.
I SHALL ENDURE!
I WILL ENDURE!

Heirs of Aztlán

In March 1969, Gonzales worked to organize the first National Chicano Liberation Youth Conference in Denver, Colorado, with more than 1,000 politicized youths from across the country in attendance. It was here that Chicana/os first explicitly articulated a cultural nationalism that defends the legitimacy of a hybrid identity and re-defines ethnic Mexicans' relation to place in the lands ceded to the United States by Mexico. This was enshrined in a cultural manifesto entitled *El Plan Espiritual de Aztlán* (The Spiritual Plan of Aztlán) after the political plans that set out the goals of the movement for Mexican independence and the reforms of the Mexican Revolution. It begins:

> In the Spirit of a new people that is conscious not only of its proud historical heritage but also of the brutal "gringo" invasion of our territories, we, the Chicano inhabitants and civilizers of the northern land of Aztlán from whence came our forefathers, reclaiming the land of their birth and consecrating the determination of our people of the Sun, *declare* that the call of our blood is our power, our responsibility, and our inevitable destiny. . . . Before the world, before all of North America, before all of our brothers in the bronze continent, we are a nation, we are a union of free pueblos, we are Aztlán.[24]

El Plan Espiritual de Aztlán claimed a spiritual as well as genealogical relationship between Chicana/os and the Aztecs, and it also proudly located the origins of Aztec civilization, the very source of Mexican national patrimony, in the American Southwest. In doing so, Chicana/os were able to make the claim that their presence in the region was more legitimate than that of Americans and also to do away with much of the stigma of being Mexicans "*de afuera*" as they now claimed to be at the very fountainhead of "*lo Mexicano*" (that which is Mexican). Just as Americans had fashioned themselves as heirs to the Southwest, following in the spiritual footsteps of the padres, Chicana/os now saw themselves as the spiritual heirs to the presumed land of the Aztecs and their southward peregrinations to Mexico.[25]

While *El Plan Espiritual de Aztlán* was drafted principally by "Corky" Gonzales, the poet Alurista (a portmanteau *nom de plume* for Alberto Urista) is credited with popularizing the unifying idea of a people of "Aztlán" that galvanized Chicano nationalism. During the Youth Conference some Chicanos were, however, initially unconvinced by Alurista's romantic use of Aztec origins and criticized the use of the Aztec myth of Aztlán as out of step with the social reality of Chicana/os. Alurista defended his promotion of Aztlán as a poetic topos that permitted the actualization of a new identity for Chicana/os. He claimed:

> We have to give ourselves the responsibility of constructing a vision of the world that is truly ours, not a colonized vision of the world. An

independent, liberated view of the world. If we paint a more humanistic view of the world to live in, we will construct that world. If we paint a nightmare we'll live in a nightmare. Therefore my poetry is not only political, it's psychological, it's spiritual. It is multidimensional. I don't think it can be called just protest poetry. I'm also trying to nurture, to cultivate my heart as well as the heart of my people so we can reconstruct ourselves.[26]

The term *Aztlán* became a multivalent concept for Chicana/o nationalists; it was employed not only to refer to the territories "belonging to the Mexican Republic before 1848" but also to "the spiritual union of the Chicana/os, something that is carried within the heart, no matter where they may live or where they may find themselves."[27]

The promotion of unity among Chicana/os fostered by the idea of Aztlán encouraged them to see themselves as "a people" or rather, in the terms of the Mexican Revolution, as a collective "*Raza*." The rediscovery of the revolutionary writings of Vasconcelos in the late 1960s offered Chicana/os further inspiration to see themselves as members of an evolving "*Raza Cósmica*." One anonymous author, citing Alurista, captured the creative tenor of the optimism and pride common to early articulations of Chicano identity:

A practical revolutionist has stated that the revolutionary must perforce fantasize the new world he hopes to create. And we, Los Chicanos, the new Aztláns, can fantasize about reclaiming the lost territories, not for Mexico, but to set up an independent republic, the New Nation of Aztlán. Why not, our observations affirm that Los Aztláns have made a complete circle encompassing prophesy [*sic*], centuries, history; now we can fantasize that we shall go beyond history, beyond prophesy [*sic*]— the cosmic race, to the space age. A unique people whose travels and travails will compose the new mythology of the space age, and beyond; Aztlánes, the Cosmic Race.[28]

Just one month after the Denver Youth Conference, a second conference was convened to further define Chicana/o nationalism and ensure its future. This conference was held in the heartland of both the "Fantasy Heritage" and Aztlán: the city of Santa Barbara. Conference organizers worked to bring disparate Chicano student groups under the standard of *El Movimiento Estudiantil Chicano de Aztlán* (the Chicano Student Movement of Aztlán, or MEChA). They drafted a crucial second document, *El Plan de Santa Barbara* (The Plan of Santa Barbara). The authors of the *Plan* stated:

> For all people, as with individuals, the time comes when they must reckon with their history. For the Chicano the present is a time of renaissance, of *renacimiento* [rebirth]. . . . Recognizing the historical tasks confronting our people and fully aware of the cost of human progress, we pledge our will to move. We will move forward towards our destiny as a people. . . . [T]hroughout history the quest for cultural expression and freedom has taken the form of a struggle. Our struggle, tempered by the lessons of the American past, is an historical reality.[29]

Most importantly, the *Plan* successfully called for the implementation of Chicano studies programs throughout the university and college systems of California. The authors of *El Plan de Santa Barbara* envisioned these academic units as places where the history and culture of Chicana/os could be learned. Indeed, some of the earliest (and to this day, most vibrant) Chicana/o studies programs at schools such as California State University at Northridge and the University of California at Santa Barbara made courses on the "History of Aztlán" (a rubric referring to a historical understanding of ethnic Mexicans in the United States) and some knowledge of Náhuatl (the language of the Mexica/Aztecs) requirements for graduation.[30]

The birth of Chicano studies provided an academic venue for the early dissemination of Chicana/o history. However, the growing sense of Chicana/os as a people, and Aztlán as a place, required a more public articulation than the classroom. Mission and later Spanish Revival architecture had served to define Southern California monumentally as an American region inherited from Spanish missionaries. Similarly, during a great flowering of mural painting throughout the United States, Chicana/os began to make use of public art to establish and reinforce their own historical narratives in the lived environment and in so doing created well-defined counterspaces.[31]

For Chicana/o artists, murals became an art form that transcended the individual and served the social function of making themselves and their culture visible without the mediation of oppressive social institutions. As the movement flourished, the act of creating street murals itself came to be seen as a distinctively progressive Chicana/o cultural practice. In religious terms, muralism offered a new medium through which ethnic Mexicans could visually articulate their own religious and cultural iconography beyond church settings and in so doing employ these sacred icons to distinguish the urban spaces they inhabited and claim them as their own.

In 1969 Los Angeles art historian Shifra Goldman initiated efforts to restore and preserve Siqueiros's *Tropical America* in Olvera Street. After years of weathering and two coats of whitewash the mural was in such disrepair that preservationists initially believed that it could not be saved. Nonetheless, the rediscovery of this politically radical mural in the heart of the city would serve as a powerful model for Chicano muralists and speak to the larger social transformation of the city.[32]

Among the first Chicana/o murals in Southern California were those painted in the early 1970s at the Estrada Courts and Ramona Gardens housing projects in East Los Angeles. Resident youths, often talented graffiti taggers, were recruited by social activists to work collaboratively with artists to create art that set up a political and religious dialogue with the surrounding city. Murals began to proliferate very quickly, becoming a commonplace element in *barrio* streetscapes that had previously been demarcated principally with *placas*—stylized gang graffiti that defined territory. By the end of the 1970s, both housing projects would be home to dozens of murals depicting religious images such as the Crucifixion, and the Sacred Heart of Jesus, side by side with genealogical portraits of Aztec and Mayan warriors, Mexican revolutionary leaders and contemporary civil rights leaders (such as César Chávez, Luis Valdéz, Reies Tijerina, Martin Luther King Jr., and John F. Kennedy) as well as simple slogans spelling out messages of social uplift.[33]

The combination of religious and political imagery made murals a locus for the expression of the experiences and conditions endured by the community. As one early commentator put it, "[The] need to have a visible identity is the very essence and reason for the Chicano mural, [it is] an art that depicts the bitter frustrations of existence in the barrio."[34] All at once, murals functioned as communal markers and, through their presentation of religious imagery, they also functioned as responses to suffering. As such, they regularly became devotional and commemorative sites. While depictions of Jesus, particularly as the man of sorrows, were common, no image better conjoined the assertion of the legitimacy of ethnic Mexican presence and the sacralization of space than that of the Virgin of Guadalupe.[35]

The ubiquity of the image of this Marian apparition in Southern California, as well as the multiplicity of forms in which it is reproduced, speaks to the power of the symbolic link to Mexico that Guadalupe provided Chicana/os as they lay claim to place in the United States. As a result, the public places where Guadalupe has been portrayed, particularly though the medium of muralism, often became sites that form religious centers in their respective communities. For example, a large-scale mural of the Virgin of Guadalupe painted in 1973 at the Maravilla housing project in Los Angeles was originally a product of the efforts of artist David Lopez and psychologist Sam Zepeda, who directed members of the Arizona Street Gang in their creation of a memorial for a fallen young gang member. The mural soon exceeded the modest intentions of its creators as it developed broad recognition as the neighborhood's signature mural and devotional shrine. Years later, when the Los Angeles County Housing Authority began to demolish large portions of the old housing complex, local activists were successful in demanding that the city preserve the mural and move it to a permanent and safe location. Today it stands at the Los Angeles County Community Development Commission offices on Mednik Avenue in East Los Angeles, near its original location, where it remains well maintained by current and former residents of the Maravilla area with flowers and candles.[36]

Similarly, in 1969 the terminus of San Diego's Coronado Bay Bridge was built in the heart of San Diego's oldest and largest Chicana/o neighborhood, Logan Heights, or "Barrio Logan," displacing a great many families and effectively cutting the area in half. The resulting geographic shift left the parish Church of Our Lady of Guadalupe, which had been at the center of the *barrio*, isolated and facing the new freeway and its cement retaining walls. Local leaders proposed the creation of a park under the bridge's spans to help to heal the community; city officials at first agreed but then proceeded to grade the land for the construction of a new Highway Patrol station. In response, residents and activist college students stormed the construction site and held a twelve-day sit-in, forming human chains around the bulldozers. Three days of heated negotiations ensued, during which one angry student proclaimed to municipal leaders,

> To you Culture means Taco Bell and the funny Mexican with the funny songs. We gave you our culture of a thousand years. What have you given us? A social system that makes us beggars and police who make us afraid. We've got the land and we are going to work it. We are going to get that park. We no longer talk about asking. We have the park.[37]

In the end, the demands were met and "Chicano Park" was born. Throughout the 1970s, enthusiastic Barrio Logan locals as well as Chicana/o artists from all over Southern California carried out an extensive muralist campaign to cover the bare concrete supports of the bridge at the park. In 1978, Mario Torero restored Guadalupe to her central place in the *barrio* by completing an eighteen-foot-tall image of Guadalupe that more than thirty years later continues to receive a great number of votive candles and *ex votos* at her feet.[38]

The longevity of these devotional mural sites, as well as that of many others like them, speaks to the success of early Chicana/o muralism as a nexus of religious and political praxis.[39] As the mural movement evolved in metropolitan areas with large ethnic Mexican populations, Chicana/o art became a regular feature of American city streetscapes. Throughout the late 1970s, murals became popular in civic renovation or so-called Barrio Beautiful campaigns that attracted support from municipal budgets, the National Endowment for the Arts, and the Federal Comprehensive Employment Training Act. While government support for mural programs would eventually dwindle, the remarkable productivity of the movement had succeeded in firmly establishing a tradition of ethnic vernacular art with a strongly religious cast.[40]

More than thirty years later, Chicano Park is now not only recognized as a historical site in the city of San Diego but is also on the National Registry of Historic Places, even as a mural within the park refers it as the only bit of land reclaimed from Americans in the aftermath of the the Mexican-American War. It is significant that the park lies in the shadow of another California historical artifact. The cement overpasses above the park channel traffic from the Coronado Bridge to Interstate 5, the southernmost section of El Camino Real—the road that Americans built to retrace the footsteps of the Spanish Franciscan conquest of the state. In one place, two legacies of the Mexican-American War and two competing understandings of Southern California have ultimately come to coexist: Commuters on the Camino Real remain largely oblivious to the symbolism of the pre-Columbian ancestors depicted on the murals on the pylons under them, and the community of Barrio Logan values this section of "the padres' highway" principally as a canvas for their community's sense of history.

Urban Transformations

Currently in the city of Los Angeles alone there are more than 1,500 registered murals under the protection of mural conservancy groups, the majority of which are the legacy of the early Chicana/o muralists. However, these are dwarfed in number by the thousands of informal murals that dot the city today, even though a legal moratorium on mural projects was in effect from 2003 until recently. As Mexican immigration rose dramatically in the 1980s and '90s, new generations faced the same intertwined issues of creating a sense of place and responding to the politics of space. Their artistic responses to these problems brought new life to the muralist tradition, with the image of Guadalupe remaining the favored and most revered standard.

According to the 2010 census, nearly half (48.5 percent) of the population of Los Angeles was Latina/o and one in three Angelenos is an ethnic Mexican. In 2013 the Latina/o population of California reached parity with the state's white population (39 percent each). These figures do not include the commonly undercounted undocumented Latina/o population. This second-largest city in the country is regularly caricatured for its urban sprawl and presumed lack of center. However, the proliferation of religious iconography, particularly Guadalupan imagery, throughout the entire Los Angeles basin and San Diego corridor creates a readable network of signs that help to demarcate and define the urban environment as well as reinforce religious and cultural norms. In short, the presence of these icons works to transform public space into ethnic Mexican and Chicana/o places. The sheer volume of Marian art produced by ethnic Mexicans in Los Angeles ensures that no list of examples could ever be complete. However, a sampling of the contexts in which these images are commonly found can provide a sense of how they fit into everyday life, the number of ways in which they manifest religious culture, and their role in the creation of these places.

At their most immediate, these images are present at the domicile. In the homes of the faithful, small-scale murals, paintings, and chromo prints depicting Guadalupe are often found displayed in prominent relation to a home altar, a common manifestation of familial faith in ethnic Mexican households. These altars range from special shrines set up for particular liturgical seasons or specific life events to permanent fixtures that are a part of ongoing daily spiritual practices. They also frequently serve as sites where family history is preserved through the placement of pictures and artifacts that commemorate loved ones. By doing so, they bring together familial identity and devotional practice, creating a symbolic intimacy with the Virgin that deepens affinity toward her image when it is encountered outside of the home.

As in many other predominantly Catholic immigrant neighborhoods, the presence of yard shrines and Marian murals is a common element in ethnic Mexican residential landscapes. These oftentimes elaborate creations range in form from home-made mosaics crafted in mixed media (usually glass, plaster, and stone), to painted or framed images, to more costly artisanal tile work. The ornateness of the display registers here as a reflection of the intensity of the piety of the shrine's proprietor. It is this setting, just beyond the front door, where the display of Guadalupe bridges the private and public spheres. On the one hand, this form of religious art allows for creative self-expression, it manifests personal belief, and it creates a sacred space that consecrates the home. On the other, it participates in a community-recognized practice that also potentially challenges the larger society's ethnic, religious, and aesthetic values.

In the northeastern Los Angeles neighborhood of Highland Park, one such home mural/shrine adorns the garage of a multi-unit dwelling and is a regular sight for thousands of light-rail commuters who pass by it daily, just as the train slows into the station. The homeowner painted the image of Guadalupe with the help of reformed Avenues Gang members largely as a devotional act, but also as a strategy to curb a near-constant graffiti problem on his property. In the ten years since the mural was painted it has remained untouched by taggers, who very rarely vandalize Marian imagery. He credits his mural and others like it with improving the appearance of the neighborhood as well as for the continued sobriety and social stability of the men who painted it with him.[41]

In the public realm beyond the home, the image of Guadalupe appears at landmarks and institutions. For example, the 28th Street Elementary School in East Los Angeles is home to a mural entitled "*Mis Raices*" (My Roots). Although commissioned at a state-funded school, the mural depicts the image of the Catholic Virgin above an ethnically diverse group of laboring women and between Martin Luther King Jr. and César Chávez. While the image's principal meanings are intertwined, in this instance it would appear that the religious significance of the icon seems intended to be overshadowed by her role as an emblem of Mexican ancestry. The artist, Maria Isabel Mora, intended that the mural serve to educate the 97 percent Latina/o student body about their heritage by depicting different local cultures as all parts of a single tree.

The heuristic potential of murals to convey cultural history is frequently tapped by instructors in the Los Angeles public school system. In many parts of the city, teachers at K–12 levels routinely take students out to tour murals to see and discuss depictions of events such as Mexican independence, the signing of the Treaty of Guadalupe Hidalgo, the American annexation of the Southwest, the Mexican Revolution, and the efforts of farm labor organizers, all to give an illustrated sense of ethnic history. In a preponderance of these murals, Guadalupe is conspicuously depicted as both the representative and divine guardian of Mexico and Mexicans.

The nostalgic portrayal of Mexican history and culture has most conventionally been articulated in *pulqueria* art as relatively small-scale interior and exterior murals depicting "typically Mexican" scenes that decorate restaurants and businesses serving ethnic Mexican communities. These works are much more abundant and typically less elaborate than earlier Chicana/o murals but make similar use of religious imagery to create an expatriate and transnational sense of belonging. Art historian Anita Brenner describes the site of this traditional art form as a place in which "painter and owner collaborate with their public to produce a national property." The murals are typically "painted in cheap brilliant oils which quickly fade and peel. They are therefore constantly changing, are always the national landscape in the present, which includes the beloved and amusing things of the past."[42] Thus, *pulqueria* art provides commercial interests with an attractive and novel décor that romanticizes the cultural vocabulary of its patrons.

Cuisine is one of the most powerful markers of identity, and Mexican restaurants commonly employ *pulqueria*-style depictions of Guadalupe to suggest culinary authenticity. For instance, Rigo's Tacos #5, on Union Street between 22nd and 23rd streets in South Los Angeles, displays the Virgin of Guadalupe on the external wall of the building facing the parking lot—making her the first thing the arriving guest sees. While it is not a typical devotional site, flowers and votive candles are occasionally left at the foot of the mural by customers. Employees tend to the offerings, lighting the candles at the beginning of the work day and extinguishing them when they leave at night. To the left of the virgin, and very much in the *pulqueria* style, a *mariachi* serenades a beautiful woman dressed in the garb of an Indigenous woman from Jalisco. This particular set of murals conveys a multiplicity of signs: It romantically depicts regional culture, it makes visual reference to Mexico's Indigenous heritage, and it attests to the piety of the restaurateurs. Ultimately, these elements work in concert to define the restaurant and, most important, its food as unquestionably Mexican.

Throughout the city, the business signage created by mobile food vendors for their catering trucks and carts makes similar use of *pulqueria* art. "Super Taco #2," a typical taco truck that parks on Eastern Avenue in East Los Angeles, sports the image of Guadalupe and a Spanish galleon on its side. On Whittier Boulevard, the *"Tacos El Guero Sexi"* truck displays the Basilica of Guadalupe as well as several large images of the Virgin herself. At MacArthur Park, a street vendor for *"Paletas Sinaloa"* pushes a cart adorned in the same manner. As these merchants, and hundreds like them, make their way around city streets, the iconography they display allows them to stand out visually to customers. In the course of their peregrinations, they also integrate the imagery into the larger urban environment; their recognition becomes a part of everyday practices like walking around the city or (more likely in Los Angeles) simply driving by.

Contemporary mural blending Marian, Mexican, and pre-Columbian imagery. Detail from John Zender Estrada and others, *Mexico-Tenochtitlan: The Mural that Talks*, 6037 North Figueroa Street, Los Angeles, California, 1996. Photograph by the author.

Small businesses of all sorts participate in this same aesthetic strategy. All imaginable forms of commerce—markets, florists, auto repair shops, guitar stores, hair dressers, and car dealerships—are often decorated with murals that feature Guadalupe. Like many corner stores in ethnic Mexican neighborhoods, Joe's Mini Market on York Boulevard in Highland Park makes itself conspicuous with a large exterior portrait of the Virgin. Even as it attracts the desired clientele, the image is also credited with preventing unwanted loitering outside of the store by local youths and inebriated customers. Thus, the public use of this sacred symbol can work to regulate and define acceptable uses of community space. It is in these settings that religious murals become quotidian but powerful.

The work that these murals do in their communities is multivalent; they are potentially all at once shrines, commercial signposts, and even formal displays of collective grief. For example, a mural entitled "*La Vida Loca*" (The Crazy Life) located among the stores of the Bonnie Brae Retail Center on 6th Street was commissioned in 1992 by the 18th Street Gang in memory of a murdered member. The visually striking mural was largely painted by Juan Carlos "Wiro" Ruiz, a prominent Los Angeles automotive airbrush artist. Its principal panel foregrounds the image of Guadalupe but does so within the context of a celebration of gang life through depictions of men with guns, a quetzal symbolizing "jail birds," and a woman depicted as a snake tempting men and posing seductively—standing as an obvious misogynist counterpoint to the Virgin.

The prominent location of the mural speaks to the gang's deep roots in and strong territorial control of the area. The gang itself dates back to the late 1960s, when newly arrived Mexican immigrant men were rejected from the then-dominant Mexican-American Clayton Street Gang because of generational differences in culture and language. While the original Clayton gang faded, the less assimilated 18th Street Gang has grown to an estimated membership in the range of 8,000 in the downtown area, to 20,000 in the greater Los Angeles basin, 60 percent of whom are estimated to be young undocumented immigrants.

This particular image of Guadalupe was defaced in 1999 during a mysterious short-lived burst of iconoclastic vandalism that destroyed a number of murals with paint splashes and tags of "666" and "*La Bestia*" (the beast). The perpetrator of the spree remains unknown, but a spokesman for the Archdiocese speculated at the time, "The nature of this graffiti makes me think that it could be coming from some non-Catholic or anti-Catholic Christian sect."[43]

The clergy's recognition and embrace of ethnic Mexican religious murals speaks to the dramatic change in the relationship of the Church to Latina/o parishioners. In the 40 years since the immigration reform of the 1960s, Catholicism in Los Angeles has been transformed. Currently, more than 60 percent of the 4 million lay members of the Archdiocese are Latina/os, all seminarians are required to learn conversational Spanish, and Spanish language masses are offered in 187 of its 287 churches.[44]

The lived religious consequences of these institutional changes are made clear in the nearly universal presence of Guadalupan shrines in Catholic churches throughout Southern California. At the very center of the city of Los Angeles, in the plaza of the original pueblo, the Our Lady Queen of the Angels Church, or "*La Placita*," is home to a large-scale outdoor tile mural depicting Guadalupe and the Mexica/ Aztec neophyte Saint Juan Diego that spans the entire side of the church. Prayer vigils and public devotion in the form of flowers and candles are a constant. Every December 12, the mural serves as the backdrop for the largest celebration of Guadalupe's feast day in the city with thousands in attendance.

One of the most striking manifestations of the influence of ethnic Mexican devotional street art on church architecture is visible at Saint Lucy's Catholic Church in East Los Angeles. The church was originally built with the same spare modernism as Saint Basil's, its exterior concrete walls adorned only with a large inset cross, all of which would be transformed. In 1993, congregants and clergy commissioned muralist George Yepes to paint a remarkable set of images that remade the church entirely. The façade of the church frames a pair of images of the Virgin of Guadalupe, but they do not reproduce the traditional *tilma* image. Instead, we see two maternal images of Guadalupe, one in which she is smiling and holding an infant in something of a Hodegetria style and another in which she is weeping and cradling a dead young gang member in the manner of a *pietà*. A ribbon draped on a cross over the images proclaims them to be *Virgen de Guadalupe madre de los desamparados* (Virgin of Guadalupe, mother of the forsaken). The work is titled *"El Tepeyac de Los Angeles,"* linking the church symbolically with the location of the original apparition in Mexico. The cradle-to-grave imagery exhibits one of the principal concerns of the local community, the tragedy of youth gang violence.

Upon the completion of the mural in 1994, the church was re-dedicated with a large street festival that attracted hundreds of ethnic Mexicans from the neighborhood and from across the city. The celebration featured food, music, and a large troupe of Aztec dancers who led the crowd into the church for the dedicatory bilingual mass. Inside, the congregation assembled before another *pietà* image and hymns were sung to an image of Jesus as a fallen Latino youth shot in the chest (in the place of the holy side wound).

The use of street aesthetics at Saint Lucy's allowed the church to make use of the social capital accrued by the practice of muralism. It employed pervasive religious symbolism to strengthen a sense of solidarity and shared devotional culture between the clergy and the now largely ethnic Mexican Catholic laity. The use of this visual idiom also integrated the church into the surrounding streetscape, connecting it to, and by extension endorsing, the network of emblems of belief created by muralists.

The impact of muralism as a lay religious practice goes beyond simple aesthetic influence in the Church. The production and public display of religious iconography have contributed greatly to the creation of recognizable ethnic Mexican places out of significant swaths of urban space in Southern California. In doing so, they offer a window into a spiritual and ethnic geography of the region that is quite different (if not fully inverted) from that created previously by American regionalists who created place by transforming the nineteenth-century idea of a Spanish spiritual conquest of California into a dominant cultural narrative that naturalizes the outcome of the Mexican-American War.

Coda

The great surge in Mexican migration to the United States following the Mexican Revolution in the 1920s, followed by early repatriation efforts in the 1930s, followed by *Bracero* recruitment of laborers to the United States beginning in the 1940s, followed by the million or so deportations enacted during Operation Wetback in the 1950s, followed by the demographic transformations effected by the Hart-Celler Act in the 1960s established a see-saw rhythm of circular migration patterns for many ethnic Mexican migrants. These patterns of flow between the two countries constantly renewed Latin cultural influences in Southern California and deepened interconnections between American and Mexican cultures.

As we have seen, invented regional traditions derived from pastoral views of Spanish history were inculcated broadly into American popular culture through the arts as well as through the lived experience of architecture and material culture. Just as significantly, the regular and proximate experience of border-crossing, both in a physical and cultural sense, resulted in the creation and articulation of new cultural forms and conventions that defined region and place among ethnic Mexicans in the United States as well.

Exterior of Saint Lucy's Catholic Church, George Yepes, *El Tepeyac de Los Angeles*, 1419 N. Hazard Ave., Los Angeles, 1995. Photograph by the author.

This chapter has shown how ethnic Mexican self-ascription evolved over the course of the twentieth century in ways that reflected a variety of experiences. The mobilization of religion, literature, and the visual arts in ethnic formation by organic intellectuals such as Corky Gonzales during the civil rights era worked powerfully to give voice to the lived conditions and cultural experiences of ethnic Mexicans living in the United States. But it also allowed for the construction of a genealogy that could claim continuity with generations of ethnic Mexicans who had experienced life in *Mexico de afuera* for more than a century before. Thus, the birth of Chicana/o identity and its academic study enabled the creation of Chicana/o literary and historical canons that would constitute a sense of heritage that included a great many ancestral figures and made creative use of a newly articulated exilic *indigenismo*.

The Virgin of Guadalupe had originally been understood by colonial *indigenistas* as a mediatrix between Spanish and Indigenous cultures. But in the context of ethnic Mexican culture in the United States, and as devotion to Guadalupe was popularized within the American Catholic Church, the iconic figure became a mediatrix between those claiming continuity with Spanish culture (Americans) and those claiming continuity with Indigenous cultures predating the Columbian encounter (Chicana/os). The widespread depiction of the Virgin of Guadalupe in public murals and devotional art in American cities is clear evidence of the power of the religions icon to connote ownership of place and history for ethnic Mexicans, just as the preserved missions and revival architectures did for Americans creating Southern California.

Conclusion

Mexico's career was given special character, and made more
difficult, by proximity to the "Colossus of the North."
—Herbert Bolton, *The Epic of Greater America*, 1932

Everyone says, "I'm doing it for the people." We say to
the people, "Compare the results and tell us who has
done it 'for the people,' and you will find those who truly
committed themselves to the people and those who did it
'to' the people.
—Rodolfo "Corky" Gonzales, "Message to Aztlán," 1975

The purpose of this book has been to bring to light the role of religion
in the creation of Arcadian and indigenist historical mythologies in the
formation of Southern California following the Mexican-American
War. It has illuminated fundamental interconnections in the development of these ways of understanding the region's past. And at a broader
level, the evidence presented has also sought to challenge commonly
perceived divides between the peoples and histories of the United States
and Mexico.

The Introduction posed a central question: "What are the ways in
which the history of the United States can be made to come to terms
with its Latin American past?" Throughout these pages we have
examined a variety of ways in which individuals and groups have
worked to define the relationship of the United States' past to Latin
America, including romantic portrayals of the past, claims of spiritual
connection to place, nationalist visions of manifest and spiritual destiny,
a variety of forms of regionalism, and the creative transformation of
public spaces. Religious culture has been fundamental to these efforts.
Therefore the overall form and content of this book has engaged these

history-making projects in a manner that makes clear their connection and contribution to the study of North American religious history.

Today, significant demographic changes mean that understanding the relationship between these two mythic ways of understanding place and past is increasingly important. The dramatic increase in the Latina/o population of the United States to approximately one in six American adults, and, more significantly, one in four American children (roughly two-thirds of whom are ethnic Mexicans) has stirred considerable nativism and anti-immigrant sentiments. As a result, the reexamination of the proximate histories of the United States and Mexico has acquired greater urgency and importance.

Religion, Place, and Ethnicity

Throughout this book, we have seen that ways of understanding both conquest and resistance employed religious language and practices to buttress claims of ownership of physical space and to define the history of extant places. Most notably, a variety of forms of sacralization allowed some historical actors to re-define military conquests as spiritual ones in public history and allowed others to define diasporic contact zones as spiritual homelands in expressions of ethnic nationalism. These divergent articulations of history resulted in the creation of social conventions and spatial imaginaries that counter one another even as they share discursive fields that frame the way they order the world. In other words, when Southern California is envisioned as either an Arcadian paradise or as a part of Aztlán, that vision relies on moral and religious discourse that understands colonial encounter and conflict from radically opposing perspectives, even as both narratives claim forms of historical continuity with Latin American and Indigenous pasts. However, these conceptions of the past have resulted in complex stances toward contemporary Latin American and Indigenous peoples.

We have seen how American fascination in the nineteenth century with Spanish colonial history resulted in a particular framing of mission history that served to appropriate the region's past. Simultaneously, American criticisms of Mexican secularization of California's missions worked to divorce the region from its contemporary connections to Latin America. A central feature of this cultural work was the commonplace racist portrayal of ethnic Mexican and Indigenous peoples as inherently obsolescent, tragic, and immoral.

The effects of these emergent historical conventions can be seen most clearly in the discussion of the American victory against the Mexican state in the Pious Fund Case. The ruling in favor of the American Catholic Church added considerable momentum in American culture to the idea of historical continuity between the original Spanish expansion into Alta California and its annexation from Mexico by the United States. By making the claim that this continuity was based on religious principles of industriousness and civility rather than on historical ties to colonial Spain, Americans accelerated the process of uncoupling the region from Mexico in their own historical understanding. This cultural project was supported by literally taking possession of the Spanish missionary enterprise through the "return" of the missions to the American Catholic Church and then by successfully suing the Mexican state for the funds to support them. As a result, the missions themselves became monumental anchors for efforts to Americanize Alta California.

The appropriation of the missions then served as a foundation for a new regional identity that was popularized and commercialized at the end of the nineteenth century. Significantly, migration to this new region offered many southern and eastern European immigrants an opportunity reinvent themselves as "white" westerners and lessen the stigma their ethnicity brought them on the East Coast.

The emerging pastoral conception of California's Catholic past was harnessed to create a tangible sense of place in the wildly popular novel *Ramona* (which finished by narrating the inevitable unmaking of Mexican and Indigenous California) and ultimately was made manifest monumentally in architecture. As a result of growing enthusiasm for the missions and the opportunities provided by construction booms, the search for a distinctive regional style in California found its iconic form through the creation of Mission Revival architecture; it repeated elements of the churches' forms in secular buildings in a manner that evoked and routinized nascent ways of conceptualizing Southern California as a part of the United States.

Religious popular culture exerted a significant influence on the Americanization of the region, and the parallel development of cultural trends in Mexico had profound consequences in Southern California. At the turn of the twentieth century, creative tensions occurring because the missions functioned as Catholic churches *and* as civic monuments in a largely Protestant dominant culture resulted in denominational ecumenism. But the cooperation between white Protestants and Catholics served to deepen nineteenth-century narratives legitimizing the American conquest of California, even as the Mexican-born population of the state increased dramatically.

Through the evolution of Mission Revival into the more ornate Spanish Revival at the Panama-California Exposition in San Diego, the establishment of the coastal Camino Real roadway "linking the missions," the radical transformation of the city of Santa Barbara, as well as in the pageantry of the Los Angeles *Fiesta* and Old Spanish Days we have seen religion work through popular culture to reinforce conceptions of Southern California as a place that was historically Iberian and contemporarily American but incongruous with Mexico and, as evidenced by repatriation efforts, often inhospitable to Mexicans.

Ethnic Mexicans living in Southern California responded to the experience of living in *Mexico de afuera* through a variety of historically contingent expressions of ethnicity and redefinitions of place through the creation of new ways of understanding the region's history.

These histories inverted dominant narratives of belonging and exclusion that have been handed down from the nineteenth century and were foundational to the creation of American Southern California. We have seen how the mobilizing mythology of Aztlán allowed for the creation of geopoetics of resistance that at once claimed place, legitimized the presence of ethnic Mexicans in *Mexico de afuera*, and encouraged creative self-expression for those living in the hyphen between the United States and Mexico. Finally, we explored the use of the image of the Virgin of Guadalupe in muralism as a dynamic locus of community that implies connections to Mexico and Mexican culture as it sacrilizes and defines place.

Assessing Historical Mythologies

Carey McWilliams's critique of the selective appropriation and romanticization of California's Spanish colonial history has long provided an important lens through which to understand the creation of popular historical conventions that reinforced racist social inequities. It is important to recognize that both the romanticism central to the idea of an Arcadian Spanish colonial past and the neo-Aztecism that gives shape to the concept of Aztlán rely upon useful fictions that are inculcated and perpetuated within social fields constituted within relations of power.[1] Much like the religious narratives they make use of, these nationalist narratives gain strength through repetition, the definition of place, and public rituals that enact commonly held beliefs.

Three-quarters of a century after his coining of the term "Fantasy Heritage" and well after the emergence of late-twentieth-century Chicana/o articulations of a borderlands heritage, a critical understanding of McWilliams's assessments of historical myth offers us the opportunity to see that these powerful narratives are not to be understood simply as rectifiable falsehoods whose "veil of fantasy" is to be easily lifted. Rather, we can see that these ways of understanding place and past undergird both powerful hegemonic structures and oppositional or counterhegemonic narratives that have great cultural and political capital. A central feature of the mythic "fantasies" we have examined is that they come to exist in dialogic relation; to use McWilliams's functional distinction, they respond to and are shaped by each others' sacred and profane "truths." However, it is important to recognize that these myths do not only emerge in binary dichotomies but often exist with linkages to any number of mythic cultural formations. In the case of early Chicana/o nationalism's mobilization of the concept of Aztlán, its historical mythos was shaped not only in relation and opposition to the dominant historical narratives in American culture but also in response to nationalist critiques of expatriates articulated within Mexican national culture.

It is instructive to examine, in McWilliams's terms, the "sacred" and "profane" components of nationalist expressions of the "Fantasy Heritage" of Aztlán. Its earliest "sacred" expressions would include the positing of a spiritual unity of Chicana/os born from an assumed common cultural experience, an investment in re-worked nationalist representations of pre-Columbian Aztec civilization as representative of Chicana/o heritage, and a concomitant investment in claims of a *primal* pre-Columbian Mesoamerican connection to the lands that became the

American Southwest. From a Mexican national perspective, this final point is noteworthy as a provocative relocation of Aztlán. It places the origin of the Mexica/Aztec people, and the wellspring of *indigenista* understandings of *Mexicanidad, outside* of the current political boundaries of the Mexican state just as writers in the United States had done after the conquest of Mexico's northern frontier in the nineteenth century. In their most naïve form, the mythic "profane" elements reinforce the occlusion of Mexican pluralism, which denies the history and cultural contributions of many ethnic and racial groups in the formation of Mexican culture. At their worst, literalist conceptions of Aztlán have encouraged the questioning of the cultural authenticity and political commitments of individuals based on linguistic ability and diction, social class, and even phenotype. Moreover, early Chicano nationalism has long been criticized for relying on masculinist heteronormativity in its celebration of the bonds of brotherhood, its privileging of the Virgin Mother, and its defense of traditional patriarchal family structures.

However, the sacred truths central to these "fantasy heritages" are not commensurate in that each has been deployed for different social functions and each has had different social consequences. The idea of an Arcadian past gained a great deal of its cultural (and legal) capital as a result of its ability to link the region's Latin American past and its American present in a manner that naturalized the outcome of the Mexican-American War through racist criticisms of Mexicans and an imagined spiritual connection to Spanish colonists. In contrast, the idea of Aztlán as described by Alurista is a poetic topos that reframes and transforms experiences of the present in relation to fluid conceptions of the past. As generations of Chicana/o writers and artists have demonstrated, the concept of Aztlán is able to powerfully create a sense of heritage within cultural interstices and national borderlands when it is understood in metaphoric terms. Its greatest potential as a tool for social justice comes from its ability to facilitate an ongoing and difficult process of self-definition.

While relatively small numbers of Chicana/o nationalists articulate a belief in an authentically historical and locatable Aztlán, the popularity of literal interpretations of the myth has waned over time, and Chicana/o studies scholars have moved toward the concept of *borderlands* as an organizing principle. It is noteworthy that the idea of Aztlán is criticized most vocally by nativist American critics who *do* understand the concept literally and as a direct threat to the sovereignty of the United States in the Southwest.

Ultimately, these intertwined "fantasy heritages" should be evaluated in terms of the real effects and relations of power they advance. The Arcadian vision we have seen take shape throughout this book informed the academic study of the region for much of the twentieth century, and it continues into the twenty-first. Its contemporary influence is felt largely in presentations of public history at the missions themselves and in elementary school curricula that make use of nineteenth-century narrative tropes.[2] As we have seen, Americans' deep cultural investment in an Arcadian Spanish past in Southern California has allowed for the creation of a form of exceptionalist American regionalism that both occludes the war with Mexico and provides a rationale for it. In doing so, the idea of an inherited Arcadian past bolsters a naturalized view of the westward expansion of the United States, one driven by a moral imperative born from an assumed industrious American character rather than from an acknowledgment of martial ambition and imperial desires. As has been demonstrated, this has had the long-term effect of sustaining biases that define ethnic Mexicans as perpetually foreign to the United States. But, even as this way of understanding the region's past denigrated ethnic Mexicans, it fostered a form of ecumenism between white American Protestants and Catholics, overcoming some very powerful prejudices even as it more deeply inscribed others.

On the other hand, Chicana/o mythologies making use of the concept of Aztlán have facilitated largely inverse phenomena. Through their indigenist claims of a primal connection to the land, they have legitimated the presence of ethnic Mexicans in the United States. They have also defined a sense of region, but of one in deep relation to Mexican and Indigenous cultures rather than Spanish ones. In practice they have promoted the creation of significant places that frame communities through public art and sacralized many of them in devotional streetscapes.

The concept of Aztlán itself has had considerable longevity. However, it has also been reinvented in the work of generations of Chicana feminist writers and artists (most notably Gloria Anzaldúa, Cherríe

Moraga, Ana Castillo, and Amalia Mesa-Bains) who have made use of auto-ethnography as a vehicle for expressions of embodied experiences of gender and sexuality. It is also significant that the early mythic construction of Chicana/o heritage gave birth to the multidisciplinary academic work of investigating and narrating ethnic Mexican experiences in the United States. However, the very existence of Chicana/o studies in academic settings has recently been legally challenged and will likely continue to be.[3]

Despite fundamental differences in ways of making sense of past and present described in this book, examining how both arose offers an opportunity for the creation of new ways of understanding history that embrace the manifold consequences of the Mexican-American War as important and constitutive elements of the secular and religious histories of the United States. In a gesture that speaks to us about the "ways in which the history of the United States can be made to come to terms with its Latin American past," Octavio Paz offers us a closing reflection on the need for a greater awareness of proximate relations in our understanding of the past, even as many histories and historical myths have been understood in opposition to one another:

> You as a Chicano and I as a Mexican . . . we can't understand each other without Mexican history and Chicano history. And in turn, Chicanos cannot understand themselves without an understanding of the history of the United States or the history of Mexico. We Mexicans cannot understand ourselves without understanding pre-Columbian history and the history of Spain. And Spain belongs to European history and the Arab world. And the history of the United States cannot be understood apart from the history of England and Puritanism and Protestantism.[4]

NOTES

NOTE TO THE INTRODUCTION

1. See Carey McWilliams, *North from Mexico: The Spanish Speaking Peoples of the United States.* New York: Lippincott, 1948: 39. While McWilliams used the phrase "the mission legend" critically, later scholars have more commonly used the term "the mission myth."

NOTES TO CHAPTER 1

1. I rely on Eric Hobsbawm's definition of "invented tradition": "Invented tradition is taken to mean a set of practices, normally governed by or tacitly accepted rules and of a ritual or symbolic nature, which seek to inculcate certain values and norms of behavior by repetition, which automatically implies continuity with the past. In fact, where possible, they normally attempt to establish continuity with a suitable historic past." From "Introduction: Inventing Traditions" *The Invention of Tradition*, ed. Eric Hobsbawm and Terence Ranger. Cambridge: Cambridge University Press, 1983: 1.

2. For a survey of Mexican nationalism and the history of *indigenismo* in Mexico, see Luis Villoro's *Los Grandes Momentos del Indigenismo en México.* México, D.F.: Secretaria de Educación Pública, 1987; and Henry C. Schmidt, *The Roots of Lo Mexicano: Self and Society in Mexican Thought, 1900–1934.* College Station and London: Texas A&M University Press, 1978. For a treatment of Mexican historiographic responses to the war, see Richard Griswold del Castillo's essay "Mexican Views of 1848: The Treaty of Guadalupe Hidalgo through Mexican History," in the *Journal of Borderlands Studies* Vol. I., No. 2: 24–40.

3. In the great debates at Valladolid (1550–51), Fray Bernal Diaz de Las Casas would argue that the Aztec had been no more or less barbaric than these earlier Mediterranean civilizations, as they all lacked the Christian religion. Las Casas, Obras Escogidas, IV, p. 434–45, cited in Benjamin Keen, *The Aztec Image in Western Thought*. New Brunswick, N.J.: Rutgers University Press, 1991: 98.

4. See Stacie G. Widdifield, *The Embodiment of the National in Late Nineteenth Century Mexican Painting*. Tucson: University of Arizona Press, 1996.

5. For the pious legend of the apparition of Guadalupe, see *The Story of Guadalupe: Luis Laso de la Vega's Huei tlamahuiçoltica of 1649*, ed. Lisa Sousa, Stafford Poole, and James Lockhart. Stanford, Calif.: Stanford University Press, 1998.

6. D. A. Brading, *Mexican Phoenix: Our Lady of Guadalupe, Image and Tradition Across Five Centuries*. Cambridge: Cambridge University Press, 2003: 204 provides a reference to Miers Obras, which is where the sermon is located.

7. "Señor, vamos a restablecer el imperio mexicano, mejorando el gobierno; vamos, en fin, a ser libres e independientes." See Brading, *Mexican Phoenix*: 229.

8. Theodore H. Hittel, *A History of California Volume II*. Pacific Press and Publishing Company, 1885: 91.

9. Lisbeth Hass, *Conquests and Historical Identities in California: 1769–1936*. Berkeley: University of California Press, 1996: 36.

10. The phrase "religiously nostalgic" in reference to these attitudes is borrowed from Jenny Franchot, *Roads to Rome: The Antebellum Protestant Encounter with Catholicism*. Berkeley, Los Angeles, and London: University of California Press, 1994: xxvi. Also see Ray Billington, *The Origins of Nativism in the United States, 1800–1844*. New York: Arno Press, 1974.

11. For a history of the Black Legend and its influence on anti-Catholic attitudes in the United States see Wayne Powell, *Tree of Hate: Propaganda and Prejudice Affecting United States Relations with the Hispanic World*. Portland, Ore.: Ross House Books, 1985. For a brief but thorough survey of nineteenth-century anti-Catholic literature, see David Brion Davis, ed., *The Fear of Conspiracy: Images of Un-American Subversion from the Revolution to the Present*. Ithaca and London: Cornell University Press, 1971, esp. 9–22 and 85–99.

12. The travel literature of the time is extensive, but for the purposes of this study see Grace Greenwood, *Haps and Mishaps of a Tour in Europe*. Boston: Ticknor, Reed and Fields, 1853; and the later Helen Hunt, *Bits of Travel*. Boston: James R. Osgood and Company, 1873.

13. Nathaniel Hawthorne, *Life of Franklin Pierce*. Boston: Ticknor, Reed and Fields, 1852: 67, 105–6. Also see Robert W. Johannsen, *To the Halls of the Montezumas: The Mexican War in the American Imagination*. New York and Oxford: Oxford University Press, 1985: 68–107.

14. See Franchot, *Roads to Rome*: 38–62, on Prescott's influence, and Johannsen, *To the Halls of the Montezumas*: 100, for American comparisons to Cortés's campaign. While the literary image of the Halls of the Montezumas existed before the war, its use became much more common afterward—consider this imagery's lingering presence in the words of the twentieth-century Marine Corps Hymn: "From the Halls of Montezuma/To the shores of Tripoli/We fight our country's battles/In air on land and sea/First to fight for right and freedom/And to keep our honor clean/We are proud to claim the title/of United States Marine."

15. *Literary World*, II, August 28, 1847: 85–86.

16. Ibid., 85.

17. It is noteworthy that General Patterson was an Irish immigrant. The war with Mexico provided many Irish Catholics with an opportunity to prove their loyalty to the United States by fighting against a Catholic country, and indeed the war changed many anti-Irish attitudes in the United States. Some Irish Catholics did, however, defect to the Mexican Army, unwilling to fight fellow Catholics. For a history of these Irishmen, see Robert Ryal Miller, *Shamrock and the Sword: The Saint Patrick's Battalion in the U.S.-Mexican War*. Norman and London: University of Oklahoma Press, 1989.

18. "Complimentary Dinner Given By The Aztec Club of 1847, To Their Honored President Major General Robert Patterson, At Delmonico's in New York, January 6, 1880": 11. Pamphlet in Huntington Library Ephemera collection.

19. See Richard Griswold del Castillo, *The Treaty of Guadalupe Hidalgo: A Legacy of Conflict*. Norman and London: University of Oklahoma Press, 1990: 18.

20. See Hubert Howe Bancroft, *History of Arizona and New Mexico: 1530–1888*. Albuquerque: Horn and Wallace, 1962: 526n13.

21. See *Notes of Travel in California*, from *The Official Reports of Col. Fremont and Maj. Emory*, James M'Glashan ed., Dublin, 1849: 179. Americans brought the wartime imagination back to many parts of the country—consider towns founded by returning veterans in Iowa, Colorado, Kansas, and Georgia that all bear the name "Montezuma."

22. See Keen, *The Aztec Image in Western Thought*: 383–85.

23. Among Americans, the expression of this trope ranged from the Mormon vision of America's religious history (echoing Bernal Diaz's seventeenth-century *History of the Indies*) that claimed Aztecs were a lost tribe of Israel, to Robert Wilson, who argued that Egypt and Phoenicia were the sources of all civilization on the continent.

24. William Gleeson, *History of the Catholic Church in California*. San Francisco: A. L. Bancroft and Co., 1872: 199.

25. Ibid.: 322.

26. See Grey Brechin, *Imperial San Francisco: Urban Power, Earthly Ruin*. Berkeley, Los Angeles, and London: University of California Press, 1999.

27. For a discussion of the transition of political and economic control in Southern California at the time, see Albert Camarillo, *Chicanos in a Changing Society: From Mexican Pueblos to American Barrios in Santa Barbara and Southern California*. Cambridge, Mass.: Harvard University Press, 1996: 33–52; Douglas Monroy, *Thrown Among Strangers: The Making of Mexican Culture in Frontier California*. Berkeley, Los Angeles, and London: University of California Press, 1990: 233–77; and Leonard Pitt, *The Decline of the Californios: A Social History of the Spanish-Speaking Californians, 1846–1890*. Berkeley, Los Angeles, and London: University of California Press, 1998: 229–48.

28. Richard Henry Dana Jr., *Two Years Before the Mast: A Personal Narrative of Life at Sea*. New York: Penguin, 1981: 101.

29. Ibid.: 189. While the Santa Barbara Mission was founded in 1786, the original mission was destroyed in an earthquake in 1812 and was rebuilt in 1815.

30. Gerald Geary, *The Secularization of the California Missions, 1810–1846*. Washington: Catholic University of America Press, 1934: 16–17; and William Taylor, *Magistrates of the Sacred: Priests and Parishioners in Eighteenth Century Mexico*. Stanford, Calif.: Stanford University Press, 1996: 83–86. It is noteworthy that Geary would be very active in the campaign to canonize Fr. Junipero Serra.

31. Ibid.: 25–34; Taylor, *Magistrates of the Sacred*: 15–17.

32. See David J. Weber, *The Spanish Frontier in North America*. New Haven and London: Yale University Press, 1992: 236–70.

33. "Reglamento De La Nueva California, 1773," in *Diario Del Capitan Comandante Fernando de Rivera y Moncada* Vol. II, ed. Ernest J. Burrus, S.J. Madrid: Ediciones Porrua, 1967: 375–89.

34. Secularization was completed and mission lands were largely redistributed and sold off by 1845, just before war broke out with the United States.

35. Dana, *Two Years Before the Mast*: 232–33.

36. Joseph Warren Revere, *A Tour of Duty in California*, ed. Joseph N. Balestier. New York: C. S. Francis and Co., 1849: 33.

37. This editorial change in the editions of Dana's work is first noted in John Ogden Pohlman, *California's Mission Myth*, unpublished dissertation, University of California Los Angeles, 1974: 22.

38. Elizabeth Hughes, *The California of the Padres; or, Footprints of Ancient Communism*. San Francisco: I. N. Choynski, 1875: 32. A counter-example can be found in Mary Cone's *Two Years in California*. Chicago: S. C. Griggs and Company, 1876: 26–48. Cone makes use of Dana's writings to support a negative assessment of the mission system and its effects on California's Native American population.

39. Hughes, *The California of the Padres*: 35.

40. Ibid.: 38.

41. Ibid.: 3.

42. Ibid.: 31 and 22.

43. Joseph A. Thompson, *El Gran Capitan Jose de la Guerra: A Historical Biographical Study*. Los Angeles: Cabrera and Sons, 1961: 63.

44. Dana, *Two Years Before the Mast*: 315–20.

45. Thompson, *El Gran Capitan Jose de la Guerra*: 220.

46. Francis J. Weber tells us that the bishop "died about midnight, probably from consumption, aggravated by acute disappointment" over the condition of the missions, in *A Biographical Sketch of Right Reverend Francisco Garcia Diego Y Moreno, First Bishop of the Californias, 1785–1846*. Los Angeles: Borromeo Guild Press, 1961: 37. Americans say he died of heartache after secularization.

47. Thompson, *El Gran Capitan Jose de la Guerra*: 222.

48. Ibid.: 93–97.

49. Ibid.: 176; also see "Jose Antonio de la Guerra, Certificates of his Spanish Citizenship, 1847, July, 13 and October, 19." Huntington Library Call Number: Fac 667 (576).

50. John Bernard McGloin, *California's First Archbishop*. New York: Herder and Herder, 1966: 90.

51. Ibid.: 133.

52. Maria Del Carmen Velásquez, *El Fondo Piadoso De Las Californias, Notas Y Documentos*. México, D.F.: Secretaria De Relaciones Exteriores, 1985, provides a documentary history of the Fund up until the beginnings of secularization in California; Antonio Gomez Robledo, *Mexico Y El Arbitraje Internacional*. Mexico, D. F.: Editorial Porrua, 1965: 3–116, provides a Mexican account of the history of appropriations of the Fund, both by the Mexican government and the American Catholic Church through the Pious Fund Case.

53. Alemany quoted in Francis J. Weber, *The United States Versus Mexico: The Final Settlement of the Pious Fund*. Los Angeles: The Historical Society of Southern California, 1969: 17.

54. Ibid.: 18–21.

55. See John T. Doyle, *Some Account of the Pious Fund of California and the Litigation to Recover It*. San Francisco: Edward Bosqui & Co. Printers, 1880.

56. "Opinion of the Mexican Commissioner": 8–9.

57. Ibid.: 10.

58. Ibid.

59. Note that when the American Commissioner cited the continued need for missionization in California as a valid reason for awarding the Fund to the American Catholic Church, he opined, "I think it is evident that the Californias are still full of heathen, and that the number has increased on the whole, since in addition to the Antochthenes [*sic*] and the Europeans dwelling there, Asia has contributed the "Heathen Chinee"(sic). See ibid.: "Opinion of the American Commissioner": 3.

60. Weber, *The United States Versus Mexico*: 25–28.

61. Howard S. Levie, "Final Settlement of the Pious Fund Case," *The American Journal of International Law* Vol. 63, No. 4 (Oct. 1969): 791–93.

62. P. J. Thomas, ed., *Our Centennial Memoir*. San Francisco: P. J. Thomas, 1877: 59.

63. Ibid.: 68.

64. Hayden White, *Metahistory: The Historical Imagination in Nineteenth-Century Europe*. Baltimore: Johns Hopkins University Press, 1973: 9.

65. Thomas, *Our Centennial Memoir*: 79.

66. Ibid.: 82.

67. Ibid.: 95.

68. Ibid.: 83.

69. Ibid.: 91–92.

70. Ibid.: 91.

71. Ibid.: 118 and 120. Emphasis in the original.

72. Ibid.: 121.

73. Note that Vallejo's speech does, however, appear in translation in the centennial memoir.

74. Alfred Robinson, *Life in California Before the Conquest*. San Francisco: Thomas C. Russell, 1925 [1846].

75. Edwin Bryant, *What I Saw in California, Being the Journal of a Tour in the Years 1846, 1847*. New York: D. Appleton and Company, 1848: 284.

76. Ibid. See Antonia I. Castañeda, "The Political Economy of Nineteenth Century Stereotypes of Canilfornianas" in *Between Borders: Essays on Mexicana/Chicana History*, ed. Adelaida R. Del Castillo. Los Angeles: Floricanto Press, 1990.

77. William Redmond Ryan, *Personal Adventures in Upper and Lower California, in 1848–9*. London: William Shogerl Publisher, 1850: 181–83.

78. Charles Loring Brace, *New West or California in 1867–68*. London: G. P. Putnam and Son, 1869: 285.

79. Revere, *A Tour of Duty in California*: 184–93.

80. Yellow Bird (John Rollin Ridge), *The Life and Adventures of Joaquín Murieta, The Celebrated California Bandit*. Norman and London: University of Oklahoma Press, 1955: 8. For studies of the myth of Joaquín Murieta, see Lori Lee Wilson, *The Joaquin Band: The History behind the Legend*. Lincoln: University of Nebraska Press, 2011; and Frank F. Latta, *Joaquín Murieta and His Horse Gangs*. Exeter, Calif.: Bear State Books, 1980.

81. Yellow Bird (John Rollin Ridge), *The Life and Adventures of Joaquín Murieta*: 9.

82. Ibid.: 10.

83. Ibid.: 12–13.

84. Ibid.: 152–59.

85. Rosaura Sanchez points out that the production of these *testimonios* allowed for the articulation of an ethnic proto-nationalism among the Californios through the clear recognition of the differences between their "*Raza*" and that of the Americans. See her *Telling Identities: The Californio Testimonios*. Minneapolis and London: University of Minnesota Press, 1995: 296–97.

NOTES TO CHAPTER 2

1. Upon arrival to the region, Helen Hunt Jackson described the insularity of Southern California as making the place like "an island in the land." Carey McWilliams lauded Jackson for providing us with "the best description of the region yet coined," including it in the title of his influential monograph *Southern California Country: An Island on the Land*. New York: Duell, Sloan & Pearce, 1946. For a history of earlier European visions of California as an island, see Dora Polk's *The Island of California: A History of the Myth*. Spokane: Arthur H. Clark Co., 1991.

2. The Union Pacific and Central Pacific rail lines were to be built on the 41st parallel, whereas the Mason-Dixon line is on the 39th parallel.

3. Most American migrants to California from 1860 to 1880 came from New York, Pennsylvania, Massachusetts, and Maine, and growing numbers of Midwesterners came from Ohio, Indiana, Illinois, and Missouri. See Robert M. Fogelson, *The Fragmented Metropolis: Los Angeles, 1850–1930*. Berkeley, Los Angeles, and London: University of California Press, 1993: 64.

4. On the drastic rise of property value in Southern California during the early 1870s, see Albert Camarillo, *Chicanos in a Changing Society: From Mexican Pueblos to American Barrios in Santa Barbara and Southern California, 1848–1930*. Cambridge, Mass.: Harvard University Press, 1996: 39; and Glenn S. Dumke, *The Boom of the Eighties in Southern California*. Los Angeles: Ward Ritchie Press, 1944: 8–9.

5. For a discussion of the transition of political and economic control in Southern California at the time, see Camarillo, *Chicanos in a Changing Society*: 33–52; Douglas Monroy, *Thrown Among Strangers: The Making of Mexican Culture in Frontier California*. Berkeley, Los Angeles, and London: University of California Press, 1990: 233–77; and Leonard Pitt, *The Decline of the Californios: A Social History of the Spanish-Speaking Californians, 1846–1890*. Berkeley, Los Angeles, and London: University of California Press, 1998: 229–48.

6. Charles Nordhoff (1830–1901) was the grandfather of the Charles Nordhoff (1887–1947) who penned *Mutiny on the Bounty*.

7. Nordhoff worked for the *New York Evening Post* during the Civil War. Truman worked for the *New York Times* (1854–59), the *Philadelphia Press* (1859–61), and the *Washington Chronicle* (1861–62). During the Civil War, Truman was a correspondent for several East Coast papers while he worked on Vice President Andrew Johnson's staff. In 1873 he became editor of the *Los Angeles Star* and served there until 1877. He was hired full time by the Southern Pacific Railroad in 1879 and worked exclusively for the rail as a booster until 1890.

8. Charles Nordhoff, *California: For Health, Pleasure and Residence, A Book for Travelers and Settlers*. New York: Harper and Brothers Publishers, 1872: 18.

9. Benjamin Truman, *Semi-Tropical California*. San Francisco: A. L. Bancroft and Co., 1874: 32.

10. For a survey of the phenomena, see Jahn Baur, *The Health Seekers of Southern California*. San Marino: Huntington Library Press, 1959. For representative examples of the literature, see Walter Lindley, M.D., and J. P. Widney, A.M., M.D., *California of the South: Its Physical Geography, Climate, Resources, Routes of Travel, and Health Resorts*. New York: D. Appleton and Company, 1888; P. C. Remondino, M.D., *The Mediterranean Shores of America. Southern California: Its Climatic, Physical and Meteorological Conditions*. Philadelphia and London: F. A. Davis and Co., 1892; William A. Edwards, M.D., and Beatrice Harraden, *Two Health Seekers in Southern California*. Philadelphia: J. B. Lippincott Company, 1897. For comparison with other similar literature promoting Florida's climate, see George M. Barbour, *Florida for Tourists, Invalids and Settlers*. New York: D. Appleton and Company, 1881.

11. Nordhoff, *California: For Health, Pleasure and Residence*: 11.

12. Benjamin Truman, *Occidental Sketches*. San Francisco: San Francisco News Company, 1881: 203.

13. Nordhoff, *California: For Health, Pleasure and Residence*: 18–19.

14. Nordhoff's promotional writings were published in Germany, France, Britain, and Spain by the Southern Pacific Railroad to attract immigrants to the West. In each European translation, readers were assured that many of their countrymen had already established settlements in California so they could live in society familiar to them. See, for example, his *La Californie pour les Emigrants*. London: Le Chemin de fer Su Pacifique du sud, 1883; and *Guia de California, El Estado de Oro*. London: La Compañia del Ferro-carril del Pacífico del Sud. [*sic*], 1883. Huntington Library.

15. Nordhoff, *California: For Health, Pleasure and Residence*: 137.

16. Ibid.: 196; Truman, *Occidental Sketches*: 161.

17. Nordhoff, *California: For Health, Pleasure and Residence*: 137–38.

18. Ibid., 196. Note that after characterizing the "Pikes" as poor southerners, Nordhoff makes the slip of referring to some Pikes as wealthy, suggesting that his portrayal of southerners' poverty has more to do with perceptions of southern culture as unrefined and crass than with material wealth.

19. Truman, *Semi-Tropical California*: 74.

20. Nordhoff, *California: For Health, Pleasure and Residence*: 162.

21. Ibid.: 155.

22. Ibid.: 149.

23. Ibid.: 156.

24. James Rawls, *Indians of California: The Changing Image*. Norman: University of Oklahoma Press, 1984: 95.

25. Ibid.: 104.

26. Nordhoff, *California: For Health, Pleasure and Residence*: 159.

27. However, northeasterners transplanted to California often understood the Spanish missions as benevolent versions of southern plantations. In *Remembrances of One Hundred Years Ago*, Mary Graham explicitly connected Spanish and southern paternalism in her portrayal of the Franciscan mission system as a utopian synthesis of America's economic systems. She wrote, "The Fathers governed [the Indians] with kindness and intelligence, directed them as to how and when they should labor; be fed, clothed and cared for them. There was wealth and abundance for all. The advantages of free and slave labor were skillfully combined in this system. Never before had the Californian Indian fared so sumptuously. He had anxiety neither for the present nor the future." See Mary Graham, *Remembrances of One Hundred Years Ago*. San Francisco: P. J. Thomas, 1876: 18.

28. Nordhoff, *California: For Health, Pleasure and Residence*: 159.

29. Ibid.: 114.

30. Ibid.: 162.

31. Truman, *Semi-Tropical California*: 27.

32. *Santa Barbara Weekly Press*, 17 January 1874, cited in Albert Camarillo, *Chicanos in a Changing Society: From Mexican Pueblos to American Barrios in Santa Barbara and Southern California*. Cambridge, Mass.: Harvard University Press, 1996: 54.

33. Editorial staff of Sunset Books, *The California Missions: A Pictorial History*. Menlo Park, Calif.: Lane Book Co., 1964: 246–47.

34. Ibid.: 234.

35. Franklin Walker, *A Literary History of Southern California*. Berkeley and Los Angeles: University of California Press, 1950: 94.

36. Benjamin Truman, *The Observations of Benjamin Cummings Truman on El Camino Real*, edited and annotated by Francis J. Weber, photos by A. C. Vroman. Los Angeles: Dawson's Book Shop, 1978: 82. The essays on the missions that Weber has collected in this volume are undated—they are a reproduction of Truman's own scratchbook of his writings on the missions. However, with the text of the essays, he dates the visits that he describes as all having occurred during the late 1870s.

37. Ibid.: 34.

38. Ibid.: 52. Francis Weber notes that Father Compala was not a Spaniard but actually a native of Italy—see footnote 6 on that same page.

39. See David Glassberg, *American Historical Pageantry: The Uses of Tradition in the Early Twentieth Century*. Chapel Hill and London: University of North Carolina Press, 1990: 7–27 for a historical and cultural discussion of Fourth of July festivities throughout the country in 1876.

40. Col. J. J. Warner, Judge Benjamin Hayes, and Dr. J. P. Widney, *An Historical Sketch of Los Angeles California from the Spanish Occupancy, by the Founding of the Mission San Gabriel Archangel, September 8, 1771, to July 4, 1876*. Los Angeles: Louis Lewin and Co., 1876: 149.

41. Ibid.: 138. Significantly, the *Junta Patriotica de Juárez* was a Mexican nationalist organization that sponsored celebrations of Mexican independence and *Cinco de Mayo*. It should also be noted that after a financially disastrous decade in the 1860s, Pio Pico invested all of his remaining capital in his Pio Pico House Hotel.

42. Ruth Odell, *Helen Hunt Jackson*. New York and London: D. Appleton–Century Company, 1939: 173.

43. Helen Hunt Jackson, *A Century of Dishonor: A Sketch of the United States Dealings with Some of the Indian Tribes*. Norman: University of Oklahoma Press, 1994 (reprint of 1885 edition): xii.

44. Ibid.: xiii.

45. See M. Le B. Goddard, "A Century of Dishonor," *Atlantic Monthly* Vol. 47, April 1881: 573; "A Century of Dishonor," *Nation* Vol. 32, 3 March 1881: 152.

46. The Poncas' condition and history were given additional literary treatment in Thomas Henry Tibbles, *Standing Bear and the Ponca Chiefs*. Lincoln: University of Nebraska Press, 1995 (originally printed in 1880).

47. For a discussion of the effect of the Poncas' tour on Women's Home Missionary Groups, see Peggy Pascoe, *Relations of Rescue: The Search for Female Moral Authority in the American West: 1874–1939*. New York and Oxford: Oxford University Press, 1990: 7–8. The Indian Treaty-Keeping and Protective Association went through several later incarnations within just a few years: It became the Central Indian Association, then the National Indian Association, and when men began to join in substantial numbers, it was split into two organizations in 1883, The Men's and The Women's National Indian Association.

48. These are the words of Julius H. Seelye, president of Amherst College, describing Jackson's sentiments in the Introduction to *A Century of Dishonor*. Jackson, *A Century of Dishonor*: 1.

49. Ibid.: 342.

50. Consider Jackson's first literary depiction of an Indian on her trip out to California in 1878:

> Toward night of this day, we saw our first Indian woman. We were told it was a woman. It was apparently made of old India rubber, much soaked, seamed and torn. It was thatched at top with a heavy roof of black hair, which hung down from a ridge-like line in the middle. It had sails of dingy-brown canvas, furled loosely around it, confined and caught here and there irregularly, fluttering and falling open wherever a rag of a different color could be shown underneath. It moved about on brown, bony, stalking members, for which no experience furnishes name; it mopped, and mowed, and gibbered, and reached out through the air with more brown, bony, clutching members; from which one shrank as from the claws of a bear. "Muckee! muckee!" it cried, opening wide a mouth toothless, but red. It was the most abject, loathy thing I ever saw. I shut my eyes, and turned away. Presently, I looked again; It had passed on; and I saw on its back, gleaming out from under a ragged calash-like arch of basket-work, a smooth, shining, soft baby face, brown as a brown nut, silken as silk, sweet, happy, innocent, confiding, as if it were the babe of a royal line, borne in royal state. All below its head was a helpless mummy,—body, legs, arms, feet, bandaged tight, swathed in a solid roll, strapped to a flat board, and swung by a leathern band, going around the mother's breast. Its great, soft, black eyes looked fearlessly at everybody. It was as genuine and blessed a baby as any woman ever bore. Idle and thoughtless passengers jeered the squaw, saying: "Sell us the papoose." "Give you greenbacks for the papoose." Then and not till then, I saw a human look in the India-rubber face. The eyes could flash, and the mouth could show scorn, as well as animal greed. The expression was almost malignant, but it bettered the face; for it made it the face of a woman, of a mother.

In Helen Hunt, *Bits of Travel at Home*. Boston: Roberts Brothers, 1878: 9–10.

51. William Henry Bishop, *Old Mexico and Her Lost Provinces: A Journey in Mexico, Southern California, and Arizona by Way of Cuba*. New York: Harper and Brothers, 1883: 423.

52. Mary Cone reported in *Two Years in California* that when she visited California in 1875 the state's inhabitants were

> divided into the two classes, Americans and Californians. Under the former are included all Anglo-Saxons, no matter whence they came or how long they have been in the country. Under the latter are embraced the Spanish and their descendants, and all mixed races, of which there are many. Under the old Spanish and Mexican rule, the pure Castilians constitute the aristocracy of the country, and they are still first among the Californians. The hybrid descendants of the Mexicans and the Indians have the additional sobriquet of 'Greasers' bestowed upon them.

Mary Cone, *Two Years in California*. New York: Griggs and Company, 1876: 62.

53. Bishop, *Old Mexico and Her Lost Provinces*: 427–29.

54. Nordhoff, *California: For Health, Pleasure and Residence*: 114.

55. Odell, *Helen Hunt Jackson*: 179.

56. "Echoes in the City of the Angels" was originally printed in *The Century Magazine* in December 1883. This quote is drawn from a reprint of the essay in a collection of Jackson's California writings entitled *Glimpses of California and the Missions*. Boston: Little, Brown, 1907: 177.

57. Ibid.: 193.

58. Ibid.: 180–81.

59. *The Century Magazine* Vol. XXVI, No. 1–May (part one) and No. 2 June (part two), 1883: 3–18 and 199–215.

60. Odell, *Helen Hunt Jackson*: 183.

61. In *Bits of Travel*, her collected travel writings from Europe, Jackson (then Helen Hunt) alternates between fascination with and contempt for Catholic Rome and more positive but condescending interest in rural Catholic piety in Germany. See Hunt, *Bits of Travel*: 1873.

62. Helen Hunt Jackson, "Father Junipero and His Work," *The Century Magazine* Vol. XXVI, No. 1, May 1883: 4.

63. Ibid., 18. Jackson claimed that a lonely caretaker at Mission Carmel discovered the location of Serra's remains in the winter of 1882. But, in fact, on July 3, 1882, a crowd of more than 400 people was in attendance for the opening of Serra's grave at Carmel, including an honor guard of "Legion of Saint Patrick" Cadets of the California National Guard. The remains were deemed to be Serra's and were re-interred. See Zephyrin Engelhardt, *The Franciscans in California*. Harbor Springs: Holy Childhood Indian School, 1897, for an account of the event.

64. Helen Hunt Jackson, "Father Junipero and His Work," *The Century Magazine* Vol. XXVI, No. 2, June 1883: 201.
65. Ibid.: 215, citing John Dwinelle's *Colonial History of San Francisco*. San Francisco, 1864: 44–87.
66. Valery Sherer Mathes, "Helen Hunt Jackson: Official Agent to the California Mission Indians," *Southern California Quarterly* Vol. 63, No. 1, 1981: 68.
67. Helen Hunt Jackson and Abbott Kinney, *Report on the condition and needs of the Mission Indians of California*. Washington: Government Printing Office, 1883: 6–7. Huntington Library: 36480.
68. Jackson cited in Evelyn Banning, *Helen Hunt Jackson*. New York: Vanguard, 1973: 200.
69. Mathes, "Helen Hunt Jackson": 75.
70. "Recent Novels," *The Nation* Vol. XL, No. 1022, Jan. 29, 1885: 101.
71. "Ramona," *Overland Monthly* Vol. V, No. 27, March 1885: 331.
72. Ibid.
73. Odell, *Helen Hunt Jackson*: 213–19.
74. For a discussion of the effect of the rate war on Los Angeles, see Robert M. Fogelson, *The Fragmented Metropolis: Los Angeles, 1850–1930*. Berkeley, Los Angeles, and London: University of California Press, 1993: 66. For a broader treatment of the effect of the rate war on the region, see Dumke, *The Boom of the Eighties in Southern California*: esp. 17–27.
75. United States Bureau of the Census, *Tenth Census: 1880*. Washington: Government Printing Office, 1880; United States Bureau of the Census, *Eleventh Census: 1890*. Washington: Government Printing Office, 1892–97.
76. See Dumke, *The Boom of the Eighties in Southern California*: esp. 17.
77. Helen Hunt Jackson, *Ramona*. New York: Signet, 1988: 12.
78. Letter from Jackson to Coronel reprinted in Lindley and Widney, *California of the South*: 198.
79. James Sandos presents a well-documented history of Camulos's influence on Jackson in "Historic Preservation and Historical Facts: Helen Hunt Jackson, Rancho Camulos and Ramonana," *California History*, Fall 1998: 168–85.
80. Richard Griswold del Castillo, "The Del Valle Family and The Fantasy Heritage," in *California History*, Spring 1980: 2–15.
81. Ibid.: 8.
82. Edward Roberts, *Santa Barbara and Around There*, Illustrations by H. C. Ford. Boston: Roberts Brothers, 1886: 143–44.
83. Ibid.: 147.
84. Ibid.
85. Del Castillo, "The Del Valle Family": 8.
86. Charles Lummis, *The Home of Ramona: Photographs of Camulos, the fine old Spanish Estate described by Mrs. Helen Hunt Jackson, as the Home of "Ramona,"* second edition. Los Angeles: Chas. F. Lummis & Company, 1888: n.p.
87. Ibid.

88. Peter Thomas Comny, *The Origins and Purposes of the Native Sons and Daughters of the Golden West*. San Francisco: Native Sons of the Golden West, 1955–56: 10. Cited in del Castillo, "The Del Valle Family": 8–9.

89. See Michael Magliari, "Free Soil, Unfree Labor: Cave Johnson Couts and the Binding of Indian Workers in California 1850–1867," *Pacific Historical Review*, August 2004: 349–89.

90. For a sampling of the many sites claiming a relation to *Ramona*, see Sandos, "Historic Preservation and Historical Facts": 168–85. For literary examples of speculation about the location of the "actual" places and people of Jackson's novel, see Margaret V. Allen, *Ramona's Homeland*. San Diego: Denrich Press, 1914; George Wharton James, *Through Ramona's Country*. Boston: Little, Brown and Co., 1911; Carlyle Channing Davis and William A. Anderson, *The True Story of Ramona: Its Facts and Fictions, Inspiration and Purpose*. New York: Dover Publishing, 1914.

91. Dumke, *The Boom of the Eighties in Southern California*: 175.

92. Lindley and Widney, *California of the South*: 1.

93. Charles Nordhoff, *Peninsular California; some account of the climate, soil, productions, and present condition chiefly of the northern half of Lower California*. New York: Harper and Bros., 1888: preface and 13.

94. Karen Weitze, *California's Mission Revival*. Los Angeles: Henessey and Ingalls, 1984: 25.

95. Nadine Ishitani Hata, *The Historic Preservation Movement in California: 1940–1976*. Sacramento: California Department of Parks and Recreation, 1992: 4.

96. More than half of the boom towns of the late 1880s became ghost towns or were adopted into other municipalities within Los Angeles County. See Dumke, *The Boom of the Eighties in Southern California*: 175–99.

97. Weitze, *California's Mission Revival*: 21–23.

98. Ibid.: 29–31.

99. Ibid.: 38.

100. "California's Exposition Building," *World's Fair Magazine*, February 1892: 62.

101. John J. Elkin, ed., *Official Guide to the World's Columbian Exposition*. Chicago: The Columbian Guide Co./John Anderson Printing, 1893: 147–48.

102. Another reproduction of a historical Spanish building was attempted in the full-scale replica of the convent of *La Rabida*, the place where Columbus "well neigh [*sic*] discouraged, sought and obtained shelter and encouragement at the hands of the Franciscan Priest, Father De Marchena, who used his influence in behalf of the explorer with Queen Isabella" (ibid.: 55). The replica of the Spanish-Franciscan-run convent was erected near the anthropology building's displays of the relics and buildings of Aztec, Mayan, and southwestern cliff-dwelling cultures, offering a striking contrast between Spanish Catholic and Indigenous architectures.

103. Frederick Jackson Turner, "The Significance of the Frontier in American History," in *The Frontier in American History*. New York: Dover, 1996: 38. For a

discussion of Turner's work in relation to Boltonian history, see David J. Weber, "Turner, the Boltonians and the Borderlands," in *Myth and the History of the Hispanic Southwest*. Albuquerque: University of New Mexico Press, 1987: 33–54.

104. *The Land of Sunshine, Southern California: An Authentic Description of Its Natural Features, Resources, and Prospects, Containing Reliable Information for the Homeseeker, Tourist and Invalid, Compiled for Southern California World's Fair Association*, Compiled by Harry Ellington Brook. Los Angeles: World's Fair Association and Bureau of Information Print, 1893: 58–59.

NOTES TO CHAPTER 3

1. See Arthur Chandler, *The Fantastic Fair: The Story of the California Midwinter International Exposition*. San Francisco: Pogo Press, 1993, for a discussion of the fair, its connections to the earlier Columbian Exposition, and the role of Mission Revival in Southern California's exhibits there.

2. Max Meyberg, "La Fiesta de Los Angeles," *Land of Sunshine*, July 1894: 34.

3. For a treatment of the birth of historical pageantry, albeit one that completely ignores the contributions of the Southwest, see David Glassberg, *American Historical Pageantry: The Uses of Tradition in the Early Twentieth Century*. Chapel Hill: University of North Carolina Press, 1990. Eliza Otis, wife of Harrison Gray Otis, the owner of the *Los Angeles Times*, was a regular participant in the organization of Santa Barbara's Floral Festival (that was itself modeled on the "War of Flowers" at Nice, France) and brought the idea of a floral procession to Los Angeles. For descriptions of the first *Fiestas* in Los Angeles, see *Land of Sunshine*, especially "*La Fiesta de Los Angeles*," in both Vol. 2, No. 5, April 1895: 83–84 and Vol. 6, No. 6, May 1897: 261–68.

4. See Karen Weitze, "Sumner P. Hunt," in *Toward a Simpler Way of Life: The Arts and Crafts Architects of California*, ed. Robert Winter. Berkeley, Los Angeles, and London: University of California Press, 1997: 184, and Karen Weitze, *California's Mission Revival*. Los Angeles: Henessey and Ingalls, 1984: 55–56.

5. Glassberg, *American Historical Pageantry*: 69.

6. "*La Fiesta de Los Angeles*": 263.

7. Although Lummis and Bandelier eventually parted ways, Lummis went so far as to name a son Amado Bandelier Lummis. For a biography of Bandelier, see Charles H. Lange, *Bandelier: The life and adventures of Adolph Bandelier*. Salt Lake City: University of Utah Press, 1996. For a discussion of Bandelier's impact on the study of Mesoamerica, see Benjamin Keen, *The Aztec Image in Western Thought*. New Brunswick, N.J.: Rutgers University Press, 1971.

8. See Ramón Gutiérrez, "Aztlán, Montezuma, and New Mexico: The Political Uses of American Indian Mythology," in *Aztlán: Essays on the Chicano Homeland*, ed. Rudolfo Anaya and Francisco Lomeli. Albuquerque: University of New Mexico Press, 1989: 172–87.

9. Charles Lummis, *Some Strange Corners of Our Country: The Wonderland of the Southwest*. Tucson: University of Arizona Press, 1989: 127.

10. Ibid.

11. "In the Lion's Den," *Out West* Vol. 18, No. 5, May 1903: 637.

12. Ibid.

13. Charles Lummis, *The Spanish Pioneers*. Chicago: A. C. McClurg and Co., 1899: 12.

14. Ibid.: 11.

15. In Bolton's bibliographical notes for *The Spanish Borderlands*, he lists Lummis's *Spanish Pioneers* among his own works and those of Herbert Howe Bancroft and Frank Blackmar as the best general sources on the history of the Southwest. See Herbert Bolton, *The Spanish Borderlands: A Chronicle of Old Florida and the Southwest*. Albuquerque: University of New Mexico Press, 1996: 298.

16. For a discussion of Bolton's influence against the Black Legend in American historiography, see David J. Weber, *The Spanish Frontier in North America*. New Haven: Yale University Press, 1992: 353–55.

17. Lummis's praise for Díaz is scattered throughout many editorials, but see Charles Lummis, "The Mexican Wizard," *Land of Sunshine* Vol. 11, No. 6, November 1899: 309–14. Also see Lummis's biography of Díaz, *The Awakening of a Nation: Mexico of To-Day*. New York: Harper, 1898.

18. Charles Lummis, "In the Lion's Den," *Land of Sunshine* Vol. 9, No. 3, August 1898: 140.

19. *California Addresses by President Roosevelt*. San Francisco: The California Promotion Committee, 1903: 38.

20. See Turbesé Lummis Fiske and Keith Lummis, *Charles F. Lummis: The Man and His West*. Norman: University of Oklahoma Press: 87–88 for a discussion of Lummis, Kelso, and the birth of the Landmarks Club.

21. Two Catholic priests interested in California mission preservation were Fr. O'Keefe and Fr. O'Sullivan—Fr. O'Sullivan was frequently listed in Landmarks Club membership rosters published in *Land of Sunshine*.

22. For a counter to restorationists' appeals, see "Restoration Undesirable" from the *Los Angeles Times*, December 25, 1910: 114.

23. See Fiske and Lummis, *Charles F. Lummis*: 88. The A.P.A. Lummis refers to is the American Protective Association, an anti-Catholic association and not a precursor to the already well-established Knights of the Klu Klux Klan.

24. Ibid.: 87.

25. Ibid.: 90. Note that Pala is not a mission; it is a chapel at an *asistencia* or branch chapel—although Lummis notes this, he continually refers to Pala as a mission.

26. *Land of Sunshine* Vol. 6, No. 4, March 1897: 83.

27. Eliza Otis, "The Romance of the Mission Period" (1905) in *Some Essays About the California Missions in Honor of the V Centenary of the Evangelization of the Americas*, ed. Msgr. Francis J. Weber. California Catholic Conference, 1992: 45. Note that the 1905 date in Weber's anthology is the date of the article's reprinting.

28. Letter from Lummis to Englehardt dated April 1, 1909, transcribed in "The Correspondence of Charles F. Lummis with Fr. Zephyrin Englehardt, O.F.M.,"

in *Franciscan Provincial Annals, Province of Santa Barbara* Vol. 3, July 1941, No. 4: 52.

29. Ibid.: 53.
30. In 1943, two decades after Lummis's death, a historical commission was convened by the Catholic Church in California to investigate the life and character of Junipero Serra. In 1988, amid contentious debate, Serra was beatified by Pope John Paul II. Herbert Bolton testified at the early historical hearings.
31. See Weitze, *California's Mission Revival*: 79–111; and Fiske and Lummis, *Charles F. Lummis*: 90.
32. Among the most damaged missions that the Landmarks Club restored were Mission San Fernando and the *asistencia* at Pala.
33. Fiske and Lummis, *Charles F. Lummis*: 90.
34. Mrs. A.S.C. Forbes, *California Missions and Landmarks: El Camino Real*. Los Angeles: Self-published, 1915: 268. The idea for a single road linking the missions had been around since the 1870s, but it was not acted upon until the turn of the century. See Charles Frederick Holder, "The Cordon of the King's highway," *Land of Sunshine* Vol. 3, No. 6, 1895: 269.
35. Ibid.: 264. The Camino Real Association was assembled with delegates from California's Chambers of Commerce, County Supervisors, Highway Commissions, Automobile Clubs, Women's Clubs, Historical Societies, Native Sons and Daughters Parlors, Pioneer Societies, Camera Clubs, Farmers' Clubs, and the Landmarks Club.
36. Ibid.: 261. The Camino Real's signature mission bell and guidepost were designed by Forbes, and in fact her husband was the first bell manufacturer west of the Mississippi and made all the bells for the guideposts. The first of these was erected at the Plaza Church in Los Angeles, where it was saluted by General Antonio Aguilar, "one of the Last of the Valiant Spanish soldiers who defended the City of Los Angeles in the early days." See Forbes, *California Missions and Landmarks*: 277.
37. Forbes mentions the missions as being "one Spanish day" apart, but mission boosters had long promoted them as being one day apart—in some instances the missions were reputedly one day's horseback ride, in others one day's walk apart. Although the advent of the automobile greatly sped travel, in boosters' minds the missions stayed one day apart. The actual distances separating the missions from their neighbors range from twelve miles between Mission San Juan Capistrano and Mission San Gabriel to seventy miles separating Mission San Fernando and Mission San Buenaventura.
38. The Motel Inn was built by the Mo-Tel Corporation in San Luis Obispo in 1926.
39. Letter from Frank Miller to George Wharton James, October 20, 1903, Huntington Library: George Wharton James collection, box 1.
40. Riverside had a population of about 9,000 when the inn was built.
41. *Historic Mission Inn*. Riverside: Friends of the Mission Inn, 1998: 22.

42. Pamphlet included in letter from Frank Miller to Henry E. Huntington, December 5, 1903. Huntington Library: HEH 9068.

43. The basements of Catholic churches were commonly halls of horrors in anti-Catholic literature—most notably in Maria Monk's *The Awful Disclosures of the Hotel Dieu* from 1836.

44. *Historic Mission Inn*: 47. Note, however, that the catacombs were closed to the public several decades later because of the occurrence of water damage to the artwork displayed there.

45. Joan H. Hall, *Through the Doors of the Mission Inn*. Riverside: Highgrove Press, 1996: 58.

46. Ibid.: 85–88.

47. *California Life* Vol. XVII, No. 3, January 24, 1920: 43–44. This was a special edition focusing entirely on "The Mission Play."

48. Ibid.: 14–26. It is also noteworthy that the soldiers do not attend the Mass in McGroarty's play—claiming that "any Mass is too long for a soldier"—maintaining the American distinction between California's secular and religious conquests.

49. Ibid.: 26.

50. Ibid.: 26, 50.

51. Francis J. Weber, "John Steven McGroarty, From the Green Verdugo Hills," *Journal of San Diego History* Vol. XX, No. 4, Fall 1974: 35.

52. Zona Gale, *Frank Miller of the Mission Inn*. New York: D. Appleton–Century, 1938: 143.

53. Gordon Dudley, *Junipero Serra: California's First Citizen*. Los Angeles: Cultural Assets Press, 1969: 17–18. Note that Lummis's doctorate was, unlike Serra's, honorary.

54. Herbert Bolton, "The Mission as a Frontier Institution in the Spanish-American Colonies," in *American Historical Review* Vol. XXIII, October 1917: 52.

55. Charles Lummis, *Stand Fast Santa Barbara*. Santa Barbara Plans and Planting Committee of the Community Arts Association, 1927: 7–8. Capitals in the original.

56. "The Correspondence of Charles F. Lummis with Fr. Zephyrin Englehardt, O.F.M.," in *Franciscan Provincial Annals, Province of Santa Barbara* Vol. 4, No. 4, July 1942: 67.

57. For a survey of the rise of Mexican nationalism, see Henry C. Schmidt, *The Roots of Lo Mexicano: Self and Society in Mexican Thought, 1900–1934*. College Station and London: Texas A&M University Press, 1978.

58. Bernard S. Myers, *Mexican Painting in Our Time*. New York: Oxford University Press, 1956: 12; Desmond Rochfort, *Mexican Muralists: Orozco, Rivera, Siqueiros*. San Francisco: Chronicle Books, 1993: 17.

59. Apart from the American occupation of Veracruz, General Pershing was ordered to pursue the army of Pancho Villa into Mexico. Villa attacked Columbus, New Mexico, on March 9, 1916, in response to the American government's

sudden support of the Carranza regime against Villa. The presence of an American army wandering throughout the northern part of the country added to Mexican concerns about a possible American invasion.

60. José Clemente Orozco, *An Autobiography*. Austin: University of Texas Press, 1962: 20.

61. From *Boletín* 1914: 74, quoted in Jean Charlot, *The Mexican Mural Renaissance: 1920–1925*. New Haven and London: Yale University Press, 1963: 69.

62. See Gabriella De Beer, *Jose Vasconcelos and His World*. New York: Las Americas Publishing Company, 1966: 290–335, for a discussion of Vasconcelos's political role as Minister of Education. On his interaction with the muralists, see Charlot, *The Mexican Mural Renaissance*. Vasconcelos's influence is charted throughout the book. On Atl's political and cultural commitments, see Myers, *Mexican Painting in Our Time*: 12. Also see Diego Rivera and Gladys March, *My Art, My Life: An Autobiography*. New York: Dover, 1991: 22, for Rivera's thoughts on Atl's connections to fascism.

63. Charlot, *The Mexican Mural Renaissance*: 73.

64. José Vasconcelos, *La Raza Cósmica*, trans. Didier T. Jaén. Baltimore and London: Johns Hopkins University Press, 1979: 10.

65. Ibid.: 40.

66. Ibid.: 20.

67. Ibid.: 32. Here Vasconcelos tells his readers:

> The lower types of the species will be absorbed by the superior type. In this manner, for example, the Black could be redeemed, and step by step, by voluntary extinction, the uglier stocks will give way to the more handsome. Inferior races, upon being educated, would become less prolific, and the better specimens would go on ascending a scale of ethnic improvement, whose maximum type is not precisely the White, but that new race to which the White himself will have to aspire with the object of conquering the synthesis. The Indian, by grafting onto the related race, would take the jump of millions of years that separate Atlantis from our times, and in a few decades of aesthetic eugenics, the Black may disappear, together with the types that a free instinct of beauty may go on signaling as fundamentally recessive and undeserving, for that reason, of perpetuation. In this manner, a selection of taste would take effect, much more efficiently than the brutal Darwinist selection, which is valid, if at all, only for the inferior species, but no longer for man. No contemporary race can present itself alone as the finished model that all the others should imitate. The mestizo, the Indian, and even the Black are superior to the White in a countless number of properly spiritual capacities. Neither in antiquity, nor in the present, have we a race capable of forging civilization by itself.

68. Ibid.: 17. Emphasis in the original.

69. For a detailed discussion of the rates of Mexican immigration to the United States from 1900 to 1930, see Matt S. Meir and Feliciano Ribera, *Mexican Americans/American Mexicans: From Conquistadors to Chicanos*. New York: HarperCollins, 1993: 103–30.

70. These included the Chinese Exclusion Act, "Gentleman's Agreement," and quota legislation passed in 1921 and 1924 restricting European immigration.

71. In a letter to his brother, Martí noted that a contemporary French translation of *Ramona* had a suggestive but apt title, *Ramona: The American Conquest in Mexico*. See José Martí, *Obras Completas, Epistolario* Vol. 20. Havana: 1965: 122. For a record of the publication of *Ramona* in Mexico, see John E. Englekirk, *Bibliographia de Obras Norteamericanas en Traduccion Española*. México, D.F.: 1944: 48.

72. José Martí, *Obras Completas, Epistolario* Vol. 20. Havana: 1965: 122, 118.

73. See José Martí, *Obras Completas, En Los Estados Unidos* Vol. 11. Havana: 1965: 133–36.

74. The *Cristero* Rebellion began in July 1926 with a protest strike by the Mexican Catholic clergy against President Calles' strict enforcement of all of the anti-clerical provisions of the Mexican Constitution. The strike lasted for three years with clergy refusing to perform baptisms, weddings, and burials, and it became violent as both clergy and liberal educators were killed—the former by anticlerical activists, the latter by supporters of the clergy.

75. See Moises Sandoval, *On the Move: A History of the Hispanic Church in the United States*. Maryknoll, N.Y.: Orbis Books, 1990: 50, and also Tarcisio Beal, "Hispanics and the Roman Catholic Church in the United States," in *Hispanics in the Church: Up from the Cellar*, ed. Philip Lampe. San Francisco and London: Catholic Scholars Press, 1994.

76. Politically, the *Cristero* Rebellion opened the door to Mexico for American Protestant missionaries—an opportunity taken up most strongly by Congregationalist groups and the Wycliffe Bible translators. For a discussion of the often warm relationship between the Wycliffe Bible translators and the Mexican government, see Ethel Wallis and Mary Bennet, *Two Thousand Tongues to Go: The Story of the Wycliffe Bible Translators*. New York: Harper and Brothers, 1959.

77. *Minutes of the Thirty Sixth annual Meeting of the Southern California Congregational Conference held with the First Congregational Church of San Bernardino, May 8, 9, and 10, 1922*. Los Angeles: T. T. Jones and Company, 1922: 26–27.

78. George J. Sánchez, *Becoming Mexican American: Ethnicity, Culture and Identity in Chicano Los Angeles, 1900–1945*. New York and Oxford: Oxford University Press, 1993: 163. Sánchez marshals an impressive amount of evidence to support this figure.

79. Francisco Balderrama and Raymond Rodríguez, *Decade of Betrayal: Mexican Repatriation in the 1930s*. Albuquerque: University of New Mexico Press, 1995: 20.

80. See John Skirius, "Vasconcelos and Mexico de Afuera (1928)," in *Aztlán* Vol. 7, No. 3, Fall 1976: 479–97.

81. José Vasconcelos, "Noches Californianas," La Opinion. 7/30/1928:3. Original text in Spanish:

> Nuestra Madre Patria habia dicho la californiana en puro ingles a su auditorio anglosajón, nuestra Madre Patria es España. Y Mexico, me ha dicho un compatriota que estaba en el publico ¿por que no se ha acordado de Mexico si ella parece ser mas Mexicana que Española? De pronto yo no supe que contestar, pero después aproposito de otro asunto diverso me dijo un Californiano: mis padres Españoles vinieron, unos por Nuevo Orleans y otros, pasadndo pr Mexico; otros son Indios de Colorado o de Neuevo Mexico influenciados en generaciones ya remotas por la cultura Española que venia de Mexico; pero lo propiamente Mexicano , casi no existe para estos Californianos que se llaman a si mismos Latinos para diferenciarse de sus compatriotas anglosajones. Por otra parte pense con cierta amargura: ¿Que razon habria para que fuesen devotos de Mexico si no fuese por la comun tradicion Española? . . . ¿Pues que otra cosa dio Mexico a estas regions en el medio siglo de su dominacion militarista? Generales entonces y generales hoy como los que han venido explotando a la pobre Baja California. En cambio ¿Le hemos mandado alguna ves a estos hermanos nuestros algun implemento de trabajo, alguna idea, siquiera alguna cancion? Casi nada de esto vino por aca ni cuando eramos Aztecas ni despuse de qye terminamos de ser Españoles. Nada les mandamus aparte de ejercitos que consumaran brutales castigos . . . ¿Como pues vamos a tener derecho de ofendernos porque no se ufandan los californianos de su extinguida mexicania, pero si se apegan patrioticamente a lo Español? ¿Si todo lo bueno que en una epoca les vino de Mexico era Español? Natural es por lo mismo que en sus horas de angustia, hayan vuelto los californianos ed corazon todo entero, no a Mexico por quien perdieron patria y destino, si a España por quien poseen y conservan la alma.

82. See Maria Josefina Saldana-Portillo, *The Revolutionary Imagination in the Americas and the Age of Development*. Durham, N.C.: Duke University Press, 2003: esp. pages 208–11.

83. Charles Lummis, "Preservation of Missions Neglected by State," quoted in John Ogden Pohlman, *California's Mission Myth*. Unpublished dissertation, University of California Los Angeles, 1974: 364.

84. *Los Angeles Times*, January 10, 1920, pt. II: 1.

85. Ibid.: 14.

86. Robert Winter, "Frederick Louis Roehrig," in *Toward a Simpler Way of Life: The Arts and Crafts Architects of California*, ed. Robert Winter. Berkeley, Los Angeles, and London: University of California Press, 1997: 115.

87. See Neil Levine, *The Architecture of Frank Lloyd Wright*. Princeton, N.J.: Princeton University Press, 1996: 126–47; David Gebhard, *Robert Stacy-Judd: Maya Architecture and the Creation of a New Style*. Santa Barbara: Capra Press, 1993; Marjorie Ingle, *The Mayan Revival Style: Art Deco Mayan Fantasy*. Salt Lake City: G. M. Smith, Peregrine Smith Books, 1984.

88. See Carleton Monroe Winslow, *The Architecture and the Gardens of the San Diego Exposition*, introduction by Bertram Goodhue. San Francisco: P. Elder, 1916; Edgar Lee Hewett, *The Architecture of the Exposition*. Publisher and location n/a, 1916.

89. Among the most influential Spanish architects of all time was José Benito Churriguera, whose baroque surface textures, decorative details, and lush ornamentation were widely imitated. Much of late-seventeenth-century and early-eighteenth-century Spanish and Spanish colonial architecture has been labeled Churrigueresque. For southwestern examples, see Rexford Newcomb, *Spanish-Colonial Architecture in the United States*. New York: J. J. Agustin, 1937. Newcomb was an influential architectural historian who helped to promote the Spanish Revival.

90. Rancho Santa Fe was established by the Santa Fe Rail company; although it was advertised as being "not for the man of means only," the minimum cost for a house built in the development ranged from $5,000 to $15,000 in 1920s dollars. Developments were advertised in many of the region's newspapers, but this copy is drawn from "The Place to Make *Your* Dreams Come True!" an ad for Rancho Santa Fe in the *Santa Barbara Morning Press*, July 28, 1925: 3.

91. David Gebhard, *Santa Barbara: The Creation of a New Spain in America*. Santa Barbara: University of California at Santa Barbara Art Museum, 1982: 17–18.

92. *Santa Barbara Morning Press*, March 23, 1922: editorial page.

93. *Santa Barbara Morning Press*, July 5, 1925: 1. Pro-development Santa Barbarans quickly portrayed the destruction of their city as a great opportunity to enact earlier proposals to unify Santa Barbara's architecture along a colonial Spanish theme. The day after the earthquake, July 30, 1925, an article on the front page of the *Santa Barbara Morning Press* reported, "Santa Barbara will rise from its ruins more beautiful and substantial than ever, businessmen of the city declared with unanimity following yesterday morning's earthquake."

94. *Santa Barbara Morning Press*, July 2, 1925: 9.

95. This board was promoted and chaired by Bernard Hoffman and several architects known for their Mission and Spanish Revival works.

96. Gebhard, *Santa Barbara: The Creation of a New Spain in America*: 18.

97. Ibid.: 21.

98. *Santa Barbara Morning Press*, July 15, 1925: 4.

99. *Santa Barbara Morning Press*, July 22, 1925: 4.

100. The closeness of Spanish Revival and Mission architecture, sometimes called "Santa Barbara architecture" by the city's residents, was perhaps best expressed by a lighthearted commentator in the 1930s who reported that "Santa Barbara is a little confusing—every building is a mission—At least that's the way the

architecture affects you when you first see it. You feel like removing your hat when you drive into a service station." From Reg Manning, *Reg Manning's Cartoon Guide to California*. New York: J. J. Augustin Publisher, 1939: 28.

101. *Official Program Fifth Annual Old Spanish Days Fiesta in Santa Barbara*, Old Spanish Days *Fiesta* Inc., 1928.

102. *Official Program Twelfth Annual Old Spanish Days Fiesta in Santa Barbara*, Old Spanish Days *Fiesta* Inc., 1935.

103. Ibid.

104. Presently, debate over the inclusiveness of the name of Santa Barbara's "Old Spanish Days" has escalated. Some have proposed changing the name to "Old California Days" in recognition of the Native American and Mexican past. However, others argue that Santa Barbara's "Fiesta is different from other fiestas, because the others, in cities like San Antonio[,] are only Mexican. We're the only ones who try to keep alive the part of Spain we all have in us." See David Amerikaner, "Under the Influence," in *Rhythms and Music of Fiesta* insert, *Santa Barbara News-Press*, Sunday, August 2, 1998: 4.

105. *Santa Barbara Perpetuates the Romance, Beauty and History of Spanish California*. Santa Barbara: Chamber of Commerce, 1926: n.p.

106. Stella Haverford Rouse, *Santa Barbara's Spanish Renaissance and Old Spanish Days Fiesta*. Santa Barbara: Schauer Printing Studio, 1974: 69.

107. Borrowed from the title of Helen Delpar's book *The Enormous Vogue of Things Mexican: Cultural Relations between the United States and Mexico, 1920–1935*. Tuscaloosa and London: University of Alabama Press, 1992. It is noteworthy that the same corporations funded Protestant missionary campaigns in Mexico and throughout Latin America. See Gerard Colby and Charlotte Dennet, *Thy Will Be Done, the Conquest of the Amazon: Nelson Rockefeller and Evangelism in the Age of Oil*. New York: HarperCollins, 1995.

108. Letter, Pearl Chase to Old Spanish Days *Fiesta* Commission, undated [but a reply is dated August 1930], in Pearl Chase Collection, University of California at Santa Barbara, Old Spanish Days *Fiesta* Box.

109. Letter, Pearl Chase to John D. Kittrell, August, 13, 1930, in Pearl Chase Collection, University of California at Santa Barbara, Old Spanish Days *Fiesta* Box.

110. See George J. Sánchez, *Becoming Mexican American*: 225–26. See Phoebe Kropp, *California Vieja: Culture and Memory in a Modern American Place*. Berkeley, Los Angeles, and London: University of California Press, 2006; William D. Estrada, *The Los Angeles Plaza: Sacred and Contested Space*. Austin: University of Texas Press, 2008.

111. Myers, *Mexican Painting in Our Time*: 12; Rochfort, *Mexican Muralists*: 119. Also see Margarita Nieto, "Mexican Art and Los Angeles, 1920–1940," in *On the Edge of America: California Modernist Art, 1900–1950*, ed. Paul J. Karlstrom. Berkeley, Los Angeles, and London: University of California Press, 1996.

112. David Alfaro Siqueiros, *Mi Respuesta*. México, D.F.: Ediciones de Arte Publico, 1960: 31–21.

113. William Deverell argues, "Surely there was some profound connection, and not just a temporal coincidence, between the rise of the Mexican Revolution, the resulting influx of tens if not hundreds of thousands of Mexicans in Southern California, and the simultaneous flowering of the Mission Play and its cousins: the mission-preservationist movement and Mission architectural boom. The Spanish Fantasy Past was reinvigorated precisely when the Anglo present needed the comfort of myth, the soothing sense that the world worked the way it was meant to. Coincidence?" in Deverell, "Privileging the Mission Over the Mexican: The Rise of Regional Identity in Southern California," in *Many Wests: Place, Culture and Regional Identity*, ed. David M. Wrobel and Michael C. Steiner. Kansas City: University Press of Kansas, 1997: 253.

NOTES TO CHAPTER 4

1. George Sánchez, *Becoming Mexican-American: Ethnicity, Culture and Identity in Chicano Los Angeles, 1900–1945*. New York and Oxford: Oxford University Press, 1993: 123.

2. When Vasconcelos was in the United States he advocated repatriation for Mexicans. See Sánchez, *Becoming Mexican-American*: 122; and Francisco Balderrama and Raymond Rodríguez, *Decade of Betrayal: Mexican Repatriation in the 1930s*. Albuquerque: University of New Mexico Press, 1995: 128–29.

3. James N. Gregory, *American Exodus: The Dust Bowl Migration and Okie Culture in California*. New York and Oxford: Oxford University Press, 1989: 164–71.

4. Emory S. Bogardus, "Current Problems of Mexican Immigrants," in *Sociology and Social Research* Vol. XXV, November 1940. Quoted in Jack D. Forbes, *Azteca del Norte: The Chicanos of Aztlán*. Greenwich, Conn.: Fawcett Premier, 1973: 109–10. The provocative mention of concentration camps refers to American concerns about *Sinarquismo*, a right-wing political philosophy with fascist German and Spanish connections that had become popular in Mexico during the 1930s. See Matt S. Meier and Feliciano Ribera, *Mexican Americans/American Mexicans: From Conquistadors to Chicanos*. New York: Hill and Wang, 1993: 165–66.

5. See Juan Ramon García, *Operation Wetback: The Mass Deportation of Mexican Undocumented Workers in 1954*. Westport, Conn.: Greenwood Publishing Group, 1980; Ronald L. Mize and Alicia C.S. Swords, *Consuming Mexican Labor: From the Bracero Program to NAFTA*. Toronto: University of Toronto Press, 2010; Deborah Cohen, *Braceros: Migrant Citizens and Transnational Subjects in the Postwar United States and Mexico*. Chapel Hill: University of North Carolina Press, 2011.

6. For discussion of the Sleepy Lagoon case and the Zoot Suit Riots, see David G. Gutiérrez, *Walls and Mirrors: Mexican Americans, Mexican Immigrants, and the Politics of Ethnicity*. Berkeley, Los Angeles, and London: University of California Press, 1995: 124–30; Sánchez, *Becoming Mexican-American*: 261–67; Meier and Ribera, *Mexican Americans/American Mexicans*: 162–65. For the Zoot Suit Riots specifically see Mauricio Mazón, *The Zoot Suit Riots: The Psychology of Symbolic Annihilation*. Austin: University of Texas Press, 1984; Luis Alvarez, *The Power*

of the Zoot: Youth Culture and Resistance during World War II. Berkeley, Los Angeles, and London: University of California Press, 2009; Eduardo Obregon Pagan, *Murder at the Sleepy Lagoon: Zoot Suits, Race and Riot in Wartime L.A.* Chapel Hill: University of North Carolina Press, 2006; Catherine Ramírez, *The Woman in the Zoot Suit: Gender, Nationalism, and the Cultural Politics of Memory.* Durham, N.C.: Duke University Press, 2009; Elizabeth Escobedo, *From Coveralls to Zoot Suits: The Lives of Mexican American Women on the World War II Home Front.* Chapel Hill: University of North Carolina Press, 2013.

7. For a history of the transformation of Murieta into Zorro, see Sandra Curtis, *Zorro Unmasked: The Official History.* New York: Hyperion, 1998.

8. *La Fiesta de Santa Barbara* was filmed at considerable expense in full Technicolor.

9. Mission San Juan Bautista's New England steeple was destroyed in a fire, and the mission now makes use of a campanile.

10. McWilliams's use of the distinction between sacred and profane serves to differentiate between sacred myths that are untrue and profane history that is true. See Carey McWilliams, *Southern California Country.* New York: Duell, Sloan and Pearce, 1946: 21–83.

11. Ibid.: 82.

12. Carey McWilliams, *North from Mexico: The Spanish-Speaking People of the United States.* Philadelphia and New York: J. B. Lippincott, 1949: 39.

13. Ibid.: 47.

14. Ibid.

15. See William E. Wilson, "A Note on 'Pochismo,'" in *The Modern Language Journal* Vol. 30, No. 6: 345–46 for an early (1946) discussion of Mexican intellectuals' concern over the hybridization of the Spanish language and the U.S. Border Patrol's training of recruits in Spanglish. For an early example of a Mexican critique of the Pochos and Spanglish, see Jorge Ulica, "Do You Speak Pocho? (1924)," in *Literatura Chicana, 1965–1995: An Anthology in Spanish, English and Caló,* ed. Manuel de Jesús Hernández-Gutiérrez and David William Foster. New York: Garland Publishing, 1997: 101.

16. Octavio Paz, *The Labyrinth of Solitude.* New York: Grove Press, 1985: 13.

17. See César Chávez, *The Plan of Delano.* New York: Random House, 1972. Article 3 states, "We seek, and have, the support of the Church in what we do. At the head of the Pilgrimage we carry LA VIRGEN DE GUADALUPE because she is ours, all ours, Patroness of the Mexican people. We also carry the Sacred Cross and the Star of David because we are not sectarians, and because we ask the help and prayers of all religions."

18. Francisco Lopez, "El Teatro Campesino," in *El Malcriado* Vol. II, No. 3, April 10, 1968: 16, cited in Marshall Rupert Garcia, *La Raza Murals of California, 1963-1970: A Period of Social Change and Protest,* unpublished master's thesis, University of California Berkeley, 1981: 55.

19. Jack D. Forbes, *The Mexican Heritage of Aztlán.* Self-published, 1962. Available at http://nas.ucdavis.edu/Forbes/mhaztlan.pdf.

20. Howard S. Levie, "Final Settlement of the Pious Fund Case," *The American Journal of International Law* Vol. 63, No. 4, October 1969: 791–93; "U.S., Mexico Settle 'Pious Fund' Dispute," *Los Angeles Times*, August 27, 1967: G2.

21. See the classic statement on the mural movements of the 1960s and 1970s in Eva Cockroft, John Pitman Weber, and James Cockroft, *Toward a People's Art: The Contemporary Mural Movement*. Albuquerque: University of New Mexico Press, 1998. For a clear discussion of the interplay between modernism and *indigenismo* in Mexico at the time, see Eric Zolov, "Showcasing the 'Land of Tomorrow': Mexico and the 1968 Olympics," *The Americas* Vol. 61, No. 2: 159–88.

22. The poem's original printing is estimated at having been more than 100,000 prior to its publication by Bantam Books and wider readership. See Cordelia Candelaria's groundbreaking analysis of the poem in *Chicano Poetry: A Critical Introduction*. Westport and London: Greenwood Press, 1986: 42–50.

23. Lee Bebout articulates the idea that the poem helped to form an imagined community quite convincingly in *Mythohistorical Interventions: The Chicano Movement and Its Legacies*. Minneapolis: University of Minnesota Press, 2011. For other helpful analyses of the poem, see Juan Bruce-Novoa, *Chicano Poetry: A Response to Chaos*. Austin: University of Texas Press, 1982; Rafael Pérez-Torres, *Movements in Chicano Poetry: Against Myths Against Margins*. Melbourne: Cambridge University Press, 1995.

24. "*El Plan Espiritual de Aztlán*" in *Aztlan: Essays on the Chicano Homeland*, ed. Rudolfo A. Anaya and Francisco Lomeli. Albuquerque: University of New Mexico Press, 1991: 1.

25. See Jorge Klor de Alva, "The Invention of Ethnic Origins and Negotiation of Latino Identity, 1969–1981," in *Challenging Fronteras: Structuring Latina and Latino Lives in the U.S: An Anthology of Readings*, ed. Mary Romero, Pierrette Hondagneu-Sotelo, and Vilma Ortiz. New York: Routledge, 1999: 55–74.

26. Bruce Novoa, *Chicano Authors: Inquiry by Interview*. Austin: University of Texas Press, 1980: 276.

27. Luis Leal, "In Search of Aztlán," in Anaya and Lomeli, eds., *Aztlán: Essays on the Chicano Homeland*: 8.

28. Anonymous, *La Palabra Alambre de M.A.S.H.* Vol. 4, No. 4, June 1972: 16, quoted in Forbes, *Azteca del Norte*: 332.

29. *El Plan Espiritual de Santa Barbara*. Santa Barbara: La Causa Publications, 1970.

30. On the birth of Chicano studies see Meier and Ribera, *Mexican Americans/American Mexicans*: 222; Ignacio M. Garcia, *Chicanismo: The Forging of a Militant Ethos among Mexican Americans*. Tucson: University of Arizona Press, 1997: 56–57.

31. See the classic statement on the mural movements of the 1960s and 1970s in Cockroft, Weber, and Cockroft, *Toward a People's Art*, 1998.

32. See Shifra Goldman, "Siqueiros and Three Early Murals in Los Angeles," in *Art Journal* Vol. 34, No. 8, August 1974.

33. Eve Simpson, "Chicano Street Murals: A Sociological Perspective," *Journal of Popular Culture*, 13:3 (1980: Spring): 516. Also see Marcos Sanchez Trauilino,

Mi Casa No Es Su Casa: Chicano Murals and Barrio Calligraphy as Systems of Signification at Estrada Courts 1972–1978. Master's thesis, Art History, 1991, UCLA.

34. David Khan, "Chicano Street Murals: People's Art in East Los Angeles Barrio," *Aztlán: International Journal of Chicano Studies Research*, 6:1 (1975: Spring): 118.

35. Shifra Goldman, "The Iconography of Chicano Self-Determination: Race, Ethnicity and Class," *Art Journal*, 49:2 (1990): 167–73.

36. "The Mural Message," *Time*, April 7, 1975.

37. See Kevin Delgado, "A Turning Point: The Conception and Realization of Chicano Park," *Journal of San Diego History* Vol. 44, No. 1, Winter 1998.

38. See Delgado, "A Turning Point"; Martin Rosen and James Fisher, "Chicano Park and the Chicano Park Murals: Barrio Logan, City of San Digeo," *The Public Historian*, 24:4 (2001: Autumn): 91–111; Eva Cockroft, "The Story of Chicano Park," *Aztlán: International Journal of Chicano Studies Research*, 15:1 (1984: Spring).

39. See Marshall Rupert Garcia, *La Raza Murals of California, 1963–1970: A Period of Social Change and Protest.* Master's thesis, University of California Berkeley, 1981; Eve Simpson, "Chicano Street Murals: A Sociological Perspective," *Journal of Popular Culture*, 13:3 (1980: Spring): 523.

40. David Arreola, "Mexican American Exterior Murals," *Geographical Review*, 74:4 (1984: October).

41. Conversation with author, Los Angeles, Ca., March 1, 2008.

42. Anita Brenner, *Idols Behind Altars: Modern Mexican Art and Its Cultural Roots.* New York: Payson and Clarke Ltd., 1929: 174–75.

43. "Revered Catholic Icon Becomes Mysterious Target of Vandals in Los Angeles," *New York Times*, October 24, 1999.

44. "Nuevo Catholics," *New York Times*, December 24, 2006.

NOTES TO THE CONCLUSION

1. See Pierre Bordieu, *The Field of Cultural Production.* New York: Columbia University Press, 1993.

2. Fourth-grade curriculum in California still includes mission history with little discussion of the Mexican-American War or how the missions came to be in the possession of Americans.

3. In 2010 Arizona Governor Jan Brewer signed House Bill 2281 into law, effectively outlawing ethnic studies courses and courses that would "promote resentments towards any race or class."

4. Octavio Paz, "Entrevista con Octavio Paz," in *De Colores: Journal of Emerging Raza Philosophies* Vol. 2, No. 2, 1975: 20. Original Spanish text translated by author: "Usted Chicano y yo Mexicano . . . no nos entendemos sin la historia de los Mexicanos y la historia de los Chicanos. A su vez los Chicanos no se entienden sin la historia de los Estados Unidos y sin la historia de Mexico. Los Mexicanos no nos entendemos sin la historia de el mundo Pre-Colombiano y sin la historia de España. Ya con la historia Española es de Europa y es del mundo Arabe. Y los Estados Unidos es de la historia de Inglatera y el perutianismo y el protestantismo."

BIBLIOGRAPHY

Allen, Margaret V. *Ramona's Homeland*. San Diego: Denrich Press, 1914.

Amerikaner, David. "Under the Influence," in *Rhythms and Music of Fiesta* insert, *Santa Barbara News-Press*, Sunday, August 2, 1998.

Armas, Jose. "Entrevista Con Octavio Paz," in *De Colores: Journal of Emerging Raza Philosophies* Vol. 2, No. 2, 1975: 11–21.

Atl, Dr. *Boletín de Instrucion Publica*. México, D.F.: 1914: 74.

Balderrama, Francisco E., and Raymond Rodriguez. *Decade of Betrayal: Mexican Repatriation in the 1930s*. Albuquerque: University of New Mexico Press, 1995.

Bancroft, Hubert Howe. *History of Arizona and New Mexico: 1530–1888*. Albuquerque: Horn and Wallace, 1962.

Banning, Evelyn. *Helen Hunt Jackson*. New York: Vanguard, 1973.

Barbour, George M. *Florida for Tourists, Invalids and Settlers*. New York: D. Appleton and Company, 1881.

Baur, Jahn. *The Health Seekers of Southern California*. San Marino: Huntington Library Press, 1959.

Beal, Tarcisio. "Hispanics and the Roman Catholic Church in the United States," in *Hispanics in the Church: Up from the Cellar*, ed. Philip Lampe. San Francisco and London: Catholic Scholars Press, 1994.

Billington, Ray. *The Origins of Nativism in the United States, 1800–1844*. New York: Arno Press, 1974.

Bishop, William Henry. *Old Mexico and Her Lost Provinces: A Journey in Mexico, Southern California, and Arizona by Way of Cuba*. New York: Harper and Brothers, 1883.

Bogardus, Emory S. "Current Problems of Mexican Immigrants," in *Sociology and Social Research* Vol. XXV, November 1940.

Bolton, Herbert. "The Mission as a Frontier Institution in the Spanish-American Colonies," in *American Historical Review* Vol. XXIII, October 1917.

———. *The Spanish Borderlands: A Chronicle of Old Florida and the Southwest*. Albuquerque: University of New Mexico Press, 1996.

Brace, Charles Loring. *New West or California in 1867–68*. London: G. P. Putnam and Son, 1869.

Brechin, Grey. *Imperial San Francisco: Urban Power, Earthly Ruin*. Berkeley, Los Angeles, and London: University of California Press, 1999.

Brook, Harry Ellington, ed. *The Land of Sunshine, Southern California: An Authentic Description of Its Natural Features, Resources, and Prospects, Containing Reliable Information for the Homeseeker, Tourist and Invalid, Compiled for Southern California World's Fair Association.* Los Angeles: World's Fair Association and Bureau of Information Print, 1893.

Bryant, Edwin. *What I Saw in California, Being the Journal of a Tour in the Years 1846, 1847.* New York: D. Appleton and Company, 1848.

California Addresses by President Roosevelt. San Francisco: The California Promotion Committee, 1903.

"California's Exposition Building." *World's Fair Magazine*, February 1892.

The California Missions: A Pictorial History, editorial staff of Sunset Books, Menlo Park, Lane Book Co., 1964.

Camarillo, Albert. *Chicanos in a Changing Society: From Mexican Pueblos to American Barrios in Santa Barbara and Southern California, 1848–1930.* Cambridge and London: Harvard University Press, 1979.

Chandler, Arthur. *The Fantastic Fair: The Story of the California Midwinter International Exposition.* San Francisco: Pogo Press, 1993.

Charlot, Jean. *The Mexican Mural Renaissance: 1920–1925.* New Haven and London: Yale University Press, 1963.

Chávez, César. *The Plan of Delano.* New York: Random House, 1972.

Cockroft, Eva. "The Story of Chicano Park." *Aztlán* Vol. 15, No. 1, Spring, 1984.

Cockroft, Eva, John Pitman Weber, and James Cockroft. *Toward a Peoples Art: The Contemporary Mural Movement.* Albuerquerque: University of New Mexico Press, 1998.

Colby, Gerard, and Charlotte Dennet. *Thy Will Be Done, The Conquest of the Amazon: Nelson Rockefeller and Evangelism in the Age of Oil.* New York: HarperCollins, 1995.

Comny, Peter Thomas. *The Origins and Purposes of the Native Sons and Daughters of the Golden West.* San Francisco: Native Sons of the Golden West, 1955–56.

"Complimentary Dinner Given By The Aztec Club of 1847, To Their Honored President Major General Robert Patterson, At Delmonico's in New York, January 6, 1880." Pamphlet in Huntington Library Ephemera collection.

Cone, Mary. *Two Years in California.* New York: Griggs and Company, 1876.

Curtis, Sandra. *Zorro Unmasked: The Official History.* New York: Hyperion, 1998.

Dana, Richard Henry, Jr. *Two Years Before the Mast: A Personal Narrative of Life at Sea.* New York: Penguin Books, 1981.

Davis, Carlyle Channing, and William A. Anderson. *The True Story of Ramona: Its Facts and Fictions, Inspiration and Purpose.* New York: Dover Publishing, 1914.

Davis, David Brion, ed. *The Fear of Conspiracy: Images of Un-American Subversion from the Revolution to the Present.* Ithaca and London: Cornell University Press, 1971.

De Beer, Gabriella. *Jose Vasconcelos and His World.* New York: Las Americas Publishing Company, 1966.

Delgado, Kevin. "A Turning Point: The Conception and Realization of Chicano Park," *Journal of San Diego History* Vol. 44, No. 1, Winter 1998.

Delpar, Helen. *The Enormous Vogue of Things Mexican: Cultural Relations Between the United States and Mexico, 1920–1935*. Tuscaloosa and London: University of Alabama Press, 1992.

Doyle, John T. *Some Account of the Pious Fund of California and the Litigation to Recover It*. San Francisco: Edward Bosqui & Co. Printers, 1880.

Dudley, Gordon. *Junipero Serra: California's First Citizen*. Los Angeles: Cultural Assets Press, 1969.

Dumke, Glenn S. *The Boom of the Eighties in Southern California*. San Marino: Huntington Library Press, 1944.

Dwinelle, John. *Colonial History of San Francisco*. San Francisco, 1864.

Edwards, William A., M.D., and Beatrice Harraden, *Two Health Seekers in Southern California*. Philadelphia: J. B. Lippincott Company, 1897.

Elkin, John J., ed., *Official Guide to the World's Columbian Exposition*. Chicago: The Columbian Guide Co./John Anderson Printing, 1893.

Engelhardt, Zephyrin. *The Franciscans in California*. Harbor Springs: Holy Childhood Indian School, 1897.

Englekirk, John E. *Bibliographia de Obras Norteamericanas en Traduccion Española*. México, D.F., 1944.

"La Fiesta De Los Angeles," in *Land of Sunshine* Vol. 2, No. 5, April 1895: 83–84 and Vol. 6, No. 6, May 1897: 261–68.

Fiske, Turbesé Lummis, and Keith Lummis. *Charles F. Lummis: The Man and His West*. Norman: University of Oklahoma Press, 1975.

Fogelson, Robert M. *The Fragmented Metropolis: Los Angeles, 1850–1930*. Berkeley, Los Angeles, and London: University of California Press, 1993.

Forbes, Mrs. A.S.C. *California Missions and Landmarks: El Camino Real*. Los Angeles: Self-published, 1915.

Franchot, Jenny. *Roads to Rome: The Antebellum Protestant Encounter with Catholicism*. Berkeley, Los Angeles, and London: University of California Press, 1994.

Gale, Zona. *Frank Miller of the Mission Inn*. New York: D. Appleton–Century, 1938.

Garcia, Ignacio M. *Chicanismo: The Forging of a Militant Ethos Among Mexican Americans*. Tucson: University of Arizona Press, 1997.

Garcia, Marshall Rupert. *La Raza Murals of California, 1963–1970, A Period of Social Change and Protest*, unpublished master's thesis, University of California Berkeley, 1981.

Geary, Gerald. *The Secularization of the California Missions, 1810–1846*. Washington: Catholic University of America Press, 1934.

Gebhard, David. *Robert Stacy-Judd: Maya Architecture and the Creation of a New Style*. Santa Barbara: Capra Press, 1993.

——. *Santa Barbara: The Creation of a New Spain in California*. Santa Barbara: University of California at Santa Barbara, 1982.

Glassberg, David. *American Historical Pageantry: The Uses of Tradition in the Early Twentieth Century*. Chapel Hill: University of North Carolina Press, 1990.

Gleeson, William. *History of the Catholic Church in California*. San Francisco: A. L. Bancroft and Co., 1872.

Goddard, M. Le B. "A Century of Dishonor," *Atlantic Monthly*, V. 47, April 1881: 573.

———. "A Century of Dishonor," *Nation* Vol. 32, 3 March 1881.

Goldman, Shifra. "Siqueiros and Three Early Murals in Los Angeles," in *Art Journal* Vol. 34, No. 8, August 1974.

Graham, Mary. *Remembrances of One Hundred Years Ago*. San Francisco: P. J. Thomas, 1876.

Greenwood, Grace. *Haps and Mishaps of a Tour in Europe*. Boston: Ticknor, Reed and Fields, 1853.

Gregory, James N. *American Exodus: The Dust Bowl Migration and Okie Culture in California*. New York and Oxford: Oxford University Press, 1989.

Griswold del Castillo, Richard. "The Del Valle Family and The Fantasy Heritage," in *California History*, Spring 1980.

———. "Mexican Views of 1848: The Treaty of Guadalupe Hidalgo Through Mexican History," *Journal of Borderlands Studies* Vol. 1, No. 2., 1986.

———. *The Treaty of Guadalupe Hidalgo: A Legacy of Conflict*. Norman and London: University of Oklahoma Press, 1990.

Gutierrez, David G. *Walls and Mirrors: Mexican Americans, Mexican Immigrants, and the Politics of Ethnicity*. Berkeley, Los Angeles, and London: University of California Press, 1995.

Gutiérrez, Ramón. "Aztlán, Montezuma, and New Mexico: The Political Uses of American Indian Mythology," in *Aztlán: Essays on the Chicano Homeland*, ed. Rudolfo Anaya and Francisco Lomeli. Albuquerque: University of New Mexico Press, 1989.

Hall, Joan H. *Through the Doors of the Mission Inn*. Riverside: Highgrove Press, 1996.

Hata, Nadine Ishitani. *The Historic Preservation Movement in California: 1940–1976*. California Dept. of Parks and Recreation/Office of Historic Preservation, 1992.

Hawthorne, Nathaniel. *Life of Franklin Pierce*. Boston: Ticknor, Reed and Fields, 1852.

Hewett, Edgar Lee. *The Architecture of the Exposition*. Publisher and location n/a, 1916.

Historic Mission Inn. Riverside: Friends of the Mission Inn, 1998.

Hobsbawm, Eric. "Introduction: Inventing Traditions, in *The Invention of Tradition*, ed. Eric Hobsbawm and Terence Ranger. Cambridge: Cambridge University Press, 1995.

Holder, Charles Frederick. "The Cordon of the King's highway," *Land of Sunshine* Vol. 3., No. 6, 1895.

Hughes, Elizabeth. *The California of the Padres; or, Footprints of Ancient Communism*. San Francisco: I. N. Choynski, 1875.

Hunt, Helen. *Bits of Travel*. Boston: James R. Osgood and Company, 1873.

———. *Bits of Travel at Home*. Boston: Roberts Brothers, 1878.

Ingle, Marjorie. *The Mayan Revival Style: Art Deco Mayan Fantasy*. Salt Lake City: Gibbs Smith Books, 1984.

Jackson, Helen Hunt. *A Century Of Dishonor: A sketch of the United States dealings with some of the Indian Tribes*. Norman: University of Oklahoma Press, 1994 (reprint of 1885 edition).

———. "Father Junipero and His Work," *The Century Magazine* Vol. XXVI, No. 1, May 1883.

———. *Glimpses of California and the Missions*. Boston: Little, Brown, 1907.

———. *Ramona*. New York: Penguin Publishers/Signet Classics, 1988.

Jackson, Helen Hunt, and Abbott Kinney. *Report on the condition and needs of the Mission Indians of California*. Washington: Government Printing Office, 1883.

James, George Wharton. *Through Ramona's Country*. Boston: Little, Brown and Co., 1911.

Johannsen, Robert W. *To the Halls of the Montezumas: The Mexican War in the American Imagination*. New York and Oxford: Oxford University Press, 1985.

Keen, Benjamin. *The Aztec Image in Western Thought*. New Brunswick, N.J.: Rutgers University Press, 1985.

Klor de Alva, Jorge. "The Invention of Ethnic Origins and Negotiation of Latino Identity, 1969–1981," in *Challenging Fronteras: Structuring Latina and Latino Lives in the U.S., An Anthology of Readings*, ed. Pierrette Hondagneu-Sotelo, Vilma Ortiz, and Mary Romero. New York and London: Routledge, 1997.

Kropp, Phoebe. *California Vieja: Culture and Memory in a Modern American Place*. Berkeley, Los Angeles, and London: University of California Press, 2006.

Lange, Charles H. *Bandelier: The Life and Adventures of Adolph Bandelier*. Salt Lake City: University of Utah Press, 1996.

Leal, Luis. "In Search of Aztlán," *Denver Quarterly* Vol. 16, No. 3, Fall 1981.

Levine, Neil. *The Architecture of Frank Lloyd Wright*. Princeton, N.J.: Princeton University Press, 1996.

Lindey, Walter, M.D., and J. P. Widney, M.D. *California of the South: Its Physical Geography, Climate, Resources, Routes of Travel and Health Resorts*. New York: D. Appleton and Co., 1888.

Lummis, Charles. *The Awakening of a Nation: Mexico of To-Day*. New York: Harper, 1898.

———. *The Home of Ramona: Photographs of Camulos, the fine old Spanish Estate described by Mrs. Helen Hunt Jackson, as the Home of "Ramona,"* second edition. Los Angeles: Chas. F. Lummis & Company, 1888.

———. "In the Lion's Den," *Out West* Vol. 18, No. 5, May 1903.

———. "The Mexican Wizard," *Land of Sunshine* Vol. 11, No. 6, November 1899.

———. *Some Strange Corners of Our Country: The Wonderland of the Southwest*. Tucson: University of Arizona Press, 1989.

———. *The Spanish Pioneers*. Chicago: A. C. McClurg and Co., 1899.

———. *Stand Fast Santa Barbara*. Santa Barbara Plans and Planting Committee of the Community Arts Association, 1927.

———. *A Tramp Across the Continent*. Lincoln and London: University of Nebraska Press, 1982.

Lummis, Charles, and Zephyrin Englehardt. "The Correspondence of Charles F. Lummis with Fr. Zephyrin Englehardt, O.F.M.," in *Franciscan Provincial Annals, Province of Santa Barbara* Vol. 4, No. 4, July 1942.

Manning, Reg. *Reg Manning's Cartoon Guide to California.* New York: J. J. Augustin Publisher, 1939.

Marin, Margueritte V. *Social Protest in an Urban Barrio: A Study of the Chicano Movement, 1966–1974.* Lanham, New York, and London: University Press of America, 1991.

Martí, José. *Obras Completas, Epistolario* Vol. 20, Havana, 1965.

———. *Obras Completas, En Los Estados Unidos* Vol. 11, Havana, 1965.

Mathes, Valery Sherer. "Helen Hunt Jackson: Official Agent to the California Mission Indians," *Southern California Quarterly* Vol. 63, No. 1, 1981.

Mazón, Mauricio. *The Zoot Suit Riots: The Psychology of Symbolic Annihilation.* Austin: University of Texas Press, 1984.

McGloin, John Bernard. *California's First Archbishop.* New York: Herder and Herder, 1966.

McWilliams, Carey. *North from Mexico: The Spanish Speaking People of the United States.* Philadelphia and New York: J. B. Lippincott Company, 1949.

———. *Southern California Country: An Island in the Land.* New York: Duell, Sloan & Pearce, 1946.

Meir, Matt, and Feliciano Ribera. *Mexican Americans/American Mexicans: From Conquistadors to Chicanos.* New York: Hill & Wang, 1993.

Meyberg, Max. "La Fiesta de Los Angeles," *Land of Sunshine*, July 1894.

Miller, Robert Ryal. *Shamrock and the Sword: The Saint Patrick's Battalion in the U.S.-Mexican War.* Norman and London: University of Oklahoma Press, 1989.

"The Mission Play," in *California Life* Vol. XVII, No. 3, January 24, 1920.

Monroy, Douglas. "An Essay on Understanding the Work Experience of Mexicans in Southern California. 1900–1939," *Beyond 1848: Readings in the Modern Chicano Historical Experience*, ed. Michael Ornelas. Dubuque: Kendall/Hunt Publishing Company, 1993.

———. *Thrown Among Strangers: The Making of Mexican Culture in Frontier California.* Berkeley, Los Angeles, and London: University of California Press, 1990.

Muños, Carlos Jr. *Youth, Identity, Power: The Chicano Movement.* London and New York: Verso, 1989.

Myers, Bernard S. *Mexican Painting in Our Time.* New York: Oxford University Press, 1956.

Newcomb, Rexford. *The Old Mission Churches and Historical Houses of California.* Philadelphia and London: J. B. Lippincott and Company, 1925.

———. *Spanish-Colonial Architecture in the United States.* New York: J. J. Agustin, 1937.

Nieto, Margarita. "Mexican Art and Los Angeles, 1920–1940," in *On the Edge of America: California Modernist Art, 1900–1950*, ed. Paul J. Karlstrom. Berkeley, Los Angeles, and London: University of California Press, 1996.

Nordhoff, Charles. *California: For Health, Pleasure and Residence: A Book for Travelers and Settlers.* New York: Harper and Brothers Publishers, 1872.

———. *La Californie pour les Emigrants*. London: Le Chemin de fer Su Pacifique du sud, 1883.

———. *Guia de California, El Estado de Oro*. London: La Compañia del Ferro-carril del Pacífico del Sud [*sic*], 1883.

———. *Peninsular California; some account of the climate, soil, productions, and present condition chiefly of the northern half of Lower California*. New York: Harper and Bros., 1888.

Notes of Travel in California, from *The Official Reports of Col. Fremont and Maj. Emory*. Dublin: James M'Glashan, 1849.

Novoa, Bruce. *Chicanos Authors: Inquiry by Interview*. Austin and London: University of Texas Press, 1980.

Odell, Ruth. *Helen Hunt Jackson*. New York and London: D. Appleton–Century Company, 1939.

Orozco, José Clemente. *An Autobiography*. Austin: University of Texas Press, 1962.

Otis, Eliza. "The Romance of the Mission Period" (1905), in *Some Essays About the California Missions in Honor of the V Centenary of the Evangelization of the Americas*, ed. Msgr. Francis J. Weber. California Catholic Conference, 1992.

La Palabra Alambre de M.A.S.H. Vol. 4, No. 4, June 1972: 16.

Pascoe, Peggy. *Relations of Rescue: The Search for Female Moral Authority in the American West: 1874–1939*. New York and Oxford: Oxford University Press, 1990.

Paz, Octavio. *The Labyrinth of Solitude*. New York: Grove Press, 1985.

Pitt, Leonard. *The Decline of the Californios: A Social History of the Spanish-Speaking Californians, 1846–1890*. Berkeley, Los Angeles, and London: University of California Press, 1998.

"*El Plan Espiritual de Aztlán*," in *Aztlán: Essays on the Chicano Homeland*, ed. Rudolfo A. Anaya and Francisco Lomeli. Albuquerque: University of New Mexico Press, 1991.

El Plan Espiritual de Santa Barbara. Santa Barbara: La Causa Publications, 1970.

Pohlman, John Ogden. *California's Mission Myth*. Unpublished dissertation, University of California Los Angeles, 1974.

Polk, Dora. *The Island of California: A History of the Myth*. Spokane: Arthur H. Clark Co., 1991.

Powell, Wayne. *Tree of Hate: Propaganda and Prejudice Affecting United States Relations with the Hispanic World*. Portland, Ore.: Ross House Books, 1985.

"Ramona," *Overland Monthly* Vol. V, No. 27, March 1885.

Rawls, James. *Indians of California: The Changing Image*. Norman: University of Oklahoma Press, 1984.

"Recent Novels," *The Nation* Vol. XL, No. 1022, January 29, 1885.

"Reglamento De La Nueva California, 1773," in *Diario Del Capitan Comandante Fernando de Rivera y Moncada*, ed. Ernest J. Burrus, S.J. Vol. II. Madrid: Ediciones Porrua, 1967.

Remondino, P. C., M.D. *The Mediterranean Shores of America. Southern California: Its Climatic, Physical and Meteorological Conditions*. Philadelphia and London: F. A. Davis and Co., 1892.

"Restoration Undesirable," *Los Angeles Times*, December 25, 1910: 114.

Revere, Joseph Warren. *A Tour of Duty in California*, ed. Joseph N. Balestier. New York: C. S. Francis and Co., 1849.

Ridge, John Rollin (Yellow Bird). *The Life and Adventures of Joaquín Murieta, The Celebrated California Bandit*. Norman and London: University of Oklahoma Press, 1955.

Rivera, Diego, and Gladys March. *My Art, My Life: An Autobiography*. New York: Dover, 1991.

Roberts, Edward. *Santa Barbara and Around There*, Illustrations by H. C. Ford. Boston: Roberts Brothers, 1886.

Robinson, Alfred. *Life in California Before the Conquest*. San Francisco: Thomas C. Russell, 1925.

Robledo, Antonio Gomez. *Mexico Y El Arbitraje Internacional*. México, D.F.: Editorial Porrua, 1965.

Rochfort, Desmond. *Mexican Muralists: Orozco, Rivera, Siqueiros*. San Francisco: Chronicle Books, 1993.

Rosales, Arturo. *Chicano! The History of the Mexican American Civil Rights Movement*. Houston: Arte Publico Press, 1993.

Roske, Ralph J. *Everyman's Eden: A History of California*. New York: Macmillan, 1968.

Rouse, Stella Haverford. *Santa Barbara's Spanish Renaissance and Old Spanish Days Fiesta*. Santa Barbara: Schauer Printing Studio, 1974.

Ryan, William Redmond. *Personal Adventures in Upper and Lower California, in 1848–9*. London: William Shogerl Publisher, 1850.

Sánchez, George. *Becoming Mexican American: Ethnicity, Culture and Identity in Chicano Los Angeles, 1900–1945*. New York and Oxford: Oxford University Press, 1993.

Sanchez, Rosaura. *Telling Identities: The Californio Testimonios*. Minneapolis and London: University of Minnesota Press, 1995.

Sanchez-Tranquilino, Marcos. *Mi Casa No Es Su Casa: Chicano Murals and Barrio Calligraphy as Systems of Signifiration at Estrada Courts, 1972–1978*. Unpublished master's thesis, University of California Los Angeles, 1991.

Sandos, James. "Historic Preservation and Historical Facts: Helen Hunt Jackson, Rancho Camulos and Ramonana," *California History*, Fall 1998.

Sandoval, Moises. *On the Move: A History of the Hispanic Church in the United States*. Maryknoll, N.Y.: Orbis Books, 1990.

Santa Barbara Perpetuates the Romance, Beauty and History of Spanish California. Santa Barbara: Chamber of Commerce, 1926.

Schmidt, Henry C. *The Roots of Lo Mexicano: Self and Society in Mexican Thought, 1900–1934*. College Station and London: Texas A&M University Press, 1978.

Siqueiros, David Alfaro. *Mi Respuesta*. México, D.F.: Ediciones de Arte Publico, 1960.

Skirius, John. "Vasconcelos and Mexico de Afuera (1928)," in *Aztlán* Vol. 7, No. 3, Fall 1976.

Sterling Cockroft, Eva, and Holly Barnet-Sanchez, eds. *Signs from the Heart: California Chicano Murals*. Venice, Calif.: Social and Public Art Resource Center, 1990.

Taylor, William. *Magistrates of the Sacred: Priests and Parishioners in Eighteenth Century Mexico*. Stanford, Calif.: Stanford University Press, 1996.

Thomas, P. J., ed. *Our Centennial Memoir*. San Francisco, 1877.

Thompson, Joseph A. *El Gran Capitan Jose de la Guerra: A Historical Biographical Study*. Los Angeles: Cabrera and Sons, 1961.

Tibbles, Thomas Henry. *Standing Bear and the Ponca Chiefs*. Lincoln: University of Nebraska Press, 1995 (originally printed 1880).

Truman, Benjamin. *The Observations of Benjamin Cummings Truman on El Camino Real*, edited and annotated by Francis J. Weber, photos by A. C. Vroman. Los Angeles: Dawson's Book Shop, 1978.

———. *Occidental Sketches*. San Francisco: San Francisco News Company, 1881.

———. *Semi-Tropical California*. San Francisco: A. L. Bancroft and Co., 1874.

Turner, Frederick Jackson. "The Significance of the Frontier in American History," in *The Frontier in American History*. New York: Dover, 1996.

United States Bureau of the Census, *Tenth Census: 1880*. Washington: Government Printing Office, 1880.

United States Bureau of the Census, *Eleventh Census: 1890*. Washington: Government Printing Office, 1892–97.

Vasconcelos, José. *La Raza Cósmica*, trans. Didier T. Jaén. Baltimore and London: Johns Hopkins University Press, 1979.

Velásquez, Maria Del Carmen. *El Fondo Piadoso De Las Californias, Notas Y Documentos*. México, D.F.: Secretaria De Relaciones Exteriores, 1985.

Villoro, Luis. *Los Grandes Momentos del Indigenismo en México*. México, D.F.: Secretaria de Educación Pública, 1987.

Walker, Franklin. *A Literary History of Southern California*. Berkeley and Los Angeles: University of California Press, 1950.

Wallis, Ethel, and Mary Bennet. *Two Thousand Tongues to Go: The Story of the Wycliffe Bible Translators*. New York: Harper and Brothers, 1959.

Warner, Col. J. J., Judge Benjamin Hayes, and Dr. J. P. Widney. *An Historical Sketch of Los Angeles California from the Spanish Occupancy, by the Founding of the Mission San Gabriel Archangel, September 8, 1771, to July 4, 1876*. Los Angeles: Louis Lewin and Co., 1876.

Weber, David J. *The Spanish Frontier in North America*. New Haven and London: Yale University Press, 1992.

———. "Turner, the Boltonians and the Borderlands," in *Myth and the History of the Hispanic Southwest*. Albuquerque: University of New Mexico Press, 1987.

Weber, Francis J. *A Biographical Sketch of Right Reverend Francisco Garcia Diego Y Moreno, First Bishop of the Californias, 1785–1846*. Los Angeles: Borromeo Guild Press, 1961.

———. "John Steven McGroarty, from the Green Verdugo Hills," *Journal of San Diego History* Vol. XX, No. 4, Fall 1974.

———. *The United States Versus Mexico: The Final Settlement of the Pious Fund*. Los Angeles: The Historical Society of Southern California, 1969.

Weber, Francis J., ed. *Some Essays About the California Missions in Honor of the V Centenary of the Evangelization of the Americas*, ed. Francis J. Weber. Los Angeles: Knights of Columbus, 1992.

Weitze, Karen. *California's Mission Revival*. Los Angeles: Henessey and Ingalls, 1984.

———. "Sumner P. Hunt," in *Toward a Simpler Way of Life: The Arts and Crafts Architects of California*, ed. Robert Winter. Berkeley, Los Angeles, and London: University of California Press, 1997.

White, Hayden. *Metahistory: The Historical Imagination in Nineteenth Century Europe*. Baltimore: Johns Hopkins University Press, 1973.

Winslow, Carleton Monroe. *The Architecture and the Gardens of the San Diego Exposition*, introduction by Bertram Goodhue. San Francisco: P. Elder, 1916.

Winter, Robert. "Frederick Louis Roehrig," in *Toward a Simpler Way of Life: The Arts and Crafts Architects of California*, ed. Robert Winter. Berkeley, Los Angeles, and London: University of California Press, 1997.

ABOUT THE AUTHOR

Roberto Ramón Lint Sagarena, Associate Professor of American Studies and Director of the Center for the Comparative Study of Race and Ethnicity at Middlebury College, has received teaching awards from the University of Southern California and Princeton University. He currently serves as Director at Large of the American Academy of Religion. His scholarship engages the role of religion in the formation of racial, ethnic, and regional identities in the Americas.